A minority and the state

MANCHESTER
1824

Manchester University Press

A minority and the state

Travellers in Britain in the twentieth century

Becky Taylor

Manchester University Press
Manchester and New York
distributed exclusively in the USA by Palgrave

The right of Becky Taylor to be identified as the author of this work has been asserted by her in accordance with the Copyright, Designs and Patents Act 1988.

Published by Manchester University Press
Oxford Road, Manchester M13 9NR, UK
and Room 400, 175 Fifth Avenue, New York, NY 10010, USA
www.manchesteruniversitypress.co.uk

Distributed in the United States exclusively by
Palgrave Macmillan, 175 Fifth Avenue,
New York, NY 10010, USA

Distributed in Canada exclusively by
UBC Press, University of British Columbia, 2029 West Mall,
Vancouver, BC, Canada V6T 1Z2

British Library Cataloguing-in-Publication Data is available

Library of Congress Cataloging-in-Publication Data is available

ISBN 978 0 7190 9126 1 paperback

First published by Manchester University Press in hardback 2008

This paperback edition first published 2013

The publisher has no responsibility for the persistence or accuracy of URLs for any external or third-party internet websites referred to in this book, and does not guarantee that any content on such websites is, or will remain, accurate or appropriate.

Printed by Lightning Source

Contents

Preface

My interest in researching and writing about the experiences of Travellers in modern Britain was only in part stimulated by the fact that there was no general history of Travellers for the twentieth century. More than this was the apparent paradox I came across whenever I spoke to someone about my proposed work: everyone always had an opinion about 'Gypsies', but virtually no one had ever met one, let alone could claim a Traveller as a friend.

Very often the first question people asked was 'do you mean the real Romanies, rather than the "didikais" or "pikies" or "tinkers"?' They would then go on to say that they have nothing against 'real Gypsies', who live in bow-topped caravans and sell pegs, but these nasty Tinkers in their chrome caravans who come and tarmac drives or 'lop and top' are quite another matter. Similarly, the stereotypes of modern Travellers as dirty, antisocial, thieving and dangerous are trotted out in the popular press on a regular basis, underpinned by the assumption that Travellers are always a 'problem'. Although one of Britain's longest established minority groups, they simultaneously suffer racism on a daily basis and are denied an ethnic identity. Unlike other, more recently arrived minority groups, they have not generally been part of the state's vision of a 'multicultural Britain'. Instead, they are commonly denigrated as social pariahs who have failed to keep up with march of modernity and now post-modernity. Yet the ubiquitous nature of Gypsies in popular imagination is contrasted sharply with the absence of both personal experience and factual information. How could I explain this disjuncture? This book is an attempt to begin to answer this question.

Acknowledgements

Over the course of the nine or so years I have taken to conduct the research and write what has become this book I have incurred a huge debt to many people. I received help, and often interest beyond the call of duty from archivists and staff at numerous record offices and archives around the country. Of particular assistance were the staff of the Romany Collection at the Brotherton Library, Leeds University and the Scott MacFie Collection at Liverpool University; Steven Hobbs at Wiltshire Record Office; staff at Surrey History Centre and Hampshire Record Office; the archivist at the Public Record Office of Northern Ireland, whose enthusiasm led to an enjoyable and profitable stay; and archivists at Perthshire and the Highlands Record Offices; and Alan from Suffolk mobile library service. The London City Mission welcomed me and allowed me access to their records. Chris Williams flagged up the contents of the Association of Chief Police Officers archive at the Open University, opened the relevant files, shared his office and provided photocopying and coffee. Thank you.

I owe much also, to long-suffering friends and family members who have let me use spare rooms, sofas, floor and car space in the course of my research, or who have provided vital childcare. Many thanks to Penni and David Taylor, my parents, for ongoing help and support of all kinds, Maureen when in Wembley, Alex and Clare in Leeds, Olaf in Sheffield, Glen, Bryony and Nickolai in Cambridge, Duncan and household in Liverpool, Richard J., Zarah, Ray and Sam in Aldershot; Sarah and Justin and Lisa for emergency childcare; and Helen B. for three years of living in her garden and material on the 1994 Criminal Justice Act.

I would like to thank David Feldman for his perspective on the state and incisive analysis when I floundered, and continued support well beyond his original role of supervisor; Pat Thane and Leo Lucassen, whose critical comments enriched both my thinking and the shape of the book; John Stewart for encouragement and advice with the proposal; and Ben Rogaly for consistent interest and genuine support, which included allowing me to encroach into our current project. Thanks also to the barrister specialising in Traveller cases who wished to remain anonymous, and who, as ever, gave generously of his time and expertise.

I owe a debt to the Travellers I met in Norfolk while conducting separate research for Sheffield University, after the main bulk of work for this book had been completed. Visiting and interviewing them by the side of the road, on official sites and in houses, their stories added flesh to what had often been the dry bones of archival material. All too often they confirmed the reality of life at the margins of British society. Thanks also, to the residents of Dale Farm for their hospitality and sociability; and to Roseanna MacPhee who took the time to talk to me about Bobbin Mill.

Finally, I would like to thank Paul, without whom it would not have been possible; and to Jack, who made it neither possible nor easier, but certainly a lot more fun.

Abbreviations

ACERT	Advisory Council for the Education of Romany and other Travellers
ACPO	Association of Chief Police Officers
CRE	Commission for Racial Equality
DoE	Department of the Environment
HMI	His/Her Majesty's Inspector of Schools
HO	Home Office
JGLS	*Journal of the Gypsy Lore Society*
LCM	London City Mission
LEA	Local Education Authority
MHLG	Ministry of Housing and Local Government
MoH	Ministry of Health
NFU	National Farmers' Union
RDC	rural district council
UDC	urban district council

Introduction

When I first started the research for this book in the late 1990s, I was motivated by the simple observation that there was no general history of Travellers in Britain for the twentieth century to parallel David Mayall's work for the nineteenth century. This in turn led me to reflect on what this said about the relationship between settled society and Travellers: in a highly literate country with what some might think of as an obsession with history, why had one of its oldest minority groups been ignored in this way? As I show in the course of the book, this was only in part the result of the strong oral tradition of the Traveller communities themselves and their lack of a consistent collective identity. To a great extent it has been the legacy of the development of 'Gypsy studies' as a field of research, as well as the deeply engrained way in which the state and settled society have treated and represented Travellers.

Reviewing the contents of this book and the material that generated it, to what extent can I claim it lives up to the subtitle, *Travellers in Britain in the twentieth century*? Anyone looking for systematic coverage of all Britain for the whole of the century will be disappointed: the lack of sustained records from any particular area, let alone nationally, over an extended period of time, rendered such an aspiration unrealisable. Instead, I was required to take a more magpie approach, chasing up leads as they emerged from secondary sources and newspapers throughout the country. Where appropriate I have included evidence from both Northern Ireland and Eire – although outside the definition of 'Britain' – owing to the flows of migration, as well as cultural and familial links between Irish Travellers and those in Britain.

This book has been shaped primarily by the way in which Travellers' lifestyles affected the settled population as the presence of a

'Gypsy problem' generated documentation, whereas a continued low-key presence of Travellers largely did not. Evidence is concentrated in times of activity or concern, and is interspersed by larger time periods and geographical areas of absence. This 'lumpy' nature of the evidence can produce a bias in the mind of the researcher, as the temptation is to listen to the noise and not to give equal weight to the silence. Throughout the book, therefore, I attempt to assess whether the existing records are an expression of the norm or of experiences that are specific to a time and/or location. Therefore, I do not claim to provide consistent documentary evidence from all parts of the country, as the in-depth research is concentrated in areas which yielded the largest bodies of archives, but I do assert that I can create a broadly national picture of the relations between Travellers and settled society and point to particularities within this.

Added to any potential bias in the provenance of sources is the fact that the bulk of the material I have used comes from the first six decades of the twentieth century, with overspill into the preceding and following years. The focus of my work on the pre-1968 period was partly strategic, as the years from the passing of the Caravan Sites Act to the end of the century have been far more studied than earlier years; and partly practical, as the thirty-year rule was still in place when I conducted the archival work for the book. Both local record offices and the National Archives, however, hold substantial material on the post-1968 period, and offer a rich and unexplored opportunity for a historian wishing to study these years.

A further challenge of the research has been to surmount the difficulty of using written sources when investigating traditionally orally-based communities. The bulk of archival material has been written about Travellers and not by them, although this is slowly being counter-balanced by publications and discussions from within travelling communities. There remains the fact that anyone writing the history of Travellers must do so primarily through the eyes of the settled population and the state. These sources, however, have their own strengths as they are ideal for unpicking how the nature and preoccupations of dominant society moulded its relationship with Travellers.

An emphasis on the interaction between Travellers and wider society rather than simply on Travellers themselves, allows the research to reach beyond the sometimes narrow world of 'Gypsy studies' and throw light on wider historical themes. It reveals, for example, the significance of the expansion of the state and the relationship between central and local government over the twentieth century, and the importance of differentiating between the various levels of the state when understanding the history of Travellers in modern Britain. It also enables an exploration of attitudes towards minorities, citizenship and the meaning of inclusion and exclusion, for example in the context of the establishment of the welfare state.

The position of Travellers in Britain, perhaps more than any other minority group, demonstrates the absence of a 'Whiggish' experience of history, with no simple progression from racism and marginalisation in the dying days of Victorianism to the inclusive and open world of late twentieth-century multiculturalism. With some justification the first decades of the twentieth century can be depicted as a time of relative stability and ease in the relationship between Travellers and settled society, while the 1950s and 1960s and the years after 1994 were periods of growing crisis and repression.

These periods themselves hide regional and local particularities, as well as broader trends affecting the whole of British society, such as increasing standards of living and changes in expectations in education, gender and generational relations, travel and patterns of settlement and home ownership.

Intertwined with these changes, both those specific to Travellers and those affecting British society more generally, have been some central continuities. Most notable, particularly when contrasted with the massive changes experienced in Travellers' lifestyles over the century, has been the continuity of stereotypes laid on Travellers by settled society. These have been key in mediating the relationship between the mainstream and Britain's travelling communities. In addition, Travellers themselves have always been actors in their own history, not simply acted upon by outsiders, and therefore their agency has always been a central component of their experiences in twentieth-century Britain.

The shape of the book attempts to reflect the dynamic relationship between these various elements of continuity and change and is consequently arranged by both period and theme. For the three main periods delineated in the book – up to 1945, 1945–68 and post-1968 – I attempt to give a sense of the reality of Travellers' lives at the time, including their economic activities, as well as how the actions of the state at its various levels affected them. This is not simply in terms of provision of or conflict over sites and stopping places, but also as it extended into the realm of education and welfare provision. History, however, is not a tidy or clear-cut business and there is an inevitable 'fuzziness' between periods, with some changes taking place in particular areas long before becoming a more general phenomenon. Therefore, the periodisation must be taken as an attempt to reveal broader trends and experiences, rather than a definitive and absolute account brooking no slippage.

Woven into this general history is an exploration of the three main themes of the book: the impact of stereotypes, the role of the British state and the agency of Travellers themselves. Before moving on to examine these themes in more detail I will clarify exactly who I am referring to by the term 'Travellers'.

Who are 'Travellers'?

Anyone writing about Britain's traditional travelling communities needs to deal with the thorny question of definition. This is not simply a matter of semantics as individuals are still routinely moved on or discriminated against on the grounds that they are Travellers, or are denied planning consent because they have 'lost' their 'Gypsy' status through being sedentary.

Recent work has confirmed exactly how problematic it is to label Britain's travelling populations, with meanings often heavily contested and 'not politically neutral'.[2] My understanding follows that set out by Liegeois and Gheorghe in 1995, in that 'Gypsy' relates to ethnic groups whose origins lie in the diaspora from India in the tenth century, and who subsequently mixed with other groups in the course of their migration north-westwards; while 'Traveller' generally refers to groups who claim a predominantly indigenous European origin, but who have traditionally been nomadic and self-employed.[3] Thus although there has been inter-marriage between the different travelling communities of Britain and with settled society, English and Welsh groups with a tradition of nomadism are commonly described as 'Gypsies', while Scots and Irish ones are seen as 'Travellers'.

While these distinctions are helpful when discussing the communities at a broad level, when attempting to construct their history using available evidence they are less useful. Writers rarely make such nice distinctions, instead either using the blanket term 'Gypsy', or, as I discuss in the following section, deploying a range of labels to denote the 'pure-blooded' or otherwise nature of the individuals under discussion. Given the fact that it was rarely possible to discern whether someone was a 'Gypsy' or a 'Traveller' from the available evidence, in combination with the fact that 'Gypsy' has historically been tied closely to racialised and often pejorative definitions, I use the term 'Traveller' in preference to any other in the course of my writing.

In doing this I refer to people who self-define as being part of the hereditary travelling populations of the British Isles. While this often means that both an individual's parents are of Traveller origin, this is not exclusively the case: someone may have one non-Traveller parent, but still live within and be seen as part of Traveller culture. Equally, a Traveller does not cease to be a Traveller as a result of living in a house. While some have used house-dwelling as a means of distancing themselves from their birth community, other individuals retain their links with wider Traveller culture and/or maintain nomadic patterns of income generation.

Additionally, given the fact that many of the sources I have used have been generated by the state, following the Dutch historians Leo Lucassen, Wim Willems and Annemarie Cottaar, I also include in the scope of my work people who have been defined *by the state* as leading 'an itinerant way of life and who are stigmatised as Gypsy or who have been given similar labels'.[4]

In contrast in the text I typically use the term 'Gypsy' to denote the racialised and romanticised idea of Travellers held by many of the writers whose work I discuss. This does not mean that some Travellers today do not self-define as 'Gypsies' – as many certainly do – simply that it is too loaded a term to use more generally. Similarly, I do not use the Romany word *gorgio* or *gorge* for non-Travellers. As a non-Traveller, not only did I feel that it would be wrong to appropriate the word for my own use, but it also has pejorative overtones, and so I have opted for the more neutral term 'settled society'. This however leaves the problem that 'Travellers' are apparently defined by their nomadism, and 'settled society' by its sedentary nature, thus hiding both the fluid nature of settled society and the increasing tendency among Travellers to settle. It is therefore with an understanding that labels always obscure more than they reveal that I use these terms in this book.

Stereotypes

A review of the literature on Travellers from the twentieth century not only delineates a historiography but it also identifies the main themes that were to govern settled society's understanding of Travellers and their relationships with mainstream society. Given the fact that Traveller culture, even today, is largely non-literate, it is unsurprising that the literature became dominated by concerns of mainstream society: 'It has been claimed that literate people have history, while non-literate people have myth, but in the case of Gypsy-Gorgio history there is a fusion of the two. The literate tradition of the dominant society has assisted in myth-making'.[5]

The assumption behind almost all writings on Gypsies from the late nineteenth century up until the 1960s was that Travellers posed a challenge to modernity and civilisation. The majority of work produced in the first decades of the twentieth century was generated or inspired by members of the Gypsy Lore Society.[6] This was a group of amateurs and scholars intent on discovering and recording the language and culture of Gypsies before they disappeared. These 'gypsiologists' were attempting to capture a life apparently threatened by the twin evils of urbanisation and industrialisation. Thus, the 1889 edition of the *Journal of the Gypsy Lore Society* (*JGLS*) contained an article on the Irish Tinkers relating some of their customs 'because they *must* gradually disappear under the pressure of modern law' (emphasis added).[7]

In attempting to record this world gypsiologists in fact created another, one which bore little resemblance to the daily reality of Travellers. Their depiction of Gypsies stemmed almost wholly from their own fantasies and prejudices, emphasising the exotic, the foreign and the natural. Their equation of Gypsies as part of the natural world, in opposition to civilisation, is one key to understanding settled society's conceptualisation of nomadism in Britain:

> Why ... are we setting ourselves the impossible task of spoiling the Gypsies? ... they stand for the will of freedom, for friendship with nature, for the open air, for change and the sight of many lands; for all of us that is in protest against progress ... The Gypsies represent nature before civilisation ... He is the last romance left in the world.[8]

The idea that Gypsies lived at one with nature was taken as given. Descriptions of them and their camps firmly located them in rural settings, using imagery stressing their similarity to the animal kingdom:

> In summer time, these dusky wanderers might be seen encamped upon the commons, or on the sprawling borders of some

quiet road, beneath a sheltering hedge ... as free as the wild
bird ... gliding about the solitudes of the land, like half-tamed
panthers ... [9]

Such writing both emerged from and fed into the wider 'ruralist' literary genre of the first half of the century. It is important not
to overstate its impact on popular thought as 'the shift *towards* a
swooning nostalgia for the rural past takes place only among a small,
articulate but not necessarily influential avant-garde'.[10] Mandler has
rightly pointed to the limited nature of the 'back to the land' and
arts and crafts movements, and the preservation and conservation
societies,[11] but it was from their constituents that many of the supporters of Gypsies and their romantic lifestyle were drawn. Augustus
John, for example, was friends with some of the leading gypsiologists
of his time and became President of the Gypsy Lore Society and
claimed Gypsy ancestry. Over several summers he 'took to the open
road with his two women and numerous children packed into a couple
of caravans'.[12]

A main theme of the ruralist genre was the benefits gained
from escaping from civilisation and its cares, and conversely the joys
gained by becoming at one with nature. These writings, sometimes
by individuals with a Traveller heritage, glorified 'the tramp' as well
as Gypsies, assuming that being in the countryside and taking part
in 'simple' activities such as walking and caravanning, automatically
brought one closer to nature.[13]

What is striking about this conceptualisation of Gypsies is how
little it changed over time. The same language and ideas were used
by the writers of the mid- and late twentieth century,[14] with their
work depicting Gypsies as one of the remaining features of a vanish-
ing rural England. Croft-Cooke, for example, saw in them:

[a] certain primitive nobility which their ignorance and naiveté
do not blunt, the secretive ways of them – their sudden comings
and goings which are unaccountable even to themselves, their
personal grace, suppleness ... their sly yet noisy humour, their
almost apish gusto, their touch of the fantastic, the exotic, both
in their appearance and in their nature, which silhouettes them
against the grey background of industrial England.[15]

Countless articles in rural interest magazines, such as *Country
Life*, *The Border Magazine* and *Yorkshire Life Illustrated* persistently
propagated a rural and picturesque view of a Traveller lifestyle.[16]
Where Travellers were featured in photographs they were in quaint

rural settings, typically engaged in peg-making or basketry, with a bow-topped caravan in the background.[17]

Another central feature of writings on Travellers was the common imagery used and preconceptions of both supporters of Gypsies and those who sought to regulate nomadism. Detractors of Gypsies' lifestyle as much as supporters deployed ideas of 'race' and 'nature' in their writings:

> The Gypsies (who are on the lowest scale of culture) should be looked upon as a community of children of nature who as yet have but a superficial knowledge of civilisation and who will long defer its adoption ... Their volatile nature and inability to consider the future, their instability and restlessness, make any approach to even the lower forms of civilisation impossible ... they have everywhere either remained untouched by civilisation or have adopted merely its worst forms.[18]

As Sibley has observed, in both schools of thought there was a tendency to 'exclude peripheral groups from urban "civil" society' through depicting them 'not simply as a rural people but as a part of nature'. He sees this as resulting in a tendency to 'dehumanise' them, arguing that relegating them to the natural world was 'symptomatic of racist thinking'.[19] In this Gypsies were treated in a similar manner to Europe's colonial subjects, where relations between colonisers and colonised were governed by two beliefs: firstly, that with help and guidance those from less advanced civilisations could be brought up to the standard of the Christian West, and secondly, the idea of a permanent physical difference between races, often emphasised by describing the colonised as animal-like and close to nature. Stuart Hall has argued 'these two discourses, that of cultural differentialism and that of biological racism, were ... not two different systems, but "racism's two registers", and in many situations discourses of both were in play, the cultural slipping into the biological and vice versa'.[20]

The racialisation of Britain's travelling communities was given an extra twist by gypsiologists who constructed the theory that there was a decline in the racial purity of Gypsies as they increasingly mixed and married with degenerate members of the settled population. Gypsiologists developed a racial hierarchy which placed 'pure-blooded' Gypsies, who were believed to speak the best Romany, at the top;[21] followed by 'didikais', half-breeds, posh-rats, or pikies – groups with varying proportions of Gypsy blood depending on which source one reads; and 'mumpers' or 'hedge-crawlers', who were vagrants with no Romany ancestry, at the bottom. This implied that while Gypsies were somehow racially suited to nomadism and so were capable of maintaining traditional codes of conduct, with vagrant drop-outs and those of mixed blood this capacity was diminished or absent.

> To confuse the 'true' Gypsy with these *posrats* of diluted blood was presented as a grave error that led to much injustice being directed towards the clean-living Romany. The latter, declining in numbers as the century progressed, were superior in manners, morals and occupations to their degenerate and impoverished 'mumply-brothers'. These half-breeds were said to have inherited all the vices of the Romany and the *Gaujo* but none of their virtues.[22]

For gypsiologists anxious to discover a Golden Age and a pure Gypsy culture, this outlook allowed them to pursue their pet theories, with any contradictory findings dismissed as the result of cultural pollution and miscegenation.[23] Such 'scapegoating' enabled gypsiologists to distance themselves from the squalid, urban Traveller encampments that existed around all Britain's major cities and any other elements that impinged on romantic notions of a rural Gypsy idyll.

The tension between the actual lives of Travellers and their popular representation of the rural picturesque Gypsy was played out in the twentieth century. This had a major impact on policy development as well as on popular imagination. In part this was the result of a lack of information held by the state about Britain's travelling communities. In 1956 preliminary enquiries on the part of a Welsh Office researcher found it 'puzzling' that it did 'not appear possible to obtain particulars of the nomadic population from the Registrar General'.[24] He was reduced to writing to Dora Yates at the Gypsy Lore Society in an attempt to establish the number of Travellers in Glamorgan and Monmouthshire.[25]

The reliance of the state on pseudo-scholarly writings and gypsiologists to inform their position towards Travellers meant there was often a very thin line between the 'state' and popular imagination. This allowed two key stereotypes to become central in mediating settled society's relationship with Travellers: the idea of the 'pure-blooded Gypsy' and the idea that a 'true Gypsy lifestyle' was incompatible with modern society. As Acton observed, the stereotypes developed by gypsiologists and others provided the state with 'an ideological tool' to justify repression, for while gypsiologists were 'fortunate in almost never meeting a Gypsy who is not "true", "the authorities" tend to claim they never meet one who is. They classify every Gypsy they meet as not being "true Gypsies" ... they are only dealing with mongrelised imitations'[26] and treated them accordingly.

The state

That Travellers presented a problem for the modern, bureaucratic state was accepted by members of the British elite:

> We cannot as a nation treat the Gypsies as though they did not exist ... They cannot be exterminated and if they disappeared their loss would be severely felt as they provide a reservoir of labour ... on the other hand ... they are generally unpopular and no one wants them to settle for long periods in any given neighbourhood.[27]

Travellers were seen as an anachronism with their perceived untidy habits, lack of regular employment and employer, and freedom from allegiance to union, church or locality. They clearly posed a question to a state where political citizenship was based on constituency residence, and social citizenship on sustained community participation within a narrow geographical context.[28] Travellers might be perceived as having an intrinsically problematic relationship with the state, but this was dynamic and historically as well as geographically contingent. Stereotypes of Travellers may have been remarkably consistent over the course of the twentieth century and throughout much of Europe, but the experiences of British Travellers were markedly different from their counterparts in mainland Europe.[29] This indicates that their lives were governed as much by the structure and ambitions of the state within which they lived as by the stereotypes that often mediated their interactions with those structures.

Over the course of the century the nature of government and understandings of citizenship shifted profoundly, and by definition so too did Travellers' relationship with the state. Painted in broad terms, the expansion of the state in the twentieth century, as it affected Travellers, might be seen as forming three waves. The first was a continuation of nineteenth-century efforts to temper the impact of laissez-faire capitalism on the environment and society through regulation and control, for example, of employment, public health and related behaviour. The second wave shifted the role of the state into more proactive efforts to improve the lives of its (particularly working-class) citizens, and was broadly associated with measures such as the 1908 Children's Act, the various national insurance acts, as well as inter-war legislation, and the reforms of 1944–48 that have been seen as creating the 'welfare state'.[30] This expansion can be measured in quantitative terms: in the 1900s public authorities spent less than 8 per cent of gross domestic product, but by the 1960s this had risen to over 50 per cent.[31] The third wave of expansion saw the state moving into regulating the attitudes and practices of its citizens towards minority (particularly ethnic minority) groups, initially through the means of race relations legislation, but by the 1990s also through the European Union.[32]

These waves of expansion must be seen as overlaying one another, adding tiers of state activity and new areas of influence over the lives of citizens. As with the rest of the population, Travellers were affected by all three waves: through public health measures, planning laws and the regulation of land use; through the expansion of education, public housing and welfare measures; and through the potential for increased legal protection and targeted services under specific discrimination legislation as well as more general anti-racist and multicultural policies. The consequences of these different areas of state action were not equal. Arguably Travellers were most affected by measures that had the greatest negative impact on their lifestyle and culture, and least affected by those with the most positive potential.

Within a general expansion of 'the state' can be traced a fluctuating balance of power between central and local government.[33] The inter-war period is often seen as the 'zenith of responsible local government',[34] with the remit of county and county borough councils in particular being vastly wider than in the later twentieth century. However, their expansion was by no means unproblematic, with active councils often coming into conflict with a parsimonious Ministry of Health, or inactivity on the part of some local authorities leading to patchy provision or an absence of certain services.[35]

The reforms of 1944–48 in some ways confirmed a trend of centralisation of power that was a feature of government during the Second World War, with legislation taking away some key services from local authorities, for example through the creation of the National Health Service. Even new or expanded services under council control, such as social services, housing and education, demanded certain minimum standards of services which were tied to Whitehall approval and grants. The move towards centralisation of power and decision-making continued in the 1980s and 1990s, but crucially for Travellers certain areas, particularly planning, education and housing, continued to retain large elements of local autonomy.

An expansion of the state must not be confused with harmony of intention and purpose between central and local government. Removed from day-to-day pressures from local taxpayers and from the need to balance service development with income, central government was typically more able to develop a vision of impartiality and equality than councils who had to deal with the nuts and bolts of delivery. Threaded through this book is the theme of ratepayer prejudice and consequent local authority reluctance in extending to Travellers those services envisaged by central government as being for all British citizens.

The competing priorities of different levels of the state were often further complicated by tensions and contradictions between the different functions and duties of government. This was most notable in the closing years of the century when race relations and human rights legislation, along with targeted education and health services, delivered by a council might often conflict with the aims of planning and development control officers.

With the extension of government at all levels came new understandings of what it meant to be both a civil servant and a citizen. State expansion was supported by a rapid increase in the professional sector and the consequent emergence of a professional ethic and more objective standards of service. This new public domain was 'characterised by the ethos of duty and service, by a genuine commitment to professionalism … [inspiring] trust and confidence in citizens at large'.[36] As evidence from the Home Office and the Ministry of Health in the years up to 1939 shows (Chapter 2), civil servants took the practice of impartiality seriously, for example through refusing to confirm local powers that specifically targeted Travellers as a group.

This new ethos has been depicted by Marquand as spilling over into ideas about the reciprocal duties of individual citizens, 'necessitating that they suspend the pursuit of their immediate wants, and instead have regard for the public interest more generally'.[37] The development of the idea of the active participatory citizen found its feet during the Second World War when even those not in active service were expected to contribute to the common cause in a myriad of ways. Individuals or groups who were seen as having failed to pull their weight were vilified and marginalised: 'increasingly, the British character was being defined as the responsible active citizen with both duties to the state and rights deriving from those duties ... shirkers and black marketers were singled out in talks, features and plays as undermining the communal national effort'.[38]

Yet Neill has argued citizenship as an idea generally received little attention from either politicians or intellectuals. For the immediate post-war decades he states that despite the publication of Marshall's work on citizenship,[39] there was little debate as 'British society seemed so clearly united ... it appeared superfluous to raise the question of what in fact defined a British citizen'. He goes on to state that 'beyond a vague contractualism that implied that the state had an obligation to secure its subjects' minimum welfare, on the basis that they had collectively paid into a common insurance fund', there was little interest in the subject.[40] Beveridge had certainly promoted this attitude to citizenship during discussions of his proposed welfare reforms.[41] However, as I discuss in Chapter 6, it was precisely this contractualist assumption that was problematic for Travellers. Perceived as failing to contribute to national insurance specifically and modern life more generally, their status as citizens and their rights in relation to the state were questioned.

In this and other ways Travellers did not relate to the state simply as unmarked citizens, but as part of a minority population and marginal group. Bauman has pointed to the role of modernity in attacking particularity and difference, and its tendency to promote the assimilation or extermination of minorities.[42] While he has discussed the cultural and ideological ambivalence created by the presence of minorities within a nation state,[43] possibly of more importance for Travellers was the physical ambivalence they presented. Police and judicial procedure, planning controls and sanitary regulation, welfare entitlement and education were all based on a presumption of permanent residence. Such developments were grounded in a fundamental assumption of inclusivity – that it was neither desirable nor possible to exclude oneself from their grasp. Individuals or groups who challenged these assumptions through recourse to a different lifestyle were depicted as social failures. In the process racial and environmental theories of nomadism were often simultaneously mobilised and conflated:

> It may be that [the vagrant] has a bad hereditary, exhibiting itself in congenital laziness and workshyness beyond his power

to rectify ... he may be a hereditary wanderer as, for instance, the tinker or Gypsy. He may suffer from mental or physical degeneracy comprising feeble-mindedness, imbecility, mental deficiency or the lesser defects of mental peculiarity or excessive dullness. He may be of dissolute or drunken habits, he may be actively criminal, or he may merely have failed to develop sufficient personal resources or initiative to enable him to hold his own in a competitive world.[44]

Nomadic lifestyles were seen as the result of failure and social inadequacy, not as a positive and desirable choice. In the words of one bureaucrat, 'the problem we are here dealing with is that of the flotsam and jetsam which has failed to fit into the ordinary framework of society'.[45] The automatic equation of living on the road with delinquency was to have a major impact on the way in which Travellers were treated by both law enforcement agencies and welfare initiatives.

Reactions to the persistence of Traveller culture in the face of an encroaching state went to the heart of Britain's image of itself as a tolerant country, and its belief of its impartial treatment of minorities.[46] Bauman sees the response of modern states as being an 'offer of assimilation *luring* its victims into a state of chronic ambivalence with the bait of admission tickets to the world free from the stigma of otherness'. In contrast to previous attempts to deal with minorities:

> What made the standing invitation particularly alluring and morally disarming was the fact that it came in the disguise of benevolence and tolerance ... a part of the *liberal* political programme ... Under the policy of assimilation, tolerant treatment of *individuals* was inextricably linked to intolerance aimed at collectivities, their ways of life, their values and, above all, their value-legitimating powers.[47]

Therefore, within a study of British Travellers lies an examination of wider historical questions concerning the nature of the state, minorities and modernity. The expansion of welfare provision became one major forum for the playing out of tensions. Revisionist accounts of the development of the welfare state have pointed to its problematic relationship with minorities, particularly the way in which it tended to confirm or exaggerate, rather than abolish, disadvantage.[48]

Critiques have exposed the way in which the aims of welfare and social agencies reveal deeper conflicts between the interests of a liberal state and marginal groups within its borders. As Liegeois has noted, part of the general characteristic of European states to move away from outright discrimination towards assimilation has been a tendency to assert control over lifestyles. This has been 'by means of more and more detailed regulations', which may in themselves be contradictory, such as legislation limiting the duration and location of stopping places versus the legal obligation on children to attend school. This created what he terms a 'web' in which Travellers were caught and for whom 'these laws [were] mutually reinforcing in their negative effects'.[49]

Within this context welfare was often deployed with the aim of achieving the 'normalisation' of persons 'perceived as marginal or deviant', but that at the same time 'the decision to assimilate has never reduced the desire to exclude', with the result being 'not integration but marginalisation' in the spheres of employment, schooling and accommodation. Travellers, in this formulation, never became full members of the state, but rather remained as twilight citizens.[50]

Traveller agency

The trouble with the term 'impact' is its connotation of passivity. No one will deny that … minority groups have been the victims of strong and perhaps irresistible pressures. Yet they have not merely endured impacts. To suggest such helpless passivity is as much a historical error as it is an insult.[51]

The formation of the Gypsy Council in 1966 marked the birth of the first active pressure group containing significant numbers of Travellers. It was launched on the back of a wave of active resistance to a number of concerted and often brutal local authority evictions.[52] This does not mean that up to this date Travellers had been submissive receptacles for the actions of the state and settled society: 'We should be careful in portraying these groups as criminals, marginals and beggars, it is equally important not to end up at the other extreme. We have to realise that the people who are hidden behind these labels were not only, or mainly, (passive) victims of repression and persecution'.[53]

One of the central ways in which Travellers have succeeded in resisting the influences of mainstream society has been through the persistence of their forms of economic activity, specifically self-employment and use of family networks in exploiting work opportunities and providing labour. While Travellers' economic activities required them to interact with non-Travellers, this typically was very much on their own terms. Secure in the knowledge that an income could be won without recourse to the formal labour market, Travellers were able to bypass two of the main routes to socialisation in modern society – the education system and the workplace with its attendant culture.

Paradoxically, while nomadism, another key feature of traditional Traveller culture, has often been a central cause of conflict with the state and settled society, it has also been one of the main tools by which they were able to maintain their independent identity. Research on the methods of resistance by groups and individuals with little social or political capital has attested to the importance of evasion as a technique of opposition, often more so than overt conflict.[54]

Central to the practice of evasion, at least among nomadic Travellers, was the ability to 'move on' in order to avoid confrontation with the authorities, settled communities or other Traveller families whenever there was potential for conflict. The case of a local medical officer of health boasting that the best way to get rid of Travellers in the district was 'to press them to send their children to school'[55] is illuminating. On one level it was an example of the state cynically using its tools to harass Travellers, but on another it demonstrated the means by which Travellers maintained their separate identity and culture in the face of an encroaching state. Such evasion was a powerful technique in avoiding state interference. The boundedness of local authority influence, limited as it was by county or other administrative borders, worked in Travellers' favour. Once outside an official's geographical area of responsibility, Travellers dropped from the view of a council that seldom had either the resources or inclination to pursue the matter.

Since the 1970s the growing shortage of stopping places in combination with a inadequate number of pitches on official sites has had serious consequences within Traveller communities. Those with sought-after official pitches were reluctant to lose them by moving away. Not only did this reduce their ability to evade agents of the state, such as school attendance officers, but also increased the likelihood of conflict with other Traveller families whom they might have avoided given the opportunity.

It has not simply been through avoidance strategies that Travellers have retained control over their lives. They also responded to the increasing constraints imposed upon them in twentieth-century

Britain through the manipulation of settled society's stereotypes and preconceptions of the meaning of a 'Gypsy' identity.

One way in which a 'Gypsy' stereotype was positively asserted was when carrying out economic practices where a 'Gypsy' identity lent a certain authority to proceedings, most commonly perhaps with fortune-telling at fairs or as part of door-to-door selling. In other cases the perception that Gypsies have 'second sight' was deployed as part of evading trouble, as in situations where horses were caught illicitly grazing:

> We might say that they'd got through the gap on their own, but sometimes it didn't work and he'd [the farmer] send for the police. When the police arrived he'd demand we paid him £2 or £3, and we had to hand it over. It was a lot of money and we didn't like parting with it, so sometimes one of our old ladies would start up a weird noise … and she'd get out a crystal ball and look into it. She'd howl about three times, and a few others would go and look in the ball, then they'd look at the farmer, then at the ground, not saying anything. The farmer would get jittery and change colour, and at the same time a good, respectful Gypsy would go up to him and say: 'It's in your interest to give us this cash back – if you don't you'll be looking back over your shoulder all your life'.[56]

On a wider level Acton has pointed to the practice of claiming to have 'pure Gypsy blood' as a means of asserting an individual's right to travel, while 'scapegoating' other travelling communities: "'I'm a real Gypsy/Traveller/Romani, and we don't do that, only the (ethnic category name with pejorative overtones)'". He observed that the effect of this 'transference of blame' was to divert the hostility of the accuser away from that particular individual to an absent outsider group which both parties could agree was fundamentally incapable of maintaining a nomadic lifestyle. While in the short term this was 'an attractive strategy for the individual Traveller', it was not without its shortcomings, as it served to confirm racialised definitions of Travellers, equating a right to travel with spurious definitions of blood purity.[57]

Travellers deployed negative stereotypes as much as superficially more positive 'romantic' images of their way of life in order to gain advantage at the expense of both the authorities and settled society. An account of resistance to an eviction in Epping Forest from the early twentieth century shows an interesting mix of overt and more subversive forms of resistance. The group of Travellers in

question decided to resist the eviction by 'chain[ing] their wives and
children to the caravan wheels'. When the police arrived and found
what the Gypsies had done, and 'saw there was likely to be a big fight
... it was decided to offer the caravan dwellers ... some pieces of
gold, which some of the Gypsies readily seized, the organized resistance soon broke down and soon the forest was cleared'. Some of
those who had received money bought land in Essex where a 'certain field was put up in plots for auction and the Gypsies bid for
most of the outside plots, knowing that the inside ones would remain unsold if surrounded by Gypsies, and the land would be useful
to them for grazing purposes'.[58]

Such self-assertion through a manipulation of settled society's
negative images of Travellers was a consistent theme throughout the
century. From the 1960s it was reinforced by the increasing social
and geographical isolation of Travellers. The location of both official sites and temporary stopping places on peri-urban land, often
far away from residential areas, reduced contact between Travellers
and the settled population. At the same time, increased harassment
from councils, the police and local residents caused Travellers to stop
in larger groups: 'if three or four families moved onto a bit of land,
they'd get pushed around ... so we started to pull on places in our
hundreds. That way they had to tread a bit more carefully.[59] The
combination of large concentrations of Travellers and geographical
isolation commonly turned sites into perceived ghettos, which the
settled population avoided unless absolutely necessary: Travellers
may have been vilified, but increasingly they were also feared and
consequently left alone.

> Toughness. That, more than anything, was what we knew them
> for. They may have been a minority group, like the Asians were
> in our youth, but no gangs took up 'gypo-bashing', or shouted
> abuse across the street to them. The truth was that we were
> scared of the gypsies, both as a race and as individuals. They
> were usually bigger, stronger and better fighters than us and
> they lived outside the laws and world that was ours.[60]

New perspectives

It was not until the 1960s and the rise of the Traveller activist movement and the Gypsy Council, coupled with changes in academic
methodology and theory, that stereotypes of Travellers began to be

challenged from within the academic establishment. Activist-sociologists such as Thomas Acton,[61] the anthropologist Judith Okely[62] and the historian David Mayall[63] were key in challenging traditional views of Travellers and in formulating new ways of articulating their experiences. In particular they rejected the view of Travellers as a separate rural group, culturally, economically and genealogically sealed off from the sedentary population.

Okely in particular has stressed the importance of the concept of 'commercial nomadism' – the fact that Travellers throughout their history sought out economic niches that were difficult for a settled worker to fill, but were viable in a nomadic context. Because past writers tended to stress only the most visible economic activities, and those which fitted into their preconceptions of Gypsy activities – peg selling, fortune telling, tinkering and casual agricultural work – the assumption was that Gypsies were adversely affected by mechanisation, mass production and the introduction of plastics. However, Okely stressed that Travellers' skills and traditions in work lay 'not in the content of their occupations, but in their form'.[64] The values of self-employment, avoidance of wage labour, occupational flexibility and the use of the informal economy have been the key features of Traveller economic activity for centuries. As a result, the decline of traditional rural occupations did not shatter Traveller identity, but rather Travellers have responded by moving into different fields.

Okely's analysis, supported by the work of the historian David Mayall, also undermined the myth of the inherent rurality of Gypsies.[65] Mayall's analysis of the nineteenth century, backed up by work by Sibley,[66] showed contemporary writers were well aware of urban and peri-urban Traveller encampments but that they did not accept that this was the Gypsies' true habitat. The urbanisation of the Travellers may have increased their visibility but did nothing to persuade commentators that they had sound economic reasons for being located there. However, as Travellers' incomes were linked to servicing the settled population, their lifestyle was intimately bound up with the wider population. Consequently, rapid industrialisation and urbanisation of the majority of the populace also resulted in an urban Traveller population. Gypsies have been portrayed as helpless in the face of industrialisation, modern technology and urban advance,[67] yet this was primarily the result of the insistence on romanticised, rural images of Travellers, rather than on any true understanding of their position in the economy.

An acceptance of Travellers' roles in the economy as commercial nomads removed the importance of a hypothesis of exotic origin in explaining the cultural and economic survival of Gypsies in the twentieth century. However, there has been a tension between this approach and that taken by more activist-oriented work, which stressed the ethnic status of Travellers, including their roots in an Indian diaspora. In the context of race relations legislation and a multiculturalist perspective which asserts the need for the rights of ethnic minorities, some writers have continued to emphasise the ethnic distinctiveness of Travellers in order to seek their protection and to assert their rights.[68]

Dutch-based scholars have generated perspectives that usefully shed light on Traveller–state relations in Britain, taking the debate away from ethnicity-based analysis.[69] Lucassen *et al* have demonstrated, through their 'stigmatisation perspective', the significance of stereotypes in the treatment of nomadic people. They stressed the importance of social construction both in the formation of minorities and in their treatment, and emphasised the role of the state in this process.[70] This perspective demands a subtle approach to state policy and attitude, requiring an analysis of the differing approaches of central and local authorities.[71]

Consequently, in this book I explore the role of stereotypes and their impact on state attitudes and policy, as well as the importance of the agency of Travellers themselves. The book also highlights the lessons Traveller history can offer in understanding modern state expansion, notably the extent of its ambitions and inherent tensions between different levels of government.

Advances made in academia and in some councils' Traveller services in recent years have largely failed to filter through to popular consciousness, and the tabloid media in particular has been central to perpetuating racist and outdated stereotypes of Travellers. In the closing section of the book I consider how it is that Travellers have lost out in 'multicultural' Britain, and indeed have seemed to lose their 'ethnic' status in the process.

Notes

1   D. Mayall, *Gypsy Travellers in nineteenth century society* (Cambridge, 1988).
2   C. Clark, 'Who are the Gypsies and Travellers of Britain?', in C. Clark and M. Greenfield, *Here to stay: The Gypsies and Travellers of Britain* (Hatfield, 2006), 11. The best overview of the debate is contained in D.

Mayall, *Gypsy identities, 1500 to 2000. From Egipcyans and moon-men to the ethnic Romany* (London and New York, 2004).

3 J. P. Liegeois and N. Gheorghe, *Roma/Gypsies: A European minority* (London, 1995), 6.

4 L. Lucassen, W. Willems and A. Cottaar, *Gypsies and other itinerant groups: A socio-historical approach* (Amsterdam, 1998), 2.

5 J. Okely, *The Traveller-Gypsies* (Cambridge, 1983), 2.

6 The Society was formed in 1888 under David MacRitchie of Edinburgh, and later became based at the University of Liverpool.

7 D. MacRitchie, 'Irish tinkers and their language', *Journal of the Gypsy Lore Society*, 1:6 (1908), 351.

8 A. Symons, 'In praise of Gypsies', *JGLS*, 1:4 (1908), 295–9.

9 E. Waugh, 'Children of the Wilderness', in J. Sampson (ed.), *The wind on the heath: A Gypsy anthology* (London, 1930), 12. See also D. Yates, *My Gypsy days: Recollections of a Romani rawnie* (London, 1953), 17; and Symons, 'In praise of Gypsies', 296.

10 P. Mandler, 'Against "Englishness": English culture and the limits to rural nostalgia, 1850–1940', *Royal Historical Society Transactions*, 7 (1997), 160, original emphasis. This piece provides a useful résumé of the recent debates surrounding the idea of Englishness.

11 This is not to argue that they had no impact on wider trends. For an analysis of the composition and impact of the folk movement, see G. Boyes, *The imagined village: Culture, ideology and the English folk revival* (Manchester, 1993). For the link between ruralism and town planning see S. Heathorn, 'An English paradise to regain? Ebenezer Howard, the Town and Country Planning Association and English ruralism', *Rural History, Economy, Society, Culture*, 11:1 (2000), 113–28.

12 Eric Rowan quoted in A. Sampson, *The scholar Gypsy: The quest for a family secret* (London, 1997), 61.

13 M. A. Crowther, 'The tramp', in R. Porter (ed.), *Myths of the English* (Cambridge, 1992). For examples of writings by Travellers in this genre see X. Petulengro, *Romany hints for hikers; by Gipsy Petulengro* (London, 1936); G. B. Evens, *A Romany on the trail* (Epworth, 1942): and *A Romany in the country* (Epworth, 1944).

14 F. I. Cowles, *Gypsy caravan* (London, 1948); R. Croft-Cooke, *The moon in my pocket: Life with the Romanies* (London, 1948); J. de Baraclai Levy (London, 1953); *As Gypsies wander*; R. Farre, *Time from the world* (London, 1962); I. Fonseca, *Bury me standing: The Gypsies and their journey* (New York, 1995); C. Hughes, *West with the Tinkers: A journey through Wales with vagrants* (London, 1954); P. McEvoy, *The gorse and the briar* (London, 1938); J. Phelan, *We follow the roads* (London, 1949).

15 Croft-Cooke, *Moon in my pocket*, 2.

16 For example R. Church, 'The raggle-taggle Gypsies', *Green Life* (1945), 92–3, and B. L. Burman, 'Gypsies: Free, romantic, mysterious', *Reader's Digest*, 70 (1957), 26 and 32.

17 See *The Countryman*, 41:1 (1950), for two such pictures.

18   A. Thesleff, 'Report on the Gypsy problem', trans H. Ehrenborg, *JGLS*, 5:2 (1911), 83–5 and continued in *JGLS*, 6:4 (1911), 266.

19   D. Sibley, 'Persistence or change? Conflicting interpretations of peripheral minorities', *Environment and Planning D: Society and Space*, 4 (1986), 65.

20   Quoted in C. Hall, *Civilising subjects: Metropole and colony in the English imagination, 1830–1867* (Cambridge, 1992), 17. For a gendered perspective on this see E. Said, *Orientalism* (Harmondsworth, 1979), 188; and M. Yegenoglu, *Colonial fantasies: Towards a feminist reading of Orientalism* (Cambridge, 1998).

21   J. Sampson, *The dialect of the Welsh Gypsies* (n.p., 1907).

22   Mayall, *Gypsy Travellers*, 78.

23   See Sampson, *Dialect*.

24   The National Archives, Kew (hereafter TNA), BD 11/3777, memo by Prosser to Barbara Adams, 13 June 1956. For the patchy efforts of the Registrar General to include Travellers in census returns see TNA, RG 19/107.

25   TNA, BD 11/3777, letter from Prosser to Yates, 14 June 1956.

26   T. Acton, *Gypsy politics and social change: The development of ethnic ideology and pressure politics among British Gypsies from Victorian reformism to Romany nationalism* (London, 1974), 84.

27   TNA, HLG 71/903, Bishop of Gloucester to Bevan, 16 October 1950.

28   D. Robbins, 'Citizenship and nationhood in Britain', Working Paper, New Ethnicities Unit, University of East London, May 1995. For a mainland European perspective see R. Brubaker, *Citizenship and nationhood in France and Germany* (Harvard, 1992).

29   A. Cottaar, L. Lucassen and W. Willems, 'Justice or injustice? A survey of government policy towards Gypsies and caravan dwellers in western Europe in the nineteenth and twentieth centuries', *Immigrants and Minorities*, 11:1 (1992), 56. For an exploration of stereotypes in German literature see D. Strauss, 'Anti-Gypsyism in German society and literature', in S. Tebbutt (ed.), *Sinti and Roma: Gypsies in German-speaking society and literature* (New York and Oxford, 1998), 81–90.

30   Inter-war measures included the 1918 Maternity and Child Welfare Act, the establishment of the Schools Medical Service in 1919, the 1921 Tuberculosis Act, the 1929 Local Government Act, and the creation of the Unemployment Assistance Board in 1934. The key reforms of 1944–48 were the 1944 Education Act, the 1945 Family Allowance and National Health Service Acts, the 1946 National Insurance Act, and the 1948 National Assistance Act.

31   Quoted in J. Harris, 'Society and the state in twentieth century Britain', in F. M. L. Thompson (ed.), *The Cambridge social history of Britain, 1750–1950, vol. III: Social agencies and institutions* (Cambridge, 1990), 64.

32   The 1976 Race Relations Act and the Race Relations (Amendment) Act of 2000, the 1998 Human Rights Act and the European Conven-

Introduction 23

33 S. Szreter, 'A central role for local government? The example of late Victorian Britain', *History and Policy*, May (2002), www.historyandpolicy.org/archive/policy-paper-01.html. For the mediation of central-local relations via the means of central government funding see G. C. Baugh, 'Government grants in aid of the rates in England and Wales, 1889–1990', *Historical Research*, 65 (1992), 215–37.
34 J. M. Mackintosh, *Trends of Opinion about Public Health* (London, 1953), 131.
35 B. Taylor, J. Stewart, and M. Powell, 'Central and Local Government and the Provision of Municipal Medicine, 1919–1939', *English Historical Review*, 122:496, 397–426.
36 D. Marquand, *The decline of the public: The hollowing out of citizenship* (Cambridge, 2004), discussed in E. Neill, 'Conceptions of citizenship in twentieth century Britain', *Twentieth Century British History*, 17:3 (2006), 424–38. For the rise of professionalism generally see H. Perkin, *The rise of professional society: England since* 1880 (London and New York, 1990), and within the civil service specifically see J. Pellew, *The Home Office, 1848–1914: From clerks to bureaucrats* (London, 1982) and C. Bellamy, *Administering central and local government relations, 1871–1919: The Local Government Board in its fiscal and cultural context* (Manchester, 1988).
37 Marquand, *Decline of the public*, 38.
38 S. Nicholas, 'From John Bull to John Citizen', in R. Weight and A. Beach (eds), *The right to belong, Citizenship and national identity in Britain, 1940–60* (London, 1998), 45.
39 See T. H. Marshall, *Citizenship and social class and other essays* (London, 1950).
40 Neill, 'Conceptions of citizenship in twentieth century Britain', 424–5.
41 J. Stapleton, 'Citizenship versus patriotism in twentieth century England', *The Historical Journal*, 48: 1 (2005), 170.
42 See Z. Bauman, *Modernity and the Holocaust* (Cambridge, 1989) and *Modernity and Ambivalence* (Cambridge, 1991).
43 Bauman, *Ambivalence*, Chapter 4.
44 *Report of the Departmental Committee on Vagrancy in Scotland*, 1936, Cmd. 5194, 13–14.
45 TNA, BD/11/377, internal Welsh Office memo, 6 April 1956.
46 For more a general consideration of this theme see C. Holmes, *A tolerant country? Immigrants, refugees and minorities in Britain* (London, 1991); K. Lunn (ed.), *Hosts, immigrants and minorities: Historical responses to newcomers in British society 1870–1914* (New York, 1980); and Weight and Beach (eds), *The right to belong*.
47 Bauman, *Ambivalence*, 102, 106–7. Original emphasis.
48 C. Pierson, *Beyond the welfare state? The new political economy of welfare* (Pennsylvania, 1998); I. Illich, *The right to useful employment* (London, 1978); P. Squires, *Anti-social policy: Welfare, ideology and the disciplinary*

state (Hemel Hempstead, 1990).

49 Liegeois, *School provision for ethnic minorities: The Gypsy paradigm* (Hatfield, 1998), 41.
50 *Ibid.*, 47.
51 H. Brody, *Maps and dreams* (London, 1981), 247, quoted in Sibley, 'Persistence or change?', 69.
52 Acton, *Gypsy politics*, 163.
53 Lucassen, Willems and Cottaar (eds), *Gypsies and other itinerant groups*, 8.
54 For accounts of the agency of the oppressed see J. C. Scott, *Weapons of the weak: Everyday forms of peasant resistance* (New Haven, CT and London, 1985); E. P. Thompson, *The making of the English working class* (London, 1963); P. Fryer, *Aspects of Black history* (London, 1993); Lunn (ed.), *Hosts, immigrants and minorities*; L. Tabili, 'The construction of racial difference in twentieth century Britain: The Special Restriction (Coloured Alien Seamen) Order, 1925', *Journal of British Studies*, 33 (1994), 54–98.
55 'Van dwellers', *Barnsley Chronicle* (22 May 1926).
56 Jack Locke quoted in J. Davies, *Tales of the old Gypsies* (n.p., 1999), 71.
57 Acton, *Gypsy politics*, 80–1.
58 A. West, 'Memories of a life's work: My friends the Gypsies', *London City Mission* (1937), 167.
59 J. Stockins, *On the cobbles: The life of a bare-knuckle Gypsy warrior* (Edinburgh, 2000), 49–50.
60 M. Knight and M. King in Stockins, *On the cobbles*, 15.
61 While a student at Oxford in the 1960s Thomas Acton worked in the summer schools for Travellers and became involved in the formation of the Gypsy Council.
62 Judith Okely lived on Travellers sites in the early 1970s and charted the impact of the 1968 Caravan Sites' Act.
63 Mayall, *Gypsy Travellers*.
64 Okely, *The Traveller-Gypsies*, 33.
65 Mayall, *Gypsy Travellers*.
66 Sibley, 'Persistence or change?', 62–4.
67 For example, see W. Kornblum and P. Litcher, 'Urban Gypsies and the culture of poverty', *Urban Life and Culture*, Spring (1972), 239–52.
68 For a detailed discussion of this see Mayall, *Gypsy identities*, Chapter 7.
69 Lucassen, Willems and Cottaar (eds), *Gypsies and other itinerant groups*.
70 *Ibid.*, 9.
71 For an expansion of this theme see Cottar, Lucassen and Willems, 'Justice or Injustice?'

Part I

The early twentieth century and wartime

1

Travellers' lives, 1900–45

The popular image of Gypsies in Britain, propagated by gypsiologists and other writers, was of a people who turned up out of the blue, camped on commons or byways in their bow-topped caravan, grazed horses, sold pegs and perhaps 'tinkering', 'here today and gone tomorrow'. This conception painted Britain's nomads as irredeemably rural, separate from the modern world and inexplicable.

In this chapter I show how this ruralist image of Travellers has only ever been one part of the story of their lives in modern Britain. Using Okely's conception of 'commercial nomadism' as central to understanding the movement and culture of Travellers, I show how the routes and employment strategies taken by travelling families had their own logic. They often aspired to be stationary in the winter, or for even longer periods, and despite appearances, Travellers were intimately tied to the concerns and trends of settled society. This is made clear in the final section of the chapter which deals with the Second World War.

More than for the latter half of the twentieth century, the years up to 1945 suffer from a lack of sources, with evidence particularly from a Traveller perspective being very limited.[1] In places, therefore, descriptions are based on perhaps only one or two individual accounts. In these cases they may be taken as illustrative of particular experiences which may have a wider resonance, rather than typical of the lives of Travellers more generally.

Patterns of nomadism

As Mayall has observed, itinerancy and migrancy were a way of life for large numbers of the population in the nineteenth century,[2] with

Travellers making up only one part of Britain's travelling population. Jan Lucassen's study on migrant labour in Europe between 1600 and 1900 demonstrates how mobility, especially seasonal labour, was functional and an essential element within the labour market and therefore for economic development. By concentrating on the function of the services provided by itinerant workers, Lucassen's work shows how migrant working cannot in general be seen as a cloak for begging or thievery, as was often believed. Hawkers and pedlars, for example, specialised in areas with a weak infrastructure and economically backward conditions,[3] while certain crops demanded intensive labour over a very short period of time for harvesting, which could not be provided by the local labour force alone. Within the wider migrant workforce of Europe, Travellers were 'made visible by their choice to live in tents or caravans which enable[d] them to move around *with* their families'.[4] In doing this, Travellers were travelling not simply to find employment, but as a way of life. Families were not only on the road to accompany a working male head of household. On the contrary, a key feature of Traveller's economic activities was the family nature of much of their work. While men dominated certain activities, notably dealing, women were central to money-making activities, commonly hawking goods and taking part in agricultural work. Children were expected to take part in field work, collect the raw materials for hawking and learn basket making and other skills alongside their parents:

> My mother had to support us with only her basket of pegs for sale, and her lace to sell to the Gorgios. As for me, I used to help out too. I used to go with my brother, with my father's pony and trap, and collect watercress, mushrooms and other things to sell ... My sister, she sold violets, snowdrops, and primroses and other wild flowers.[5]

The importance of children in the Traveller economy, and the emphasis placed on learning skills integral to this way of life from an early age, often placed Travellers at odds with mainstream society and the state over the issue of education.

Contemporary accounts of Traveller's economic activities indicate a wide range of occupations and services performed by Travellers. These included what are thought of as 'traditional' activities such as fruit picking, horse and donkey dealing, peg making and hawking, knife grinding, umbrella and chair mending, fortune telling and working the fairs. However, it is important to sound a note of caution. The difficulty in relying on outside observers in detailing the occupations of Travellers is the tendency to record only these visible 'Gypsy' occupations, where being identifiably 'Gypsy' was useful as a marker of legitimacy or expertise. There were times when a Traveller identity could be inhibiting and therefore might be hidden. It is largely only through personal accounts of individual Travellers that we know of times when they worked in mills or factories, joined the army, or otherwise took employment where their identity was invisible.[6] In some cases Travellers were able to integrate factory work into their lifestyle. For instance, at Bobbin Mill in Perthshire up to the 1920s, Travellers engaged in piecework at the mill, while being permitted to camp in its environs.[7]

Central to Travellers' economic activities were the twin tenets of flexibility and self-employment. Together these allowed Travellers to maximise the opportunities and minimise the precariousness of life out of the economic mainstream and to ensure that they remained in control of income generation. Economic activity may have required interaction with the settled population, but Travellers aimed to ensure that it was conducted as far as possible on their own terms. As a result, piece work rather than an hourly wage was preferred when engaged in agricultural labour, as Travellers could control how long a task took; for example, through using children and other relatives to complete the work. Equally, the flexibility of hawking and dealing were favoured over regular waged employment: 'January we sold firewood. And when we weren't selling firewood, flowers or wool, there was the hens and the hoss [horse] trade. We used to break horses too'.[8]

> All around the house were stacks of old iron and special sorts of timber collected by Johnny on his tinkering rounds. There was also a shed at the back crammed always with drying sheep and rabbit and mole skins ... they tried to sell mats or brushes or clothes pegs or buckets or crocks when there was no work to be done ... they also offered to buy sheep and other skins, to remove unwanted scrap-iron, to barter worn or disused harness for screws, spanners or other tools[9]

A flexibility and versatility in dealing meant that notwithstanding contemporary fears over the disappearance of true Gypsies in the face of industrialisation and urbanisation, Travellers were able to make the transition relatively easily. Gypsies did not die out with the decline in wooden peg making and horse selling, they simply shifted into other areas, such as to scrap and motor dealing, both these activities becoming more common by the 1930s.

Additionally, contrary to the impressions of settled society, Travellers did not move at random around the countryside. Instead, they tended to travel in fairly small groups of family and extended family, on well-known circuits, keeping to the same parts of the country. Betsy Whyte, who grew up in Scotland in the inter-war period, followed a regular circuit of work governed by the seasons. In the spring her family went pearl fishing in Speyside, followed over the summer by potato picking, fruit picking and harvesting on a number of farms that they visited every year. They over-wintered in a small town, where her father made baskets and her mother hawked when the weather was too severe for winter farm work.[10] The pattern of sticking to certain routes and activities is echoed in accounts by other Travellers: 'We have what we call our "runs", you know – at one time we do a bit of potato planting and cleaning, afterwards we travel to the strawberry country, then we go on to haymaking and field pea-picking'.[11] Travellers in the Caithness region were largely boat-based in the summers, which they spent whelking and hawking on the west coast of Scotland, while the winters were spent in Oban.[12]

For virtually all Travellers a central part of their 'run' were certain horse fairs, such as Barnet, Yarm or Appleby; or race meetings, most notably Epsom; or some of the larger harvesting events, such as strawberry picking in the Fens or hop picking in Kent and Hampshire. As well as presenting opportunities to earn large sums of money, they also acted as social occasions, with Travellers from all over the country converging for the duration.

After 1918 Travellers became increasingly affected by improved transport which made hawking less profitable, and during the Depression, increased competition from unemployed workers who had taken up door-to-door selling.[13] At the same time, the growth in the mass production of kitchenware and other household items was leading to the beginnings of a throw-away society. Leitch has concluded that seasonal work consequently became more important to counteract the decline in peddling and tinkering.[14] By the 1930s the horse trade was well past its peak, although the horse fairs and horse dealing continued to be both economically and socially important. Scrap, car and lorry dealing began to take over as central activities along with hawking and casual agricultural work.

The seasonality of many Travellers' lives and the nature of many of their activities, which were subject to the vagaries of the weather, the mood of householders or fairgoers, as well as micro and macro changes in the market meant that their livelihoods were precarious. Establishing a seasonal round and diversifying their activities reduced this insecurity, through ensuring that they did not rely on one particular crop or good, and by building up relationships with farmers, dealers and householders, as well as creating a network of known stopping and grazing places. Travellers' migration patterns, which to the settled population might have appeared as random 'here today and gone tomorrow' movements, had in reality their own logic.

While Acton has seen the pre-1945 period as being relatively stable, with 'a community of craftsmen, agricultural workers, horse-dealers and entertainers existing in a fairly stable symbiosis with Gaujo society',[15] in fact many of the changes which were to make a major impact after the Second World War had their roots in this period.

Evidence of the impact of the First World War on Travellers is limited, with the most detailed account stemming from a government investigation into 'Tinkers' in Scotland in 1918. It found that substantial numbers of Travellers had joined up, and that a nomadic lifestyle had been made more difficult for their families, not only as a result of their absence but also through the Defence of the Realm regulations that prevented camping and lighting fires in certain areas: 'The families were driven into towns; but on account of the prevailing scarcity, only slum or derelict houses could be obtained by them ... Separation allowances enabled them to pay rents'. In Caithness the Duke of Portland gave £100 to help the women buy utensils and furniture: 'Their life in these houses has been relatively comfortable. They have kept the houses and themselves fairly clean and have given little cause for complaint'. Women were able to supplement their allowances through engaging in begging, hawking and collecting rags and old iron, for which there were high prices: 'practically all the young women are engaged in this now lucrative occupation'.[16]

There is some evidence that the pattern of men joining up and women settling for the duration of the war was repeated south of the border: '[Granddad joined up and] when he went away Portsmouth Corporation housed Grannie and the children and saw to it that the children went to school'.[17] The trend of war promoting settlement and increased contact with settled society was to be repeated, but on a larger scale, during the Second World War.

This is not to argue that prior to this Travellers were cut off from mainstream society. On the contrary, one of the most notable features of Travellers' economic activities was the degree of face-to-face interaction with the settled community. Far from being a 'secret people', many Travellers had daily contact with householders, other dealers, farmers and land workers in the course of their economic activities.[18] Arthur Harding's account of Travellers in the East End, for example, presents them as an integral part of the legal and underground economy of the area, as well as living with and among the general population.[19]

Unlike interactions with officials where there was an obvious power imbalance, in these economic dealings what is often most clear is the reciprocal nature of the relationship. While there were undoubted instances of Travellers being unwelcome, if these had formed the majority of interactions then their livelihoods would not have been sustainable: Travellers provided a range of services for the settled community, and would often be welcomed for doing so.

> Some people gave us a welcome. If they were living on the side of a mountain, or in a real lonely place, they mightn't get to town for six months, and they loved to see the Travellers coming so that they would get their pots and kettles mended and buy little things ... we were sort of newspapers and radio as well as everything else.[20]

Not only in isolated areas were Travellers welcomed, just as they might have been in the early nineteenth century; they performed useful functions in urban areas too. In the absence of easily obtainable second-hand clothing, Traveller women commonly sold on unwanted clothes and bedding to families in the poorer areas of cities.[21]

Travellers also came into contact with the settled, usually working-class population as they worked alongside both rural and urban labourers, most notably at harvest time. Just as the hop fields of Kent and Hampshire held both East Enders and Travellers, and the fruit and vegetable farms of the Welsh Borders had Travellers and workers from the West Midlands conurbation, accounts of fruit picking in the Scottish berry fields show that working alongside Travellers at harvest times were people from Glasgow and other urban areas.[22] Other intensive farm work, such as planting and harvesting, could see Travellers working with other hired farm workers on farms, sharing accommodation as well as entertainment in the evenings.[23]

But contact through work did not automatically lead to lots of social mixing. During the berry harvest, which like hop-picking entailed large numbers of people camping over a few weeks, Travellers pitched in a separate field and adults as least did not generally associate with the other pickers:

> Few Travellers really liked the way we had to live at the berry-picking, so near to the many hundreds of town-dwellers ... We did not feel completely at ease with so many of them around. Sometimes they would start strikes and marches from one berry farm to another, getting all the other berry pickers to strike as well ... We wanted no part of this, but we were forced to stay away from work under threat until they had come to some agreement.[24]

While Travellers may have worked alongside settled, mainly working-class people, the above extract indicates the divergent attitudes they held towards employment. Betsy Whyte felt that the settled population's attitude to life was 'silly. They start to work at fourteen, or even earlier, and go on working right up till they are old men, never taking any enjoyment to themselves'. This she contrasted to the attitude of Travellers who, she felt worked hard 'as long as they felt they were working for themselves', hence their keenness to accept piece-work rather than an hourly rate of pay. She also believed that the 'scaldies', as the urban poor were called by Travellers, were far more badly hit by unemployment and the Depression than Travellers 'as few of them could turn their hand to anything that would bring a few coppers'. In one case Betsy's mother helped a penniless single woman, young and pregnant, to receive poor relief and aid from the Salvation Army; and at another time the family helped a group of young men from the city, who had no money or work, by giving them food and showing them how to call for, and sort, rags.[25]

Whyte's observations highlight some of the key features of Traveller attitudes to employment: a willingness to work hard and be flexible in their choice of employment, so long as they were their own boss, and an unwillingness to work for the sake of it. Not investing so much of their identity in formal paid employment, and aware of their marginal position, Travellers saw collective bargaining as irrelevant, and instead relied on their reputation as hard workers to find and keep employment. It is clear from Whyte's account that the settled population was something they interacted with on a daily basis, often at arm's length and with mistrust, although also with friendship or even pity.

Sites and winter quarters

Traveller sites and stopping places differed widely depending on how long they were used, the numbers of people using them and where they were located. However, they tended to have a number of common features. Ideally they were sited somewhere where the Travellers would experience little or no harassment; be close either to raw materials for creating goods, to places where goods might be sold, or paid work obtained; and for Travellers still reliant on horses, grazing and water needed to be easily obtainable. Given this range of requirements it is unsurprising that alongside the use of commons, green lanes and other rural stopping places, areas of urban and peri-urban wasteland were also attractive to Travellers. This was particularly the case over the winter, when Travellers generally sought a long-term site to mitigate the worst of the weather, and where cities provided them with greater opportunities for income generation.

Gordon Boswell, born in 1895, describes spending the summer season at South Shore in Blackpool, which was a permanent encampment with people working on the entertainments of the town, and moving round different parts of northern England, before finding a winter park-up, often by a rubbish tip in Preston. They would start getting ready for spring travelling in mid-February, and move off after the horses had been shod and the wagon cleaned. His family would stop on green lanes and commons where there was grazing for their horses and gleanings of firewood, staying a few days and working an area before moving on.[26] This appears to have been a fairly typical pattern for the times and was the basis for settled society's image of Travellers with bow-topped caravans parked on the 'windy heath' that has proved so enduring.

However, there were many times when Travellers did not have the luxury of choosing when and where to go. Maintaining a life on the road commonly consisted of seeking out marginal land in the context of limited choice, regular eviction and negotiation with farmers and other members of settled society:

> [Around] Brechin alone there were five old byways which many Travellers had wintered on ... All of these camps were within one day's travelling of each other ... A policeman or perhaps two would come to Old Trinity Road, and tell them that they would have to move on the next day. So they would shift to Green Tree, perhaps, and live there for a few days before being told to move on again ... This went on the whole time, and in spite of having to rake their tents down in freezing weather

and go on for five or six miles ... Many farmers were quite agreeable to allowing us to live on their land, provided that we helped with the many jobs which were at that time needing done on the farm.[27]

In other cases Travellers would move to a town, where winter quarters might consist of a privately rented house, a regular park-up in a yard or field, or on one of the larger permanent sites that existed throughout the country. While the ideal was to stay in one place for the whole of the winter, this might not be possible if the authorities in an area actively made an effort to move on van-dwellers: 'In the wintertime we used to live in the wagons. We'd spend about six months travelling all around the North [of Ireland], and then when the real bad weather came we'd go back to Belfast and we'd be hunted from one mucky field to another.'[28]

Others abandoned tents and vans altogether in the winter and moved into houses. Before 1939 the availability of cheap private housing in areas which did not object to Travellers renting was aided by the continued existence of slums, and condemned houses that were only available for short lets.[29] As Sibley has argued, for Travellers poor housing was not necessarily seen as bestowing status in the terms understood by mainstream society, but may have been viewed as an 'adaptable space' and a base from which they were able to exploit aspects of dominant society.[30] The importance of housing, providing a flexible space from which Travellers could conduct a range of livelihood occupations, is revealed in reflections on being provided with a new council house, after the 'hovel' in which they used to over-winter was condemned:

> we could not do the things that we had been used to doing. We could not [sort] rags, Daddy could not get making his baskets. The old house had had sheds and a wash house which we could use for this purpose ... We used to play horn gramophone and make fun dancing and carrying-on in the evenings, but the complaints from the neighbours soon put a stop to that ... To make it worse, very few of our Traveller friends visited us. They said that they didn't want to come in-about the new house, and shame us up.[31]

The ambivalence felt by many Travellers to moving into houses meant that they often preferred to move onto one of the 'van towns' that by the beginning of the twentieth century had become a permanent feature of the urban landscape. For significant numbers of Travellers, urban sites became a haven not just in winter but all year round. By the end of the nineteenth century, these sites existed in many parts of London and its periphery, as well as the newer cities of the midlands and north. The tendency of Travellers to settle was in part the result of the increasingly urbanised and industrialised nature of Britain. A concentration of the settled population in urban areas meant it was less necessary for Travellers to move widely to reach and service different populations. In addition, enclosure of the commons – reducing the area of common land in Britain from eight million to just over two and a half million acres by 1873[32] – and the expansion of urban areas, meant there was less marginal land where it was acceptable for Travellers to halt, so sites that were safe attracted permanent populations.

The observations of contemporaries[33] and presence of the London City Mission Gypsy missioners testified to the number of Travellers in and around the capital. By 1918, the mission was visiting camps in Barking, Leytonstone, Higham's Hill, Edmonton, Cheshunt, Abbey Wood and Bexley Heath. A note from 1922 observed that some of the camps visited had upwards of two hundred people on them.[34] Outside London similar sites could be found in and around all major cities.

By the inter-war period these sites were increasingly being viewed as a problem, on both sanitary and social grounds. A 1933 survey of moveable dwellings conducted by the three local government associations revealed that Travellers were commonly encamped either during the winter or more permanently, on long-term sites, making them almost indistinguishable from other shanty site dwellers: in Royton, they 'plant[ed] themselves on a spare piece of ground in the centre of the District and remain[ed] there for months together until they have worked the District from end to end'.[35] Bromley council had a longstanding battle with a site, which had been rented to Travellers in 1930. Three years later there were sixty structures, and the council complained that while it had been partly successful in removing the 'scum' of the Travellers, 'many still remain'.[36]

As well as these van and shanty sites in urban areas, in some villages such as Kirk Yetholm in Northumberland and many around the New Forest,[37] Travellers had moved into houses in significant numbers, either permanently or using them as a winter base. Elsewhere in rural areas 'colonies' or 'plotlands' had been formed after Travellers and others had bought up land from speculators trying to cash in on the building boom that accompanied the expansion of

London and the supporting suburban rail network, but had found that for some reason their land was unsuitable.[38] This trend led to the creation of some of the largest and most long-lived sites, with Travellers alongside other plot owners creating stable communities, such as Belvedere Marshes in Kent and Marks Tey in Essex.[39]

In contrast, the concentration of Travellers in 'compounds' in the New Forest was the result of official intervention, when in 1926 seven areas in the Forest were set aside for Travellers to camp, so long as they complied with bylaws. They were able to move freely between the seven areas, but not to camp outside the compounds. Before this, Travellers used to camp in small groups throughout the Forest, moving on every forty-eight hours as bylaws demanded, to prevent the claiming of squatter rights. By the Second World War, the seven compounds were reduced to five and contained 411 people.[40] It is not clear what prompted the creation of the compounds, but it may have been the result of increased holiday camping and leisure use of the Forest, and an increasing concern by the Verderers[41] to control use of the area.

Collective myth of both the travelling and settled populations of Britain held that before 1939 Travellers stopped in out-of-the-way places, and moved on regularly, with little harassment from the local people. While there is an element of truth in this, it is far too simplistic. The majority of Travellers may have been largely nomadic, but this was by no means the case for their entire population, and that where possible virtually all Travellers found, or attempted to find, winter quarters where they could remain throughout the worst of the weather. As I show in Chapter 2, even in this period Travellers were by no means invulnerable to harassment and eviction.

Travellers and the Second World War

The popular perception of Travellers living a timeless rural existence almost inevitably led to a contemporary belief that Travellers were barely affected by the Second World War.[42] In contrast, since the late 1960s writers have often tied Traveller history to today's political agenda in an attempt to fight for the improved position of Travellers in contemporary society. Unsurprisingly, the focus of this literature has been the experience of European Roma during the Holocaust,[43] while in Britain, Travellers have been depicted as patriotic, only failing to do their duty through bureaucratic incompetence and despite continued persecution.[44] While usefully highlighting the invisible role played by Travellers during the Second World War, it has done little to illuminate the range of roles and experiences of the community. In the remainder of this chapter I begin by considering how the state on a broad level dealt with its travelling communities before moving on to explore the impact of the war on Travellers, and how they were perceived by settled society during the conflict.

How a state treats minorities during times of crisis is one indication of its commitment to values such as equality and impartiality. Superficially, Travellers were treated in the same way as other British citizens, being issued with no special identity cards or ration books,[45] nor were separate records kept about their enrolment in the Forces.[46]

Immediately following the outbreak of war the government embarked upon registering Britain's entire population, both for rationing purposes and in preparation for mobilisation. Enumerators experienced some practical difficulties in both finding and recording Travellers, especially as some did not know their date of birth.[47] However, it is important not to overstate this: '[people] with pens and paper in their hands appeared in every doorway, taking a very methodical census. Almost overnight or so it seemed, every living soul had been issued with an identity card, and, little later, ration books'.[48] Only small numbers of people were missed, the majority of whom were registered at a later date. This is not to claim that some Travellers did not deliberately hide to evade being counted, or take advantage of a lack of a birth certificate to lie about their age to avoid conscription. Despite widespread perceptions, Travellers were not unreachable by the bureaucratic state, and when necessary the state was fully able to reach its population.

Throughout the war there was a tension between a position of insisting that Travellers were simply normal citizens, and an underlying feeling that somehow they were different, and should therefore be treated differently. Thus, although Travellers were British citizens, this did not stop the Home Office from seriously considering the possibility of internment, along with aliens and other suspect groups:[49]

> *it is considered impracticable* to treat the Gypsies as aliens by obliging them to report regularly to the police ... It is also being considered whether they should be restricted to certain sites by Defence Regulation Acts. At present they can be excluded only from certain coastal areas or the neighbourhood of certain establishments [emphasis added].[50]

A further observation on the reasons for internment of Travellers never taking place suggests that it was more than simply practicality that stopped the legislation from being passed. There were a range of issues: 'how to define a Gypsy to the exclusion of the legitimate camper ... and the fact that it was doubted if public opinion would accept restrictions on Gypsies which would limit their freedom and put them in a worse position than the aliens.[51]

These statements indicate a departure from pre-war assertions of central government impartiality, and paradoxically suggest that it was public opinion rather than the professionalism of civil servants that in part acted as a break on repression. While internment plans were not enacted, the fact they were considered puts into question the Home Office's inter-war commitment to equality (see Chapter 2).

The experience of Travellers shows that even when not explicitly discriminated against, impartial actions of government could have negative consequences for this minority group. Treating Travellers as normal members of the population meant that government made no particular efforts to reach them despite, for example, their high levels of illiteracy.

In one case a Traveller woman was fined £25 for 'unlawfully retaining' duplicate food and clothing ration books that she had been sent in error. The reason given for the heaviness of the fine was that these 'offences went to the very heart and security of rationing', despite the fact that the woman was illiterate, had never used the books, and had not fully understood the implications of her actions.[52] In such a case it is impossible to tell whether it was a genuine mistake, or whether the woman tried to take advantage of her illiteracy and use it as a defence despite knowing the implications of her actions.

The classification of Travellers as commercial travellers for the purposes of rationing allowed them to use their coupons wherever they went. This could present its own problems:

> We likes tea, sugar and bacon the same as you, and it's even more difficult for us to get. We've got them travelling ration cards, and as we can't read nor write we didn't get anything for several weeks because we didn't know what to do. We go from place to place and only get the bare leavings, because it stands to reason that the shopkeepers are going to serve their regular customer gents with all the best stuff first.[53]

Such difficulties did not mean that Travellers were not able to occasionally take advantage of the existence of coupons. Betsy Stanley tells how her mother, who used to be given clothes while she was out hawking, sold her clothing coupons 'because they didn't need them. The young women – I suppose they wanted a nice new blouse for the weekend – they used to ask my mother for her clothing coupons'.[54]

The most obvious way in which Travellers engaged with the state was through service in the Forces, although the absence of statistics makes it impossible to quantify their involvement. Travellers were very conscious of their ambiguous status in the eyes of the public, and could take great pains to assert their patriotism. As one Traveller woman stated: '[My] two sons are in the Army, my husband was in the last war, my grandsons will soon be in this one. We live in England, we are protected by England's laws, we love England and are ready and proud to fight for her'.[55] Similarly, immediately the war broke out there were newspaper articles stressing the patriotic response of Travellers to the situation:

> The Gypsies are rallying to the nation's call. At recruiting depots all over the country they are registering for military service. Soon they will be in khaki. And Britain will never have better soldiers than they ... A life close to nature has made them good scouts ... 'They are anti-Nazi', says Miss Yates, Secretary of the Gypsy Lore Society, 'and they have a score to settle with the Germans for the persecution of Gypsies in Germany'.[56]

It is clear that some Travellers deliberately attempted to avoid going to war, to the extent of buying fake identity cards and false exemption classifications. The difficulty is in determining the extent to which Travellers' actions during the war were a result of their *Traveller* identity. As there were many deserters who weren't Travellers, there were obviously reasons other than Traveller identity that could cause an individual to avoid military service.[57] However, for those who did desert, it is likely that they experienced a greater level of support than a house-dweller might typically have expected:

> Lots of cousins, friends and other relatives came home on leave. Quite a few of them had lost the taste for soldiering, and just didn't return to their units. One young friend let his hair grow and when the police or any other authority came looking for deserters, he would don a skirt and play with a skipping rope, chanting rhymes in a girlish voice.[58]

Similarly, when a Traveller deserter was arrested in Horton, near Slough, other residents of the camps are reported to have attempted to prevent the police from entering the van, and had warned him that they were approaching.[59]

Between extremes of heroism and desertion, the reality for most Travellers was much more prosaic. A number of accounts show how a spell in the Services increased the literacy of individual Travellers. For the Welsh Traveller Corgi Powell, 'the Army had instilled into him by brute force the elementals which the village schoolmaster had failed to do. It was not until he had gone into the Army that Corgi had learned to tell the time properly'.[60] Another Traveller, upon demobilisation, could 'write tolerably well and had gained an extensive vocabulary through the reading of Westerns'.[61]

Life in the Forces created a forum in which personal relations between Travellers and other communities could develop. Some accounts confirm how individual Travellers were valued by their units and comrades, and others the challenges they faced when dealing with discipline and authority.[62] For Tony Butler, this resulted less in friendship than in a reduction of antipathy: 'in action, he lost a little of his gorgio-hating spirit, having seen many of that despised race display great courage in battle'.[63] In some cases contact led to an increased sympathy for the social and political situation of Travellers on the part of their comrades:

> I made a chum in the Navy, who, when he told me that he was a Gypsy, expected me to be ashamed of him. Ashamed of a Gypsy, who joined the Navy as a volunteer, who was willing to fight (and perhaps die) for a country which had pushed his people around!?[64]

The war also increased both the amount and density of contact between the settled and Traveller populations on the home front. Their involvement in waged employment in Britain must be set against a background of massive labour shortages. Often for the first time Travellers worked alongside the rest of the population as waged employees in factories and similarly unfamiliar surroundings:

> Their old, familiar, everyday occupations are diverted into War production ... Gypsy girls ... quickly become expert in the complicated wiring of electrical equipment for aircraft and knife grinders naturally gravitate into different branches of metal-working ... [A] gang [of fifty Travellers are] employed by a firm of demolition contractors, cleaning up 'blitzed' areas with a fair amount of rescue work thrown in ... In one heavily bombed town they worked right through nights of consecutive raids shoring up walls, tunnelling through debris, and releasing trapped people.[65]

As well as opening up opportunities for Travellers in waged employment, the war provided the chance to make money in the traditional areas of the economy they occupied, such as scrap-dealing. They 'already have a flying start in this trade because, when horse dealing went out of fashion, they began business in old cars and spare parts'.[66] Gordon Boswell had moved into scrap at the end of the Depression, buying when prices were low, and when the Beaverbrook appeal[67] was launched he sorted the metal collected by the Women's Voluntary Service.[68] Involvement in the scrap trade was not, however, without its pitfalls. With the public also collecting old metal, children were given it for free rather than householders saving it for passing Travellers.[69] At least one council found itself forced to issue a warning that 'proceedings will be taken against anyone stealing from scrap iron dumps'. This was directed 'against Gypsies and others who have been seen to sort over the junk and take certain items away'.[70]

Some growth areas of business attracted public complaint and the suggestion that Gypsies were profiting from the misfortunes of others: '[Gypsy] women who show a strip of lace or some clothes pegs are more anxious to tell the lady's "fortune" than to part with their goods ... as so many wives are parted from their husbands by evacuation, or by the fighting Services, a certain class of Gypsy is finding door-to-door business very lucrative just now'.[71]

While some forms of business, such as scrap collection, could be seen to be both profitable and working with the rest of the population for the war effort, there was a fine line between that and profiteering. Then Travellers were depicted as feeding off, and profiting from, the anxieties and conditions generated by the war.

In some cases the engagement of Travellers in the war effort was the result of directed and specific attempts to mobilise them. In the early years of the war Edward Harvey had been among those who had deliberately set out to bring Travellers into vital areas of employment suffering from labour shortages. As a member of the Gypsy Lore Society he knew some Travellers and spoke Romany, two things that he felt were important in bringing them into the war:

> [Where] the ordinary public can be called up by posters and newspaper advertisements, are told when and where to report, the system fails with people who can't read. Consequently, Gypsies have to be dug out; we have to go and fetch them, and that's another reason why people suspect them of shirking. I go to their camps and talk to them in their own way.[72]

His observations confirmed how the authorities needed to actively engage with the Travelling community in order to fully involve them in the war effort. It was not enough to expect them to be reached through the normal public information channels and to come forward. Harvey's actions also suggest that it remained up to private individuals to ensure that this 'outreach' took place.

This was demonstrated in the summer of 1943 when the Ministry of Labour and National Service were criticised for failing to integrate Travellers into the war effort.[73] Instead of taking official steps to mobilise them, it took advantage of the services of 'Gypsy' Ernest Williams,[74] who created a scheme to engage Travellers in agricultural work. Williams was appointed to 'assist Gypsies in finding agricultural and other work of national importance in Surrey ... Farmers wanting extra labour [were] to contact him through the local Ministry of Labour office'.[75] When publicising his scheme, the image of Travellers he promoted reinforced prevailing stereotypes about their lifestyle and relationship to the war:

> I want to contact those who are wandering around making pegs and selling them door-to-door. I hope to be able to persuade them to take up agricultural work and benefit not only themselves, but also the farmers and the country ... They know there is a war on, they don't know what it is about ... Farmers need have no fears of being burdened with Gypsies when the work is completed. They just notify me, and I can arrange for the Gypsies to go on to someone else.[76]

If newspaper reports were to be believed, a year later the Williams scheme was having a big impact as 'hundreds' of Travellers took part in the harvest.[77] Yet, deeper analysis suggests that the scheme's impact was superficial and largely irrelevant, as it ignored the already active role of Travellers in agriculture. Travellers' own accounts of war work, particularly that of women, showed how they continued to engage in seasonal agricultural labour throughout the war, and in fact found their role expanded due to labour shortages, both in the farming industry and forestry.[78]

In Warwickshire, a county unaffected by Williams' work, the chief labour officer to the war agricultural executive committee stated that Travellers had done 'a great deal': 'They have always made and continue to make a valuable contribution to the war effort'.[79] Six months before Williams' scheme got the go-ahead, the *Evening Standard* ran an article praising Travellers' input into agriculture. A Shropshire farmer was quoted as saying 'if it hadn't been for the Gypsies, half of my beet crop would still be lying in the fields ... They pulled twelve acres of beet and loaded it with no extra help. They are still with me, working hard and regularly'.[80]

The presence of deserters at hop and other farms at harvest times indicates that farmers, forced to rely largely on women and older men, were willing to turn a blind eye to the legal status of young men in order to get the work done. In at least one case, the labour shortage led to a farmer speaking out against the introduction of tougher bylaws in his area, stating, 'there would not be a place in the country where [Travellers] could live, and farmers would have difficulty obtaining labour'.[81] While Travellers had always engaged in seasonal agricultural work, and this continued to be an area of continuity in their lives, the labour shortage changed the context. More work and regular work was available, with the opportunity for reliable wages, putting Travellers in the rare position of being in a seller's market.

The significance of Williams' scheme did not lie in the numbers of Travellers it brought into the war effort. Instead it highlighted how the government failed to actively engage with Travellers. Although Whitehall gave support to the scheme, there was no indication that it was to be extended, nor that civil servants saw it as meriting manpower or bureaucratic involvement. The implication was that where Travellers failed to engage in the home front it was their fault and not that of the state.

The combination of the opportunities presented by stable employment and the uncertainties of wartime conditions resulted in an increase in settlement of Travellers. Those resident in Thirsk in the winter of 1939–40 were typical of many in their response to the new conditions: 'Probably on account of the war and the danger of air raids, the caravanners have decided to winter in the country'. The women of the site were engaged in potato harvesting and the men on public-works schemes.[82] Some Travellers were forced to settle after their hawking licences were revoked causing them to fall back on claiming dole.[83] With many Travellers moving into the scrap trade, some found it more convenient to find a permanent base from which to work, as they could store greater quantities of metal before weighing it in. Settlement was also attractive for Travellers with relatives in the Forces as 'we can get letters easy and have them read to us'.[84] Additionally, some Travellers who had been organised into land labour brigades had sites established for them by the local authority.[85]

Along with the advantages of economic and social stability brought by settlement, it was also a way of avoiding the increased disadvantages of being on the road. Reports of Travellers worried about breaking blackout regulations, combined with many families having men in the Forces, led local authorities in Scotland to turn a blind eye to, or in some cases positively encourage, the re-occupation of condemned houses. When Travellers did try to move, they found it more difficult than they had in pre-war times, owing to the closure of some sites and a lack of available transport: 'The old camping sites which we had intended staying on were fenced off and had notice boards threatening prosecution to anyone disregarding the signs. At the time Travelling people feared to offend authority'.[86]

A tendency for settlement was partly counteracted by other forces. Some Travellers moved to Ireland for the duration of the conflict to escape bombing regulation and conscription.[87] Many camping grounds in or around large cities were under threat from air raids,[88] leading Travellers to leave their permanent homes.[89] The heavy bombing of 1940 generated reports that Travellers had moved to more rural areas,[90] but in Wiltshire at least, they were kept on the move 'on account of the acquisition by the War Department of a considerable number of old-established camping grounds' on Salisbury Plain.[91]

Despite the active role that the majority of Travellers took in the war, either in the Forces or on the home front, and the major impact of the conflict on Travellers' nomadic lifestyles, the public reaction to Travellers during the war was often at best ambivalent, and at worst downright hostile. While Travellers adapted, mainstream society did not respond by changing its stereotypes of Gypsies. Instead, people fell back on the old, polarised images that had been popular for at least a century. Supporters of Travellers tended to depict them as a remote, picturesque people who were unaffected by the trials of modernity, while their detractors saw them as shirking, thieving layabouts. Neither of these images were a useful means of highlighting the important roles that Travellers adopted.

As Britain allegedly united in the war effort, those who were seen as failing to do their duty were vilified and marginalised, as they were undermining the communal national effort.[92] Throughout the war there was a consistent stream of articles in newspapers that suggested how Travellers remained fundamentally unaffected by the conflict. This message was particularly popular in articles about food rationing: 'Many people wonder how Gypsies get off with food rationing. It is understood however, that hedgehogs are not rationed'.[93] Although there were attempts by Travellers to challenge this stereotype: 'some gents think we live on baked hedgehog and berries, but I'm thinking that most of us would be pretty sick if our wives didn't give us tea with sugar in it'.[94] Such articles assumed Gypsies were able to circumvent the strictures of rationing, and simply confirmed for the settled population that the free and easy life of Travellers avoided the responsibilities and difficulties of modernity.

As Britain reached the low point of the war in 1941–42, anti-Traveller voices increasingly interpreted this 'freedom' as shirking. This was bolstered by a long-running myth that Travellers avoided conscription:[95]

> It is odd to realise that the once-persecuted Gypsies are probably the most carefree race in Europe today. They have no territory of their own for Hitler to plunder. Even in Nazi-occupied countries, the Gypsy tribes are still 'free' minorities, who live primitive lives in remote places ... [In Britain] few Gypsies are conscripted for the fighting forces ... [there are eight thousand Travellers of fighting age but] the majority are below Army education standard.[96]

As the war progressed, the press increasingly ran stories of desertion, draft dodging and, preferably eventual capture:

> Scores of young nomads – some with call-up papers already on their pockets – have eluded the Army authorities and the police for months. Many of military age have not even registered, and in these cases no call-up is possible ... Call-up letters are left at the nearest Post Office to be called for. Sometimes they are not collected for a month. Even when a Gypsy collects his summons to a medical examination there is nothing to prevent his driving off to another part of the country. In this case he can be 'missing' for months ... To those of us that have sons fighting it is most painful to see these young fellows going free ... and in the meantime [they] do a bit of poaching and a bit of pinching whenever they get the chance.[97]

The summer and autumn of 1944 saw an increase of interest in Traveller desertions following a police and Army raid on a hop-pickers' camp in Alton, Hampshire. A dawn swoop picked up 27 deserters and men who had avoided registration, as well as several others who were holding false identity cards. The event was reported widely in the press,[98] and even though Travellers only formed part of the hop-picking labour force, with the majority of workers coming from the East End, no reports suggested that non-Travellers may have been involved. Nor did the papers mention the fact that the farmers, desperately short of labour, had obviously employed these able-bodied young men on their farms. The stories were set up to emphasise the difference between the wily shirking Gypsy and the heroic Tommy, to highlight the lengths to which anti-social elements would go in order to undermine the war efforts of decent citizens.

Travellers who were caught deserting were typically hauled up in front of a magistrate. The legal representative of two Travellers who were caught at Melford fair, and charged with holding false identity cards, was faced with the difficult task of trying to put the best light on their actions: 'The case must strike the magistrates as being a bad one ... But Bird was a Gypsy who had been brought up casually in caravans. He had not enjoyed the advantages of education and [his counsel] had no doubt that he had no proper understanding of patriotism or even of duty to his country'.[99] It is significant that the only defence their solicitor could muster was that the defendant was inherently asocial and unpatriotic due to his nomadism and Gypsy identity. Statements such as this only served to reinforce the stereotype that Travellers had no interest in the course of the war.

The theme of Travellers undermining the war effort also emerged in incidents of ration fraud, black market dealing and smuggling. Travellers in Lancashire, for example, were accused of being 'a source of trouble to Lancashire police and food authorities. Travelling from town to town they are claiming rations on Travellers' ration books in several places on the same day' and thus 'illegally obtaining their food'. A police official was reported as saying 'it seems likely that some of these Gypsies have also obtained additional petrol, but although their quick movements from place to place adds to our difficulties, we hope to complete our checks very soon'.[100]

Despite the widely held beliefs of contemporaries, the conflict had a major impact upon the lives of Travellers. Along with the settled population their lives became circumscribed by regulations put in place by government. Rationing caused problems for those who were mobile, and those who were illiterate were likely to have found the new systems more difficult to work and understand. Bombing raids, combined with the increase in regulations, caused some Travellers to leave for Ireland, others to move to less vulnerable areas of the country, and still others to settle down in their local area. For those who served in the Forces, the war was the first opportunity to live and work closely with the Gorgio population, to improve literacy skills, and to face prejudice or sympathy at close quarters from their superiors and comrades. The labour shortage and consequent increased engagement of Travellers with the mainstream economy had the possibility of opening up a new basis for Traveller–Gorgio relations, with the former for once being valued for their contributions. While the Travelling population found itself adapting to challenges, what is most remarkable about settled society's attitude towards Travellers was how little it altered as a result of the war. Positive opinions tended to stress how Travellers were free from the taint of hostilities, while negative ones focused on how they deliberately shirked responsibilities and undermined the war effort. While there was some attempt by those who supported Travellers to stress their practical involvement, it failed to counteract popular opinion. Central government, although expressing doubts, maintained its commitment to impartiality, with Travellers being included in the mainstream of policy development and the implementation of regulations. However, it failed to acknowledge that this was not sufficient to draw Travellers into the war effort. Their nomadism, illiteracy, and cultural identity made it difficult for officials to reach them fully, yet typically it was Travellers and not the state who were blamed for any failures. The result of this was that Travellers emerged from the war with their position in modern Britain at best ambiguous. Nomadism served to reconfirm Travellers as outsiders, and suggested that they were working against the collectivist ethos that had emerged during the war, and was to be such an important part in the formation of the welfare state.

Notes

1 The two main Traveller biographies for this period are B. Whyte, *The yellow in the broom* (Edinburgh, 1979) and J. Seymour (ed.), *The book of Boswell, autobiography of a Gypsy* (Harmondsworth, 1975).

2 Mayall, *Gypsy Travellers*, 13.

3 J. Lucassen, *Migrant labour in Europe, 1600–1900: The drift to the North Sea*, trans. D. A. Boch (London and Sydney, 1987), quoted in Lucassen, Willems and Cottaar (eds), *Gypsies and other itinerant groups*, 135–52, especially 143–4.

4 *Ibid.*, 1. Original emphasis.

5 J. Sandford, *Gypsies* (London, 1973), 14.

6 See, for example, Davies, *Tales*, for various accounts of relatives joining the Army and other employment strategies; also Whyte, *Yellow in the broom*, 139.

7 Author's conversation with Roseanna MacPhee, Bobbin Mill resident, 28 November 2006.
8 Dick Harrison, quoted in Davies, *Tales*, 165.
9 C. Hughes, *West with the Tinkers: A journey through Wales with vagrants* (London, 1954), 11.
10 Whyte, *Yellow in the broom*.
11 F. Cuttriss, *Romany life, experienced and observed during many years of friendly intercourse with the Gypsies* (London, 1915), 68–70.
12 *Report of the Departmental Committee on Tinkers in Scotland* (Edinburgh, 1918), 10.
13 R. D. Sexton, 'Travelling people in the United Kingdom in the first half of the twentieth century', Ph.D. dissertation, University of Southampton, 1989, 54.
14 R. Leitch (ed.), *The book of Sandy Stewart* (Edinburgh, 1988), xxviii.
15 Acton, *Gypsy Politics*, 131.
16 *Tinkers in Scotland*, 4, 13 and 16.
17 Eli Frankham quoted in Davies, *Tales*, 28.
18 I might also add the rash of gypsiologists and middle-class writers who latched themselves onto Traveller camps with apparent ease and frequency.
19 R. Samuel, *East End underworld: Chapters in the life of Arthur Harding* (London, 1981).
20 N. Joyce, *Traveller: An autobiography* (Dublin, 1985), 3. See also *Tinkers in Scotland*, 13.
21 See Whyte, *Yellow in the broom*, 122; and Joyce, *Traveller*, 37.
22 Whyte, *Yellow in the broom*, 38–9.
23 E. MacColl and P. Seeger, *Travellers' songs from England and Scotland* (London, 1977), Introduction.
24 Whyte, *Yellow in the broom*, 102–3.
25 *Ibid.*, 45, 49 and 122.
26 Seymour, *Book of Boswell*.
27 Whyte, *Yellow in the broom*, 94–5.
28 Joyce, *Traveller*, 20.
29 See, for example, *Tinkers in Scotland*, 18–21.
30 D. Sibley, *Outsiders in urban society* (Oxford, 1981), 88.
31 Whyte, *Yellow in the broom*, 139–140.
32 Mayall, *Gypsy Travellers*, 20.
33 F. H. Groome, *In Gipsy tents* (East Ardsley, 1973); C. G. Leland, *The Gypsies* (Boston, 1924); T. W. Thompson, 'Affairs of Egypt', *JGLS*, 2 (1911), 113–34.
34 'The Gypsy's Vision', *London City Mission Magazine* (1922), 153.
35 TNA, HLG 52/394, Urban District Council Association memo, 10 October 1933. Other councils with similar complaints were Erith, Hazel Grove and Bramhall, and Northwick.
36 Similar complaints were made by seven other district councils throughout the country and by ten county councils.

37 Mayall, *Gypsy Travellers*, 19.
38 Evidence of Dr H. Franklin Parsons, *Minutes of Evidence of the 1909 House of Lords Select Committee on the Moveable Dwellings Bill* (H.L. 199), 253–4.
39 A detailed analysis of the genesis and culture of plotland developments can be found in D. Hardy and C. Ward, *Arcadia for all: The legacy of a makeshift landscape* (London, 1984).
40 Mayall, *Gypsy Travellers*, 33 and B. Vesey-Fitzgerald, *Gypsies of Britain* (Newton Abbott, 1973), 203–7.
41 The Verderers were the legal body established to protect and administer the agricultural commoning practices of the Forest. They derived their office, powers and responsibilities from the 1877 New Forest Act.
42 J. de Baraclai Levy, *Wanderers in the New Forest* (London, 1958); Hughes, *West with the Tinkers*; Farre, *A time from the world*.
43 D. Kenrick and G. Puxon, *The destiny of Europe's Gypsies* (London, 1972), K. Fings, H. Heuss, F. Sparing and H. Asseo, *From 'race science' to the camps: The Gypsies during the second world war* (Hatfield, 1997).
44 D. Kenrick and S. Bakewell, *On the verge: The Gypsies of England* (London, 1990), 10.
45 'But the Gypsies solve their problem', *News Chronicle* (2 January 1940).
46 TNA, HLG 71/2267, memo from Ward to B. M. Somerville, 5 November 1957.
47 See as an example 'Registration snags in Gainsborough', *Lincolnshire Echo* (2 October 1939).
48 B. Whyte, *Red rowans and wild honey* (Edinburgh, 1990), 163.
49 A. Calder, *The people's war: Britain 1939–1945* (London, 1999 edn), 130–3.
50 TNA, HO 45/25001/8, 'Gypsies: Legislation to deal with vagrant children etc.', 1944; and 'Gypsies and other itinerant van dwellers', 23 August 1944.
51 TNA, ED 11/234, Home Office (hereafter HO) note, 'The Gypsy problem', July 1944.
52 'Ration books – Hopton Gypsy gets duplicate', *Bury Free Press* (16 February 1945). For a similar case see also 'Gypsy defaced ration books – Fined £20', *Romford Times* (8 August 1945).
53 A. S. Jenkinson, 'What the Gypsy told me', *Tit-Bits* (1 March 1941).
54 B. Stanley, *Memories of the marsh: A Traveller life in Kent* (Romany and Traveller Family History Society, 1998), 45.
55 Letter to editor from E. Winter, 'Patriotic Gypsies', *Daily Telegraph* (13 March 1944). For accounts of Travellers' wartime activities see Whyte, *Red rowans*, 162–207; E. Harvey 'Wartime work of the English Gypsies', *JGLS*, 21:3–4 (1942), 81–7; Acton, *Gypsy politics*, 131–2; 'Rokkeripen', *Tatler* (30 July 1941).
56 'Gypsies are joining up', *Daily Mirror* (27 October 1939). Also 'Gypsies are rallying round the recruiting offices', *News Chronicle* (13 October 1939).
57 By October 1944 80,000 men had gone AWOL from the Army, with

about 20,000 unpardoned deserters still at large by the end of the war, Calder, *People's war*, 337.

58 Whyte, *Red rowans*, 205–6.

59 'Police at Horton Gypsy camp', *Slough Observer* (20 April 1945).

60 Hughes, *West with the Tinkers*, 65.

61 D. Strange, *Born on the straw: A Gypsy life* (London, 1968), 14.

62 F. I. Cowles, *Gypsy caravan* (London, 1948), 136–8.

63 Strange, *Born on the straw*, 14.

64 A. Burgin, *HMS Triumph*, letter to the editor, *Illustrated* (31 August 1946). See also 'Ovano', Pembroke, letter to editor, *Western Mail* (8 February 1956).

65 E. Harvey, 'Wartime work of English Gypsies', *JGLS*, 21:3–4 (1942), 84–7. See also 'What the Gypsies are doing', *The Listener* (31 December 1942).

66 A. S. Jenkinson, 'The war affects the Gypsies', *The Listener* (25 July 1940).

67 On 10 July 1940 Lord Beaverbrook issued a manifesto through the newspapers promising to 'turn your pots and pans into Spitfires and Hurricanes, Blenheims and Wellingtons'. He asked for people to hand in any articles 'made wholly or partly of aluminium' to their local Women's Voluntary Service headquarters; Calder, *The people's war*, 149.

68 Seymour, *Book of Boswell*, 150–1.

69 Jenkinson, 'The war affects the Gypsies'.

70 'Warning to Gypsies', *Swindon Advertiser* (26 July 1940). Also 'Gypsy brothers in court again', *Letchworth Citizen* (5 April 1940).

71 'The man at the door', *The Weekly Telegraph* (7 October 1942). For an example of Travellers being accused of profiteering from selling decrepit horses see 'Old horses scandal', *Yorkshire Post* (7 July 1941).

72 Harvey, 'Wartime work of English Gypsies', 84.

73 'Gypsies: War work difficulties', *Evening News* (1 April 1943).

74 Ernest Williams was from a Traveller family and had previously been a missionary with the London City Mission.

75 'Finding work for Gypsies', *Surrey Advertiser* (9 October 1943).

76 'A man with a mission', *Slough Observer* (22 October 1943).

77 'Gypsy chief rounds up Romanies to help bring in the harvest', *Reynold News* (20 August 1944).

78 Stanley, *Memories of the marsh*, 46; Whyte, *Red rowans*, 195–205; 'Down in the forest the Gypsies run factory', *News Chronicle* (30 September 1943); and 'Forest Gypsies and the services', *Southern Daily Echo* (6 April 1943).

79 'Romany's part in county's war effort', *Coventry Evening Telegraph* (9 October 1943).

80 'Gypsies stop roving and dig for victory', *Evening Standard* (8 February 1943). Also H. C. Metcalfe, letter to the editor, 'A word for the Gypsies', *Somerset County Gazette* (June 1942).

81 'Ban on Gypsies wanted', *The Star (Surrey)* (15 January 1946).

82 'Thirsk's caravan colony', *Darlington Times* (28 October 1939) and 'Gypsy camp in Thirsk', *Darlington and Stockton Times* (16 March 1940).

83 D. Yates, *My Gypsy days: Recollections of a Romani rawnie* (London, 1953), 112.

84 Jenkinson, 'The war affects the Gypsies'.

85 Acton, *Gypsy politics*, 132.

86 Whyte, *Red rowans*, 173–4, 199–200.

87 Sexton, 'Travelling people', 82.

88 'Bombs on Gypsy encampment', *The Star* (14 November 1940). See also C. Sherred, *A Romany Life* (n.p., n.d.), 3.

89 Jenkinson, 'What the Gypsy told me'.

90 'Gypsies in search of peace in the north west', *Lancashire Daily Post* (9 October 1940): 'Concession to Gypsies', *Walsall Observer* (15 January 1944).

91 'Gypsies', *Salisbury Journal* (25 May 1940).

92 S. Nicholas, 'From John Bull to John Citizen: Images of national identity and citizenship in the wartime BBC', in Weight and Beach (eds), *The right to belong*, 45. For an account of the lack of consensus during the war, and how in particular criminals profited from conflict see D. Thomas, *An underworld at war: Spivs, deserters, racketeers and civilians in the second world war* (London, 2003).

93 *South Wales Evening Post* (19 January 1940).

94 'The Gypsies are lucky', *The Sheffield Weekly Telegraph* (25 April 1942); Jenkinson, 'The war affects the Gypsies'.

95 This myth continued throughout the war despite statements by the Ministry of Labour to the contrary. The Ministry had a special team working to catch national service dodgers, including Travellers who were liable for service.

96 'The Gypsies are lucky'.

97 'Army dodgers on the run find hide outs in Gypsy caravans', *Daily Express* (26 June 1941); 'These men keep vigilant watch on national service dodgers', *Sunday Sun* (9 February 1941).

98 'Deserters live as Gypsies', *Sunday Chronicle* (27 October 1944); 'Swoop on Gypsies', *Evening News* (12 October 1944); 'Gypsy deserters', *East Kent Gazette* (28 October 1944). The following year, a similar raid was conducted at the same camp, see 'Deserters hunt in Gypsy camp', *Daily Telegraph* (31 May 1945).

99 'Changed their identity to avoid military service', *Sussex and Essex Free Press* (28 April 1944). See also 'False pretences at North Huish', *Western Guardian* (1 March 1945).

100 'Gypsies in ration book racket', *Manchester Evening News* (7 August 1941). Similar sentiments were revealed over the arrest of Travellers smuggling tea and rubber between Eire and Northern Ireland, 'Caravan cavalcade: 232 lbs. of tea hidden by Gypsies', *Daily Sketch* (8 November 1944).

2

The state and its legal responses

In this chapter I consider the relationship between Travellers and central and local government, and in particular the tension between central government's ideology of impartiality and local authorities' desire to remove Travellers from their areas.

Unlike parts of continental Europe, which from the early twentieth century generated legislation specifically targeting Gypsies,[1] the British state was much more circumspect about taking this path. After the repeal of laws outlawing Gypsies in the eighteenth century, there was no legislation targeting them as a specific group. Instead, as part of a wider legislative trend of the nineteenth century it was certain *behaviours* rather than types of people that had become regulated. So, for example, the 1824 Vagrancy Act attacked vagrancy as a way of life and not Gypsies specifically. The 1899 Commons Act enabled local authorities to take over management of commons and to enact bylaws prohibiting camping or lighting fires, while the 1885 Housing of the Working Classes Act allowed a sanitary authority to make bylaws for 'promoting cleanliness in, and the habitable condition of tents, vans, sheds and similar structures' and generally for preventing 'nuisances'.[2] Bylaws stemming from these and related Acts[3] created a new patchwork of regulation affecting Travellers, but their effectiveness was dependent partly on whether a particular locality enacted and enforced the legislation.

While these legislative tools could have the cumulative effect of outlawing sizeable parts of Travellers' lifestyles in particular areas, they did not in themselves target Travellers as a specific group. British lawmakers could, and did, make the argument that their intention was to treat everyone equally, and to require everyone to behave in certain, standardised ways. That such legislation had a disproportionate impact on certain groups was rarely, if ever, acknowledged.

One consequence of central government assertions of impartiality was that its interference in the lives of British Travellers was characterised by indifference, or sometimes vaguely benign statements moderating the sporadic calls for repression stemming from certain areas. In part this was the product of the much smaller 'Gypsy' population in Britain, compared in particular to central Europe, but it was also due to the nature of the British state itself. Of particular importance for state–Traveller relations were developing trends within government administration. The first was a tendency, typified in the Home Office, towards greater professionalism and a culture of impartiality within Whitehall.[4] The treatment of Travellers by central government therefore tested the extent of and commitment to impartial and even-handed government that had increasingly characterised the civil service by the late nineteenth century.

The second trend was the expansion of the state itself, as greater intervention was seen as necessary to solve problems caused by urbanisation and industrialisation.[5] John Davis's work demonstrates that this was a contested area as the dynamic between central and local government continually altered in reaction to new responsibilities and constraints. An acceptance by central goverment of the inevitability of relatively autonomous local bodies was tempered by a commitment to minimum standards in those services that had been subject to national regulation, the result being 'highly detailed statutory codes applied with a light hand'.[6] At the same time local authorities, hampered by an uncertain fiscal situation, 'became notably resistant to new duties [especially those] which they considered intrinsically "national"'.[7] This indicates how the development of state regulation over Travellers was not necessarily one of relentless expansion, but might instead be tied up in arguments over what constituted the proper form of regulation, and over who was willing to accept the responsibility and costs for new powers.

The ambiguous and contested position in which Travellers found themselves at the start of the century is well illustrated by the efforts of Surrey County Council to extend their powers in order to control the 'Gypsy problem'. In 1907 it lobbied the County Council Association to support new legislation controlling the 'nuisance' of Travellers. How Surrey presented and supported its argument illustrates both the county's unique position, but equally the extent to which it was part of a wider dissatisfaction with Travellers. Central government's reaction provides an insight into the relationship between Whitehall and local government, and how seriously the Home Office in particular took the issue of impartiality. Archival evidence reveals that calls for greater regulation were typically geographically and socially specific.

Surrey was close to London and to the vegetable, fruit and hop gardens of the south-east, and had much wasteland and common land. These factors combined to make it a popular area for Travellers. In the late nineteenth century the county started experiencing new pressures which made its 'Gypsy problem' much more visible. From the 1890s the Metropolitan police developed an active policy of moving on Travellers in their district, resulting in many Travellers shifting to the non-metropolitan areas surrounding London, including Surrey.[8] At the same time, along with the other counties encircling London, Surrey experienced a housing boom.[9] The rash of new mock-Tudor villas in semi-rural locations such as Boxhill and Epsom, as well as causing resentment from local residents, also had serious implications for Travellers. Inevitably, much of the new building took place on the periphery of existing settlements and on waste ground, that is, sites habitually used by Travellers. A county council representative acknowledged, 'the place has come more populous, and [Travellers] have come more into evidence. Before there were not so many houses about, and I suppose these Gypsies did what they like and were not so much noticed'.[10]

An increased number of Travellers at a time of greater pressure on land upset a balance that at best had only ever been precarious. A survey conducted by Surrey County Council in 1897 attempted to discover whether these problems were a feature throughout England,[11] but the replies suggested that, 'the evil complained of does not exist to so great an extent' in the rest of the country.[12] There were, however, certain hot spots: East Suffolk, Bristol, Southampton and Dorset all supported Surrey in calling for fresh legislation. The main areas of complaint regarding Travellers were summed up in the following report from Dorset:

> It is an everyday occurrence to find a party of these people en-
> camped ... generally near some plantation within easy reach of
> some good field of clover, where they do not hesitate to run
> their horses ... The unsanitary condition of their vans is de-
> plorable, and the immorality in the midst of which the chil-
> dren are brought up is abominable in the extreme ... the
> offspring of these lawless people are trained almost from birth
> in the art of pilfering.[13]

Answers to a questionnaire sent out by Surrey to other county councils in 1907 indicate a similarly patchy picture. Of the 36 council replies, only 10 supported calls for new legislation, and of these, only 4 – Southampton, Worcestershire, East Suffolk and Essex – were enthusiastic.[14] These councils were the exception, and attitudes of the remaining local authorities fell into two distinct patterns. The first, most simply, were from councils such as Bedfordshire and Northumberland stating that they had few Gypsies in their county and therefore did not see the need for legislation.[15] The second group consisted of counties that had no 'problem' as they took steps to move on or harass Travellers out of their area. In Cheshire, for example, van-dwellers received 'the attention of the police in order to prevent them from committing any depredations'.[16] Such concerted harassment seems to have been limited to specific areas of the country where there were particularly high concentrations of Travellers, particularly when they remained encamped for prolonged periods.

Evidence generated by Surrey indicates that ill-feeling towards Travellers might be found among all classes of people. In Chessington, for example, statements of complaint were filed from labourers as well as the parish overseer and the foreman of the local manor.[17] However, in general, resentment tended to be concentrated within two particular classes – the landed gentry and the emerging class of local authority officials. Landowners, especially those who had rights over wastes and commons, felt unable to keep Travellers off their land and disliked paying for their removal. From the growing body of local government officials arose a more general feeling of indignation directed at Travellers. These officials resented the way Travellers avoided the legal controls and responsibilities that were the hallmark of the expanding modern bureaucratic state. And it was from these two groups in particular that pressure for new legislation stemmed.

The moveable dwellings bills

From the 1880s there had been a series of attempts to pass legislation aimed specifically at those living in 'moveable dwellings'. Mayall's work has shown how, in classic Victorian style, the original impetus for the first wave of the moveable dwellings bills, in the 1880s and 1890s, came from one vociferous campaigner, George Smith of Coalville.[18] These proposed a combination of sanitary control measures and registration of dwellings in order to control and regulate the van-dwelling population.

The second wave of agitation for moveable dwelling legislation, from 1906 to 1913, was different in that the legislation was repeatedly introduced in the House of Lords rather than the Commons,
and originated from a combination of landed gentry and local government officials. Their twin influences can be seen in the proceedings of the 1909 House of Lords committee which considered the
case for moveable dwelling legislation. The Committee numbered
among its members many landowners who supported the Bill –
notably the Lords Farrer and Chudleigh – who were continually at
pains to emphasise the desirability of new regulations. They stressed,
for example, the fact that the 'police decline to deal with these people
if they are on common land';[19] advanced the idea that the number of
Travellers had been increasing over recent years;[20] and took evidence
from landowners who had experienced difficulties with Travellers.[21]

These men stressed that current legislation failed to allow
prompt removal of Travellers, and gave landowners the financial and
physical responsibility of evicting Travellers from their land.[22] It is
difficult to escape the conclusion that they desired the benefits of
landowning without the attendant disadvantages: the removal of
Travellers from their land was something they felt the state should
undertake. The moveable dwelling bills, with their sanitary regulations and registration provisions, would allow the police to remove
and prosecute Travellers without landowners having to bear any expense or inconvenience.

The motivations of the public officials, in contrast, were very
different:

> Now, under modern ideas and regulations and so forth, natu-
> rally the people who live in ordinary dwellings resent people
> who do not. Those who live in dwellings have to observe strict
> sanitary regulations, and these people observe none ... They
> do not seem to me to pay any tax on their vehicles ... [these]
> chaps seem to go free.[23]

Local authority and health professionals who gave evidence had one
common theme: that action was needed to control this class of people,
irrespective of whether or not they were a health or public order
risk. For example, Dr Fosbroke, the county medical officer for
Worcestershire, admitted that while they were a 'healthy and robust
lot', they were not 'cleanly' and thought 'that everybody should be
washed', irrespective of whether they were causing sanitary problems.[24]

As Christine Bellamy has indicated, this period saw the expansion of the state at both central and local government level in a wide range of matters, 'particularly those relating to social welfare and the physical environment'.[25] Many new state functions dealt with controlling the physical, and often by implication, the moral environment of the nation's poor under the auspices of either a local authority or the Local Government Board. In this context, Travellers were simply yet another class of persons who had failed to keep pace with the changes wrought by modernisation, and along with their brethren were to be cajoled into the twentieth century. Thus, in discussions over new legislation they were commonly grouped with pea- and hop-pickers, vagrants and show-people more often than they were considered as a racially distinct entity.

To local government officials the lack of concrete proof that Travellers were a public health risk was irrelevant: they *might* pose a risk if allowed to continue unchecked, and their habits offended modern notions of hygiene and propriety. More than this, if they were able to exist happily without sanitary regulation then they were challenging the assumptions on which modern public health policy was based. Interference by the state was not only necessary in order to assert the importance of the regulation of public health but also to reaffirm the professional status of the inspectors and sanitary officials.

Given the fact that moveable dwellings legislation was generated and supported by the elites of the old regime as well as local representatives of the expanding bureaucratic state, it is surprising that it consistently failed to become law. This is even more remarkable considering the fact that Travellers had no representative body of their own to fight their case. The formalisation of government bureaucracies had seen the concurrent emergence of bodies representing certain sectional interests, be they trade unions or charitable lobbying bodies, which pushed to ensure that their minority interests were heard. For example, the Board of Deputies was vital for the representation of Jewish interests to government in the nineteenth century and early twentieth century.[26]

In his brief analysis of the progress of Chudleigh's moveable dwellings bills, Sexton points to the action of the showmen, and the campaigning of the embryonic Showman's Guild as decisive in the Bills' failure.[27] However, even a cursory reading of the evidence shows this to be a limited explanation at best. Lobbying done by the Guild was done with the sole purpose of arguing for the exemption of showmen, as it consistently accepted the wider principle of regulation for the remainder of the travelling population. In evidence to the select committee the showmen's representative, Thomas Horne, stressed how the majority of showmen were 'well educated' and 'respectable', how there were 'not more than half a dozen' instances of Gypsies becoming showmen, and on those grounds 'wanted an exemption clause'. The Guild's representative agreed with Earl Russell that it was 'fighting merely [its] own battles ... and not for other nomads'. The Showman's Guild successfully gained exemption for its members, but it cannot be credited with more, and the answer to the Bills' failures lay elsewhere.[28]

Part of the reason, of course, lay in the fact that the mind of government, and the country in general at the time, was more preoccupied with wider issues, notably educational and poor law reform. Beyond this, however, evidence from the Home Office and Local Government Board reveal the importance of consistent opposition on the part of civil servants in blocking the bills. This challenges any belief that central government was committed either to the systematic harassment of Travellers, or even to passively acquiescing to such a policy. However, as was demonstrated in many areas of administration, the government's position was 'reactive and negative, not positive and strategic: and the central bureaucracy operated compromised, partial and pragmatic controls, which largely failed to secure a grip on local policy'.[29]

Opposition by the Local Government Board might be seen as unexpected, given its role as overseer of sanitary regulations. Yet the official position was that the legislation 'seem[ed] to go rather far'.[30] The reason behind this reluctance lay in the culture and working practices of the Board. It was fantastically overworked, covering as it did a huge range of areas of concern, maintaining a number of inspectorates, conducting audits of local authorities and compiling massive statistical records. Added to this was its work culture, epitomised by top-level officials whose position seemed to have been based on the 'frustration of social policy', rather than its advancement. Bellamy has attributed this to the dynamic between central and local government, particularly the 'prolonged and unresolved fiscal tension' accompanying the expansion of the domestic functions of the state, which placed a disproportionate burden on the rates.[31] The Board's response to the Bills was therefore a product of its desire to maintain the bureaucratic status quo rather than an indication of its attitude towards Travellers.

Significantly, while its medical and sanitary officers lobbied for greater regulatory control for Travellers, they were not particularly committed to the concept of moveable dwelling legislation. Rather, they were interested in regulation by any means available. Thus, a more consistent implementation of existing bylaws and measures were just as acceptable in their eyes as a specific Bill. It was therefore only the landed gentry who were especially committed to the creation of regulations in a specific 'moveable dwellings' form.

The Local Government Board's attitude shows how the modern state did not automatically grasp every opportunity to expand its sphere of influence. Evidence from the other Whitehall department concerned with this legislation, the Home Office, confirms this and highlights another side of the emerging bureaucracy. Key to the actions of the department was its belief that it existed as a professional and impartial body, free from the influence both of the old elites and new interest groups. For the moveable dwellings bills it sustained three lines of objection: that existing legislation, if properly enforced, was sufficient; that the Bills tended to be poorly drawn and were largely impracticable; and that they were potentially unnecessarily repressive.[32]

Home Office civil servants consistently argued that if local authorities enforced existing regulations properly there would be no problem. This can be seen in the department's dealings with Middlesex, which had gained bylaws to control nuisances for certain districts in 1895.[33] In 1904 it tried to have them extended to all urban districts,[34] complaining of 'the great amount of damage and intolerable nuisance ... in consequence of Gypsies camping in the neighbourhood and the thefts which are constantly being perpetrated at night time'.[35] Not accepting this argument, the Home Office demanded to know if bylaws had been enforced in areas where they applied and what else had been done to counter the nuisance.[36] It made enquiries and found that in fact 'no proceedings have been taken by the Police' under Middlesex's bylaws.[37]

Additionally, following contact with Scotland Yard it transpired that the situation was not as acute as portrayed by the petitioners. In the preceding eighteen months there had been two complaints of theft, five of horses being turned out to graze and five of damage: 'In no case did the amount of damage exceed a few shillings, and in neither of the cases of theft was there any evidence that the Gypsies were the perpetrators'.[38]

The second criticism of the Home Office was that the moveable dwellings bills were poorly drafted and potentially unclear in their execution. One of the main problems was that the legislation was based on the 1875 Canal Boats Act, which specified minimum standards of sanitation, ventilation, and cubic feet of space per person required on such a vessel. However, it was quickly realised that such requirements could not be enforced, and were not even appropriate, for tents made up of 'boughs of trees with some old cloth fastened over them'.[39] Equally, the transient nature of the population meant it would not be 'a simple matter to carry out an efficient machinery for identification' of Travellers, even if their vehicles were registered.[40]

Clause 2 of the 1910 Moveable Dwellings Bill provided for police to evict Travellers from private property, and was objected to by the Home Office as it introduced 'a novel and doubtful principle' regarding 'a wide and most questionable extension of the functions of the police', as in civil trespass the landowner, or their agents, had the responsibility for removing individuals.[41] Significantly, civil servants expressed fears that it would be undesirable to change 'the ordinary law of trespass in respect of a particular class, the vandweller, and to subject that class alone to arrest and prosecution for trespass'.[42] This reflected less a concern for Travellers than for wider notions of justice and consistency within the law.

Home Office civil servants also demonstrated a desire not to identify the law with the interests of a particular class, and the idea that Travellers were being singled out for repression offended notions of equality before the law. Senior bureaucrats predicted that through the bill's measures 'every convenient place would soon be closed to Gypsies. If Gypsies are to be suppressed, Parliament should at least do it with its eyes open'.[43] As with reservations on the technical drafting of the Bills, this was more the product of the department's emerging sense of identity than the result of any specific concern for Travellers.[44]

A desire to target a particular group, however, was what the drafters and supporters of the bills intended. Mr Justice Bray, a Surrey landowner, proposed that 'moveable dwellings should only be allowed in specified places provided or sanctioned by the local authority' where 'they would be easy to inspect and watch'.[45] His idea of official sites was adopted and became the centrepiece for the new versions of the bill, along with new powers to prohibit camping on any land outside the official sites in those areas where such sites were provided – what would later in the century be termed 'designation' (see Chapter 7). The chief clerk at the Home Office, however, was deeply unhappy with these proposals, which would 'involve a serious interference with Gypsy life and will probably entail hardship':[46]

> I do not feel, on reading the evidence, that a case has been made out for such restrictions. The evidence is composed of a number of allegations, often rather vague of (a) insanitary habits; (b) petty thefts; (c) damage to hedges, etc.; (d) the habit of turning their horses into other people's fields; and (e) bad language and rough manners. The only point on which the evidence is at all strong is (a). As for the other points, the witnesses say that they suppose the Gypsies are the culpable persons, but they emphasise the difficulty of proving cases ... Of course, it is quite possible that the existence of a regular nomad class is becoming really incompatible with the conditions of modern civilisation, but I think we ought to have stronger and more comprehensive evidence before it is decided to tie these people down ... it is clear that a great number of persons, particularly landowners, object strongly to the presence of all nomads, but one cannot help suspecting that their objections are often largely confused [with] the prejudice naturally felt by the respectable person towards the vagrant.[47]

The resistance of both the Local Government Board and the Home Office to various forms of the moveable dwellings bills indicates the importance of adopting a nuanced approach to state expansion and the treatment of minorities. While certain interest groups wanted greater authority over Gypsies merely because they were Gypsies, these departments resisted such pressure. Instead, their officials accepted the need for greater regulation of certain types of *behaviour*, seeing it as part of a wider framework of social regulation that was targeted at the poorer classes in general. Civil servants exhibited discomfort over harassing a particular section of society, and reacting to the bill as 'a bad piece of class legislation',[48] commenting that this 'is the sort of Bill the Lords can pass as often as they like. It has no chance in the Commons'.[49]

A reaction against an elite trying to consolidate their position of privilege can be seen from other classes of government officials. Captain Sant, the Chief Constable of Surrey, made plain his annoyance with the privileged Lords of the Manors who derived 'certain advantages from their position' but were unwilling to pay for a sufficient number of commons keepers.[50] Thus, there was no guarantee that the police were in the pockets of the gentry, instead, they too could assert their independence and stick to the letter of the law to the advantage of Travellers. The treatment of Travellers by the state said as much about the tensions between different aspects of the emerging bureaucracy and the old centres of local power as it did about the attitude of officials towards Travellers.

It was a combination of lack of concerted political interest in the issue except from a few sectional interests, firm and detailed resistance from the Home Office, and apathy from the Local Government Board that caused the failure of the second wave of moveable dwellings bills. The third and final attempt to pass this form of legislation in the inter-war period shows yet again how the preoccupations of and developments within settled society were at the heart of the failure of the bills.

The years 1918 to 1939 saw a major shift in the physical and social environment of Britain, resulting in Travellers becoming sidelined from the debate on moveable dwellings as their role was taken over by unregulated campers and shanty site dwellers. After 1918 there was a meteoric rise in rambling, camping and caravanning, and this period also saw an increase in the use of caravans as homes by poorer house-dwellers. On coastal resorts and in the countryside during the summer holiday periods, people in caravans and chalets escaping the city filled fields and waste areas.[51]

The local authority association reports of 1933 revealed how the situation had changed from the pre-war focus on 'Gypsies'.[52] Of the 30 urban district councils (UDCs) with caravan problems, the majority of these were long-term shanty sites or were due to unrestricted seaside development.[53] Of the county councils, 21 had complaints ranging from concern over 'increased risk from fire' from Travellers living in the yards of public houses, to unrestrained shack development along the Lincolnshire coast.[54] Replies from the rural district councils (RDCs) showed some of the same trends, but additionally there were problems caused by unregulated leisure camping, 'which has taken upon itself an entirely new and different complex from the days when a few scattered Gypsies or homeless people lived in tents and dilapidated huts'. The RDCs also raised concerns over their inability to remove offending dwellings that did not breach bylaws but contributed to the 'spoilation of the scenery'.[55] The problem was in:

> [The] great mixture of the structures and the classes of dwellers in them ... some are clearly homes of cleanly and law abid-

ing persons ... some are in the occupation of violent, unhy-
gienic and unsocial persons (which term is said frequently to
include Gypsies); some are in built up areas; some remote from
towns and nor readily discovered until they are too numerous
or until the powers for an Order of Court are barred; some
spoil coasts and cliffs and beauty spots; some are an offence to
persons, some to property; some are extremely mobile and some
are fixed; some are big aggregations of tents, respectable enough
but straining the local water supply and possibilities of sanitation ... [in any new legislation] the balance to be preserved is
between practically uncontrolled disorder, insanitariness and
damage to property, personal and even quasi-national, and the
reasonable enjoyment of quite commendable form of life, either permanent or as part of a holiday.[56]

Local authorities initially responded by seeking local bylaw
powers to deal with nuisances, and continued to lobby for national
legislation. However, not only might magistrates or the police inter-
pret bylaws in a number of ways unfavourable to the authorities,[57]
but in some cases bylaws were insufficient owing to the limited nature of their scope. Rural authorities were rarely granted the same
powers as their urban counterparts, giving rise to localised problems: 'so long as the powers are in force in some districts ... evicted
dwellers move [to] a Rural District'.[58] In other cases residents of a
site might comply with the bylaws, for example through providing a
water supply, meaning they could not be evicted.

Such difficulties led councils to lobby for national legislation,
initially in the form of moveable dwellings bills, but increasingly
through public health regulations. The moveable dwellings bills of
the 1920s were still framed in similar terms to their pre-war prede-
cessors, aiming to regulate Travellers through sanitary measures and
by controlling access to camping grounds.[59] Despite these continuities, the changed situation on the ground meant that, by definition,
unregulated shanty sites as well as leisure camping and caravanning
would have been brought within their remit. This was not necessarily a problem as all moveable dwelling use brought difficulties in
certain locations. However, the drafting and provenance of the bills
implied that their intention was solely to regulate Travellers, while
in practice affecting a wide range of people. Therefore, while central
government rejected the bills partly on the grounds that they unfairly targeted one section of the population,[60] certain outdoors
organisations complained the measures were too broad and that they
would be unfairly affected by proposed regulation.[61] Their complaints

were accepted by central government, who used it as one of the reasons for opposing the 1926 bill.[62]

Yet, increasing numbers of local authorities became attracted to moveable dwellings legislation as they saw it as an answer to their shanty site problem. The support of councils, indicated by the fact that the moveable dwelling bills of the 1930s were sponsored by the RDC Association rather than private landed individuals, changed the composition of the legislation. In fact, the new form of the bills no longer targeted Travellers, confirming that officials no longer saw them as the sole, or even main, source of difficulty. In line with developments on the ground, the 1932 draft exempted a tent or a van, 'which is used as the sole means of habitation by a Gypsy not in the locality for more than three months in any calendar year',[63] assuming that 'Gypsies and hawkers are outside our province ... We cannot press for restrictions on them'.[64]

A shift in focus away from Travellers and towards shanty sites removed the Home Office's main concern with the legislation. Regulations that targeted unacceptable and anti-social behaviour generally, rather than Travellers specifically, were entirely in keeping with more general bureaucratic attempts to regulate public health and the built environment. At the same time as the moveable dwellings bills changed in their focus, the Ministry of Health came to accept that existing legislation was insufficient to control the ever expanding shanty problem.[65] The confluence of these two factors – acceptance of a need, combined with an acceptable means of resolving the issue – paved the way for national legislation.

The consequent 1936 Public Health Act must not be read as Whitehall accepting responsibility for the issue of moveable dwellings. Instead, it did nothing more than confirm the two key threads of national government thinking: the importance of treating all equally before the law while legislating against certain unacceptable habits, and firmly placing enforcement at the door of the local authorities. The key difference in 1936 was that for the first time central government took on the responsibility of moving forward the debate, and with it, national policy.

The 1936 Act was extremely wide-ranging in its scope, dealing extensively with environmental health matters as well as local authority provision of public health facilities. Through measures attacking dirt, disorder and squalor, in essence it aimed to control and improve the nation's physical environment. Seen in this light, Section 268, which dealt with insanitary moveable dwellings, was part of a general attack on unregulated forms of living that created a public nuisance, and was not a specific attack on Travellers' lifestyles. Section 269 allowed councils to issue licences for siting moveable dwellings, but a licence was not needed for land not occupied for more than 42 consecutive days or for over 60 days in any one year.[66] It attempted to deal with both the problems caused by the estimated half a million campers and leisure caravanners as well as 'badly organised shanty sites' in coastal areas.[67] The terms were 'the product of an intensive but protracted try-out of almost every conceivable conception, device and precedent' and aimed 'not to be oppressive and destructive of reasonable freedom'.[68]

Travellers, or rather 'Gypsies', may have been excluded from the legislation in intention, but in actuality they felt its impact. The Ministry of Health believed that Section 269 did not 'touch true nomads'.[69] While the law did not affect Travellers when they were mobile, typically from March to October, this did not mean they were unaffected. The 1933 Local Authority Association reports had made it abundantly clear that large numbers of Travellers were semi-sedentary. The fact that policy makers believed in the perpetual nomadism of Travellers confirmed the depth of the romantic conception of Gypsies as wanderers, held by civil servants. The mobilisation of the stereotype of 'true' nomads allowed government to believe that it was legislating against those who created a 'nuisance' without persecuting a minority.

What was true was that this law did not target them as *Gypsies* but merely as people who were perceived to be living in unsanitary and substandard accommodation. By insisting that Travellers were treated as individuals in relation to the state, and not part of a collective entity with any right to particular consideration and representation, the measure confirmed the state's avowal of impartiality. It also denied Travellers the right to assert that their culture demanded a certain level of recognition and understanding by government, which might, in some cases, lead to the need for special treatment. In essence, the Public Health Act served to confirm the invisibility of Travellers in the eyes of policy makers.

Epsom Downs, 1937

The period up to 1939, despite the common depiction of it as a 'golden age', routinely saw evictions of Travellers from both temporary and permanent sites. In general these evictions were small-scale, largely unopposed by Travellers and received little attention from the press. One major exception to this was the battle to keep Travellers from Epsom Down during the racing season in 1937 and subsequent years. This episode saw not only Travellers and officials in conflict, but sections of the settled population marshalling arguments and taking sides, in what can be seen as a foretaste of post-war eviction controversies.

In April 1937, under the Epsom and Walton Downs Regulations Act, 1936, camping and other activities were banned from the area of the Downs surrounding the racecourse.[70] The normal complaints against the Travellers were heightened by the fact that large numbers were concentrated in a relatively small area, arriving up to six weeks before the beginning of the spring meeting.[71] This was also in the context of a prestigious race meeting and right in the heart of the commuter belt. The Conservators' solution was to pass a series of bylaws banning a range of activities that essentially barred Travellers from the area.[72]

Despite the ban, many Travellers, either because they had not heard or because they thought they should have the right, arrived and tried to camp as normal on the commons around the racecourse. Many of them were simply moved on, while three were 'summonsed for driving and placing caravans on the Downs without lawful authority'.[73] The new regulations did have the result of removing Travellers, but they were not an unqualified success, as most Travellers simply moved onto land outside the restricted zone, choosing commons such as Tattenham Common, a mile and a half from the racecourse. One reporter found 200 Travellers and 30 vans parked up in 'little used roadways' and on open land in the Banstead and Tadworth residential areas of Epsom.[74]

On the day three summonsed Travellers were in court one source suggests there was a protest march to the court, with a Traveller declaring: 'We shall not give up without a fight. For generations our people have used the Downs for a camping place'.[75] While there is no indication of whether or not this march actually took place, there was certainly some resistance, including a group of fifteen vans that remained until 'motor lifting gear arrived to remove them'.[76]

In contrast to everyday evictions, the high profile nature of the location and the numbers of Travellers involved meant the imagination of the press and sections of the public were captured,[77] and the Travellers were, for once, well represented in court.[78] Those who were anti-Traveller depicted the move as a triumph of ordinary, long-suffering locals over outsiders. In contrast, their sympathisers saw the new law as being foisted upon the populace by an elite group of landowners. Inevitably the two main stereotypes of Gypsies – as romantic nomads and as thieving scoundrels – were mobilised, often side by side, by those debating on both sides of the argument.[79]

Beyond the rhetoric, Travellers received practical support, with Lords Derby and Ebbisham protesting to the Conservators and proposing that they be allowed to camp on the Downs from the Thursday to the Sunday of the race week.[80] Lady Sybil Grant, a keen caravanner and daughter of an important local landowner, allowed Travellers to camp in a field on her land for the duration of the summer meeting, although restricted the privilege to more 'respectable' Gypsies.[81] She was supported by Dora Yates, Secretary of the Gypsy Lore Society,[82] and together they drew up, and began circulating, a petition asking that the bylaws *'need not be enforced during Derby Week'*.[83]

The protests of these high profile supporters did little to alter the enforcement of the new regulations, and the bylaws were applied in the years up to the Second World War. However, during and after the war Travellers were back on the Downs. This was partly as a result of the tendency of local authorities to gradually relax their vigilance as the problem diminished, thereby allowing Travellers to return in smaller numbers. The continued presence of Travellers on the Downs was also a result of the unclear legal position, as there was some confusion over the extent of Epsom Common and where the bylaws were actually operative.[84] This had the effect of removing Travellers from the central part of the Downs, while failing to ban them from the periphery or surrounding downland.[85]

While the situation on the Downs during Derby Week brought very particular challenges to the local administration, more general lessons can be drawn from the episode. The cries of sympathy for Travellers were confined to particular sections of the public, mainly those 'who write so romantically about the Romanies', but very few others. 1937 was not a year when the 'ordinary' members of the public became particularly moved by measures against Travellers. Nor did it see the mass mobilisation of Travellers in defence of their rights, as on other occasions while some actively resisted, the majority used the time-honoured avoidance tactic of simply shifting camp. Their continued presence on the Downs after 1937 can largely be attributed to a quiet and persistent pursuit of their goals, combined with a small measure of legal confusion, rather than any short-term and piecemeal attempts by their supporters to speak up for their rights. However, in the mobilisation of sections of the public to the Travellers' cause through the use of the media, the episode was a foretaste of the post-war era.

The Second World War

As shown in Chapter 1, the greater involvement of Travellers in the mainstream economy and war work during the years 1939–45 produced at best an ambivalent response from the general public, with stereotypes being reconfirmed rather than challenged. Local authorities equally failed to respond positively to the new or expanded roles adopted by Travellers. The war years saw a tension between the aspirations of local authorities that wished to see their area free from Traveller encampments and their ability to enforce the new legislation of 1936, hampered as they were by a shortage of resources.

The Bilston area of Nottingham was characterised by vans being 'tucked away in courts and backyards'. Sanitary officials acknowledged that the vans themselves were kept clean yet complained of the lack of water and sanitation provided. The years 1942–44 saw over one hundred vans being evicted, with many others leaving voluntarily.[86] In other cases, councils, with over-stretched resources, were forced to substitute strong words for action. Sites, such as one in Tadworth, which housed sixty people for over two years, were able to exist for long periods despite complaints.[87] The creation of hundreds of shanty sites on the outskirts of towns, peopled by caravan-dwellers of all sorts and the bombed-out homeless, on top of all the other strains imposed upon them by the war, meant many councils simply did not have the resources for constant evictions. This was to prove of major significance for both Travellers and local authorities in the post-war era.

While many of the conflicts between Travellers and local authorities during the war continued to be in urban and peri-urban areas, the closing months of the war saw the rise of complaints from the countryside, and specifically from farmers. One particular hot spot was Gloucestershire. A combination of intense enemy bombing of the urban parts of the West Midlands and the opportunity for seasonal agricultural work had led to an influx of Travellers in the area. By December 1944 the chief executive of the local National Farmers' Union (NFU) had drawn the attention of the Chief Constable to cases of damage thought to be caused by Gypsies.[88] The local organisation advocated the 'control of movement' of Travellers and extended police controls as a means of combating damage, theft and nuisance. [89] Pressurised by its strong stand, the local MP promoted the idea of van registration,[90] although he refused to support a suggestion to reclassify Gypsies as aliens. He believed this step would be 'impossible' as they had been 'citizens of this country for hundreds of years'.[91]

The concerns of Gloucestershire farmers were echoed in the statements of NFUs around the country, with some farmers banding together to form their own patrols to prevent trespass and damage,[92] and the national executive demanded new legislation in order 'to get every possible ounce of food to the consumer'.[93] Much to the dismay of the NFU, the Home Office held to its position that 'the present law was adequate, if enforced'.[94] This indicates that while local authorities and certain pressure groups attempted to use the war to push through further repressive measures, central government was both too busy and too unconvinced to move from its stated position of impartiality.

These tensions can be seen in even greater relief in Northern Ireland where the relative weakness of the central government gave the voices of the counties and landowners more weight.[95] In the Province the problems generated by the war were compounded by its proximity to Eire, as many Travellers moved across the border in an attempt to make a living.[96] Fundamentally, however, the councils and farmers of the region had the same complaints as their counterparts across the Irish Sea. In one incident, where a group of Travellers were burned out of their benders, the farmer in his defence in court said that he was reacting to repeated damage to his gates, crops and grazing.[97]

As a result of the 'representations received from local authorities and other sources as to the injury and annoyance caused to the community by itinerant Gypsies', the Ministry of Home Affairs established an informal committee to investigate their grievances.[98] The issue it identified as causing most grievances was the difficulty in 'catching the culprits', when Travellers were believed to have committed an offence: 'One Gypsy (using the term generally for nomads of this kind and not in a purely racial sense) is much like another, and once the wrong-doer has escaped from the scene of his delinquency, it is most difficult for the injured party to identify the person accused'.[99]

Many of the report's recommendations were based around

improving methods to control nomads. The Association of RDCs of Northern Ireland suggested that registration of Travellers at local barracks should be enforced, and that steps should be taken 'to compel the Gypsies to settle in permanent dwellings and share in the responsibilities of modern civilisation'.[100] The Committee took up part of this suggestion, believing that Travellers should be required to report to the police whenever they settled on a new pitch, or when they entered a new police area. In this way 'it should be possible without difficulty for an offence committed by an itinerant to be traced to the offender'. They also believed that the police should have powers of summary arrest as regards itinerants 'as otherwise it might involve very considerable delay in bringing him to trial'.[101] The report formed the basis for a bill intended specifically to control 'Gypsies and like itinerants', which was presented repeatedly between 1948 and 1954.

In the context of the closing years of the war and its immediate aftermath, with the massive increase in state involvement and control of people's lives, calls for the registration of Travellers may have been less draconian than they now sound. However, the fact that they were willing to consider measures that applied to certain members of the community and not others suggests that contemporary claims of working towards a fair and just society for all, was not a commitment felt equally by all members of the government. The reactionary voices were far stronger and more influential in Northern Ireland than in England, but this did not mean that officials and landowners were more liberal on the mainland, merely that central government was able to keep a stronger rein on their actions.

In summary, it is important to unpick the idea of 'the state' when considering Britain's treatment of Travellers up to 1945. The period saw Travellers experiencing harassment and evictions, but these were mainly confined to certain locations, were mainly small-scale and attracted little attention. The level of resistance to the extension of bylaws to Epsom Down in 1937 was exceptional for these years, but might also be seen as a precursor to conflicts in the post-war period.

Local councils were considerably more repressive in their intentions than central government, but even here we must distinguish between localities, with only a very few that persistently made attempts to control their Traveller populations. Central government, in the form of the Home Office and Local Government Board (the Ministry of Health after 1919), showed no desire to extend their control over the travelling population, arguing until the early 1930s that current legislation was sufficient. These departments expressed distaste for regulations that either targeted a specific community or were seen to favour a particular sectional interest, and this commitment to impartiality was central to the failure of the moveable dwellings legislation. The shift towards targeting certain types of behaviour through public health regulation, rather than Travellers as a specific group, allowed nationally based legislation controlling moveable dwellings. However, once again, central government made it quite clear that regulation would remain firmly in the hands of local government.

Notes

1 See, for example, G. Lewy, *The Nazi persecution of the Gypsies* (Oxford, 2000); Fings, Heuss, Sparing and Asseo, *From 'race science' to the camps*, 22–3; and L. Eiber, 'The persecution of the Sinti and Roma in Munich, 1933–1945', in S. Tebbutt (ed.), *Sinti and Roma*. Archival evidence of pan-European concern with 'international Gypsies' can be found in TNA, MEPO 3/2047.

2 Mayall, *Gypsy Travellers*, Appendix 1, provides a summary of legislation affecting Travellers from 1530 to 1908.

3 For example, the 1891 Public Health (London) Act, section 95 made similar provisions for the Metropolitan area.

4 See Pellew, *The Home Office*, p. 200.

5 F. M. L. Thompson, 'Town and city', in F. M. L. Thompson (ed.), *The Cambridge social history of Britain, vol. 1: Regions and communities* (Cambridge, 1990), 78.

6 J. Davis, 'Central government and the towns', in M. Daunton (ed.), *The Cambridge urban history of Britain, vol. III: 1840–1950* (Cambridge, 2000), 265–8.

7 *Ibid.*, 275.

8 TNA, HO45/10995/158231/5, letter from Commissioner of the Metropolitan police to HO, 1 January 1909.

9 For a discussion of this see P. L. Garside, 'London and the Home Counties', in Thompson (ed.), *Cambridge social history of Britain*, 516.

10 Evidence of Dr Chester, *Report from the Select Committee of the House of Lords on the Moveable Dwelling Bill*, 1910, 840.

11 Surrey History Centre, Woking (hereafter SHC), CC28/101 'Surrey county council: Regulation of Gypsies, Travellers and van dwellers etc'.

12 *Ibid.*, letter from Bedfordshire County Council to Surrey County Council, 12 February 1898.

13 *Ibid* , Chief Constable of Dorset's, 'Report', 13 April 1898, enclosed in letter from Dorset County Council to Surrey County Council, 5 May

1898.
14 SHC, CC28/158. The counties expressing their support with reservations were Berkshire, Herefordshire, West Suffolk, London and East Sussex.
15 *Ibid.*, replies from Bedfordshire, 15 January 1907; Buckinghamshire, 29 January 1907; and Northumberland, 18 January 1907.
16 *Ibid.*, reply from Cheshire, 1 March 1907.
17 SHC, CC28/101.
18 For a full discussion of Smith's efforts see Mayall, *Gypsy Travellers*, Chapter 6.
19 Evidence of Lord Farrer, *Select Committee on Moveable Dwellings*, 100.
20 *Ibid.*, 132–6.
21 See, for example, evidence of Hon. Charles Drummond, *ibid.*, 1258.
22 For example, the Agent for the Rolle Estate in Devon noted that injunctions were the main means of forcibly removing Travellers from commons, and these were expensive and took a fortnight to obtain, evidence of Mr Chamier, *ibid.*, 661.
23 Evidence of Dr Chester, *ibid.*, 840, 843, 900.
24 *Ibid.*, 496–7 and 515. There were exceptions, see evidence of Dr Farrar, *ibid.*, 393 and 364.
25 Bellamy, *Administering central and local government*, 1.
26 D. Feldman, 'Jews and the state in Britain', in M. Brenner (ed.), *Two nations: British and German Jews in comparative perspective* (Tubingen, *c.*1999).
27 Sexton, 'Travelling people', 121.
28 *Select Committee on Moveable Dwellings*, iii, 1603–4, 1609, 1667 and 1670.
29 Bellamy, *Administering central and local government*, 155–6.
30 Evidence of Mr Munro, *Select Committee on Moveable Dwellings*, 3.
31 Bellamy, *Administering central and local government*, 11–12. For a more in-depth consideration of this point see Davis, 'Central Government', 268.
32 Mayall points to these same reasons for the failure of the earlier wave of moveable dwellings bills; Mayall, *Gypsies Travellers*, 145.
33 For Middlesex's attempts to gain bylaws in the early 1890s see TNA, HO45/9825/B790/A, C, E, F.
34 This was the result of a petition sent to the Justices of Brentford by seven prominent landowners. The bylaws were to cover Greenford, Heston and Isleworth, Norwood and Hamdell, and Brentford, and effectively prohibited Travellers from camping within the vicinity of any built-up areas, TNA, HO45/14096/3, Clerk of Middlesex county council to HO, 2 February 1904.
35 TNA, HO45/14096/3, Clerk of Middlesex county council to HO, 2 February 1904.
36 TNA, HO45/14096/4, minutes, 23 March 1904.
37 *Ibid.*, letter from Scotland Yard to the HO, 24 July 1909.
38 TNA, HO45/14096/7, New Scotland Yard to HO, 2 June 1904.

39 *Report of the Select Committee on the Temporary Dwellings Bill* (London 1887), 45–6.
40 TNA, HO45/10529/14762/5, HO memo, 1909.
41 TNA, HO45/10529/14762/7.
42 TNA, HO45/10529/147162/12.
43 *Ibid.*, HO minute, 30 March 1908.
44 See Pellew, *Home Office*, for an account of the department's growing commitment to impartiality, and D. Feldman, *Englishmen and Jews: Social relations and political culture, 1840–1914* (New Haven, CT, 1994), 355–8, for how this could work against minorities in particular cases.
45 Evidence of Justice Bray, *Select Committee on Moveable Dwellings*, 8–10.
46 TNA, HO45/10529/147162/12, HO memo, February 1911.
47 TNA, HO45/10529/147162/7, Pedder's notes on Select Committee, 24 October 1910.
48 TNA, HO45/10529/147162/18, note by Pedder, 17 May 1911.
49 TNA, HO45/10529/147162/22, note by Pedder., 20 March 1913.
50 TNA, HO45/10995/158231/25, letter from Sant to HO, 1 July 1910. More broadly he also questioned the idea that Travellers were particularly worthy of police attention, see TNA, HO 45/10995/ 158231/9.
51 N. Wilson, *Gypsies and Gentlemen: The life and times of the leisure caravan* (London, 1986), 167.
52 These reports were the result of a conference between the various local authority associations and Whitehall in February 1933. A parallel report covering the whole of Scotland also revealed a similar range of nuisances and concerns, see TNA, HLG 52/396, Department of Health for Scotland, 'Report of the Consultative Council In Regard to the Statutory Provisions and Regulations Necessary or Desirable to Secure the Proper Regulation of the Erection and Use of Tents, Vans, Sheds and Similar Structures', July 1934.
53 TNA, HLG52/394, UDC association memo, 'Replies to circular letter on the subject of moveable dwellings sent to members', 31 July and 10 October 1933.
54 *Ibid.*, county council association, 'Caravans, moveable dwellings and camping grounds: Summary of observations', n.d.
55 *Ibid.*, RDC association, 'Moveable Dwellings and Camping Grounds Bill: Memo with reference to replies to the circular letter issued to members of the Association on the 28th February 1933', n.d.
56 *Ibid.*, Ministry of Health (hereafter MoH) memo, 'Caravans, moveable dwellings and camping grounds – reaction to local authority Associations' evidence', 1 February 1934.
57 See TNA, MEPO 3/2047 for a discussion of Barnet magistrates' unwillingness to uphold police attempts to use local bylaws against Travellers.
58 *Ibid.*, further MoH notes, 19 December 1929.
59 TNA, HLG/52/411, 'To provide for the regulation of moveable dwellings'.

60 As with its pre-1914 criticisms of the legislation, there were also complaints over the poor technical drafting of the Bills. The HO and MoH between them consistently blocked the Bills of the 1920s; TNA, HLG52/411, notes, 27 and 30 March 1926. The HO also rejected or modified sections of local Acts on the same grounds. See TNA, HLG 52/393, HO, 'Report on The Surrey County Council Bill, 1931', 4.

61 The Secretary of the Liverpool and District Ramblers Federation feared farmers would no longer allow ramblers to camp in their fields and so believed 'legitimate campers' should be excluded from the Bill, TNA HLG/52/411, letter from Secretary of the Liverpool and District Ramblers Federation, 16 April 1926.

62 TNA, HLG 52/411, Eccles Motor Caravans Transport Limited, Birmingham to MoH, 14 April 1926.

63 TNA, HLG 52 /394, 1932 Moveable Dwellings and Camping Grounds Bill.

64 TNA, HLG 52/395, suggestions by Council for the Protection of Rural England, n.d.

65 TNA, HLG 52/393, MoH memo, 17 December 1929.

66 TNA, HLG 52/1150. The council could attach conditions to its issue regarding provision of water, sanitation, the number and type of dwellings allowed, and the space between them. There were to be two different sorts of licences – for site owners running camps existing over 42 consecutive days or 60 total days; and for when 'a particular person stations and uses a particular structure on a piece of land in excess of the 42 or 60 days'; in this case the individual occupier was required to apply for the licence.

67 N. Wilson, *Gypsies and gentlemen: The life and times of the leisure caravan* (London, 1986), 173.

68 TNA, HLG 52/1533, minutes on shortcomings of 1936 Public Health Act, 14 February 1947.

69 *Ibid.*

70 The bylaws prohibited, without lawful authority, enclosing of any part of the Down, erecting any tent, or shed or other building and allowing of animals, except dogs on leads, onto the Down. They also covered cutting or damaging turf, trees, flowers, shrubs, plants or grass, constructing a road or parking place, camping or lighting fires, littering, or to cause annoyance or an obstruction.

71 'The Gypsies – will they see this year's Derby?', *Epsom Herald* (5 February 1937).

72 TNA, MEPO 2/3242, Police minutes regarding new Epsom bylaws, 8 April 1937. The Conservators Association was created as part of the 1933 Act. This body was given the responsibility and powers to manage the use of the Downs.

73 'Gypsies on Epsom Down', *Huddersfield Examiner* (19 April 1937).

74 'Gypsies defy Epsom ban', *Daily Sketch* (13 April 1937).

75 *Daily Mirror* (19 April 1937).

76 TNA, MEPO 2/3242, Epsom Police Station to S. D. Inspector, 26 April 1937.

77 See for example, letters to editor, *Morning Post* (23 April 1937 and 27 April 1937); 'Gypsies on Epsom Downs', *West Sussex Gazette* (22 April 1937); Gypsies on Epsom Downs', *Huddersfield Examiner* (19 April 1937); 'Lord Derby's protest', *The Times* (26 April 1937); and 'Camping on Epsom Down', *Halifax Daily Courier* (22 April 1937).

78 'Gypsies on Epsom Downs', *West Sussex Gazette* (22 April 1937).

79 See 'A Romany reverse', *Southern Daily Echo* (18 February 1937), and *Time and Tide* (24 April 1937).

80 'Lord Derby's protest', *The Times* (26 April 1937).

81 'Gypsies at Epsom', *The Times* (2 June 1937).

82 Letter to the editor from D. E. Yates, Gypsy Lore Society, *The Observer* (2 May 1937).

83 Brotherton Library Romany Collection, letter from Yates to D. U. Ratcliffe, 5 May 1937. Original emphasis.

84 TNA, MEPO 2/6984, Inspector of Epsom police station to S. D. Inspector, 10 November 1944.

85 *Ibid.*, S. D. Inspector to Superintendent, November 1944.

86 'Bilston trying to get rid of remaining van-dwellings', *Nottingham Guardian* (6 July 1944).

87 'Gypsies at Tadworth', *Surrey Mirror* (17 December 1943). For a similar case in Kent see 'Stone Street Gypsy encampment', *Folkestone Herald* (20 April and 18 May 1940).

88 'Too many Gypsies in Gloucestershire?', *The Citizen, Gloucester* (26 September 1945).

89 'County NFU and control of Gypsies', *Cheltenham Chronicle* (15 December 1945).

90 'Damage by Gypsies: NFU concern', *Gloucester Echo* (15 April 1946).

91 'Gypsies cannot be made aliens', *Birmingham Gazette* (15 April 1946). The suggestion seems to have come from one individual member of Gloucester NFU, rather than being a mainstream opinion.

92 For example, 'Day to day', *Nottingham Journal* (4 May 1945); 'Nottinghamshire Farmer's Union', *Retford Times* (15 June 1945); 'Menace of the Gypsies', *Darlington Times* (11 May 1946); 'Farmers fight Gypsies', *Sunday Chronicle* (n.d. 1946).

93 'Gypsies', *Farmer and Stock Breeder* (23 April 1946).

94 'Gypsy nuisance', *Wiltshire News* (17 April 1946).

95 For the impact of the partisan and corrupt nature of local government, and the relative weakness of Stormont on the implementation of social policies see R. Lowe, *The welfare state in Britain since 1945* (London and New York, 1999), 92–3.

96 'Ministers reply to complaints about Gypsies', *Irish News* (6 November 1944), and Joyce, *Traveller*, 3.

97 'Burnt out like rats', *Belfast Newsletter* (16 October 1945).

98 It took evidence from the Ulster Association of County Councils, the

Association of District Councils of Northern Ireland, the RUC, and the County Down Committee of Agriculture. Public Record Office of Northern Ireland, Belfast (hereafter PRONI), CAB /9B/224/1, 'Report of Committee on Gypsies and like itinerants', 1948, Appendix III.

99 Note the racist belief that all Travellers look the same. PRONI, CAB/ 9B/224/1, 'Report of Committee on Gypsies', 3.
100 'New law for Gypsies', *Sunday Chronicle* (10 November 1946).
101 PRONI, CAB/9B/224/1, 'Memorandum for the Cabinet submitted by the Minister of Home Affairs in regard to the control and supervision of Gypsies and like itinerants', 1 September 1948.

3

Education and missions

The twentieth century saw informal and legislative attempts to bring Travellers within the embrace of education, yet Traveller culture remained determinedly non-literate. Unlike in majority society where illiteracy was a stigma, amongst Travellers it was seen as part of nomadic identity and a symbol of their continuing independence.[1] This chapter looks at how the state and voluntary agencies, often missionary in origin, attempted to engage Travellers in education and welfare efforts more generally. Within this I raise the possibility that education was used, although often inefficiently, as an instrument to destroy the cultural independence of Britain's Travellers.

As with the divisions between central and local bureaucracies over Traveller encampments, the provision of education brought out inherent conflicts of interest at different levels of government. It was important for a state that saw itself as liberal to treat all children equally and require all to attend school, yet it was local, and not central government that was expected to implement the 1908 Children's Act, and subsequent legislation,[2] revealing how pressures at the local level could contradict the expectations of the centre. On one hand was a desire to see Travellers educated and integrated into mainstream society, and on the other was a reluctance to expend time and money on a group that were seen as having no claim on council resources. More than that, as Gypsy children were depicted as a potentially polluting influence there was often a question mark over their presence in schools. While segregated education may, for some, have been the answer, it did not solve the problem of socialisation – for how were Gypsies to learn the ways of mainstream society if they only mixed with their own kind?

While in many ways the history of Traveller education is distinct, it would be a mistake to ignore parallels with attempts to bring other groups into full-time education. Compulsory education had not been long extended to the working classes, and in many ways the resistance of Traveller parents and culture to education mirrored that of elements of the settled poor. The general success of normalising education within mainstream society contrasts sharply, however, with the failure of formal learning to find acceptance among Travellers. A comparison of the two experiences sheds light on the official tendency to blame this failure on Travellers themselves.

Attempts to bring Travellers into the education system fell into two categories: proactive measures, in which special efforts were made to cater for their needs; and punitive sanctions, where the police, local authorities and the courts prosecuted parents under the 1908 Children's Act. I begin by considering the motivation behind state education for Travellers and the impact of the 1908 Act, and locate its failure in the context of the expansion of education to the working classes more generally. I then move on to examine the experience of Traveller children in mainstream education, and three examples of special education schemes. Through exploring the role of voluntary initiative in providing education for Travellers, I discuss more generally the intentions and actions of missions towards Britain's travelling communities during the period.

Compulsory education

The arguments both for and against bringing Traveller children into schools were based on the same presumption: education was not a neutral tool, but the vanguard of civilisation. As a result, discussions over the education of Travellers often widened to include the desirability of settling and integrating Travellers. In common with more general depictions of the role of Travellers in modern society, the same few stereotypes were mobilised to justify opposing positions. Romantics believed that Gypsies, as representatives of 'nature' and freedom, should be allowed to roam without the burden imposed by compulsory schooling. Equally, there were those who firmly believed that education was the best means at the disposal of government for the integration of a marginal and backward group.

Calls to leave Travellers alone tended to assert that any educational efforts would irreparably destroy them, or conversely that they would be ultimately useless. Many gypsiologists believed that 'the Gypsy' was impermeable to any attempts to bring him into the modern age: 'They are changeless: the world has no power over them.

They live by rote and by faith and by tradition which is part of their blood'.[3] While romanticists felt that education was damaging and/ or useless, reformers marshalled environmentalist arguments to support their case. It was necessary to believe that Travellers were capable of change, and that their characteristics were not inherent, in order to promote education as a prime tool in their reformation.

Even those who were keen that Travellers should become integrated into society often accepted that something would be lost. Newspaper articles featuring Gypsy children in schools commonly stressed how innate Romany characteristics could still be seen under their newly acquired veneer of civilisation, and ended with a note of nostalgia, asking for example, 'if they have lost the taste for basket-making by a shady stream?'[4] These pieces sum up the ambivalent attitudes mainstream society held towards the educating of Traveller children. On the one hand, school attendance by these children was seen as good in itself, although they often gained little in the way of formal education. Yet on the other, there was a wistful harking back to the 'romantic' roots of their lifestyle, and a sadness that this was being drummed, or encouraged, out of them. Overlying this was the basic assumption that socialisation through education was desirable, even if it did not produce anything of particular value for the children concerned – the fact that they would become more malleable citizens was enough.

The Children's Act of 1908, unlike earlier educational legislation, made specific provision for children whose parents 'habitually wander[ed] from place to place' to be included in the mainstream school system. Section 118 required these children to attend school, or the parents be fined 20 shillings, with the additional possibility of the child being sent to an Industrial School. Through lobbying by the Showman's Guild, when such children made two hundred attendances between October and March, they were free to travel for the rest of the year.

Although this exemption had been put in to allow show-families to travel between fairs during the summer, it could apply to any travelling family. In effect, if a family was stationary during the winter months, sent their child to school, and received a certificate of attendance at the end confirming they had made two hundred attendances, they were free to spend the months from April to September without any schooling.

As well as giving the showmen what they wanted from the legislation, the wording also set the minds of civil servants at rest, who had wanted to promote compulsory education, but did not want to interfere with the liberty of people who chose to travel. They had had 'grave objections to any legislation that would render migration, which to other men is lawful, a crime in the case of one particular class, or which would deprive parents belonging to that class of rights of guardianship of their children which other parents enjoy'.[5]

Despite the flexibility that was built into the legislation, it threw up a number of issues regarding the education of Traveller children: who took overall responsibility for Traveller children's attendance at school; the level to which local authorities would be proactive in seeking out and providing for such children; and how Travellers' peripatetic lifestyle fitted with mainstream sedentary schooling.

Educationalists feared that the education received through such a system would prove to be 'inefficient'. Experience gained through implementing the Canal Boats Act suggested that, 'intermittent education ... has very great drawbacks to it. A child who attends the school merely one day here and there does not derive the full benefit of the instruction given in the school'.[6] A travelling lifestyle was commonly seen as the reason for irregular attendance, rather than any shortcomings in the system itself.

Newspaper reports of early prosecutions of Travellers under the 1908 Act give the impression that throughout the country there was general enthusiasm for its implementation.[7] The Director of Education for the New Forest district, for example, wrote to the Guardians of the Forest and asked their keepers to inform him of any Traveller encampments so that he could send his officers to check if there were any children of school age present.[8] Dorset Education Committee was so keen to educate its Travellers that before the legislation was even passed it was sending its attendance officers to camps and 'harassing' parents to send their children to school.[9]

The most sustained evidence for implementation of the legislation comes from Scotland, which was perhaps a result of the longer history of elementary education. Even here Travellers in the north and western isles of Scotland remained fairly untouched by the Act, owing in part to a lack of accommodation for them in the winter months, and witnesses to the *Report on Tinkers* made it clear that Section 118 was not being fully implemented. Yet, a number of local authorities, in combination with the police, had made strenuous efforts to enforce the two hundred attendances rule. In those areas this had led to the increased settlement of Travellers in towns over the winter months, and to children being sent to industrial schools if

their parents did not comply with the legislation. Oral evidence of
Travellers also points to children in this period being sent to naval
training ships instead of industrial schools, and being selected for
emigration programmes to Australia and Jamaica.[10]

In 1918 there were 171 Traveller children in 30 industrial
schools in Scotland with reports suggesting that in general they were
'backward' and 'slow to learn', while the effect of institutional life on
their character was described as 'beneficial'. Some superintendents
of the schools advocated severing all links between children and
parents in order to stop them 'reverting' to a nomadic life when they
left school. Records of the employment destinations of 58 Traveller
pupils who had graduated from industrial schools since 1900 found
that all but two of the girls had gone into domestic service, while of
the boys some became mill workers, while others joined the Forces
or engaged in 'various trades'. In all, over a quarter had 'relapsed
into tinkerdom', 18 per cent were described as having made 'fair'
progress, and 55 per cent 'good progress'. This reveals how the aim
of such schooling was not primarily to provide an education but rather
to develop their 'capacity for usefulness' and to end their 'social para-
sitism which at present seems their destiny'.[11]

In England there was a much stronger pattern of failure to use
the Act to school Traveller children. In many court cases defendants
denied that they had heard of the legislation, while others, who had
heard, were unable to find a school willing to take in their children.[12]
The impression given from the press is that in most cases neither
Travellers nor the schools particularly wanted the children in school,
and that it was left to keen policemen, attendance officers and courts
to push through a change in attitude and practice on both sides.
This was confirmed in Surrey's implementation of the Act. In 1910
the Home Office received a petition from some of the county's dig-
nitaries complaining that it was 'largely inoperative in the county'
and that in some cases the Education Committee had 'authorised
managers to exclude from school children of nomads who apply for
admission'. It was also asserted that the Committee was 'reluctant'
to enforce the law because of the 'heavy expense' of sending the children to industrial school.[13]

Surrey's 1913 survey of other county councils showed that the
Act was largely moribund in the rest of the country, with only four
county councils replying to the questionnaire. Both the West and
East Ridings of Yorkshire reported that 'very little action' had been
taken with no prosecutions,[14] while Kent reported one in which the

father was let off with a caution.[15] Berkshire replied that it had so far left the police to initiate proceedings, and stated rather ambiguously that 'no difficulty of any kind has yet resulted'. There had been a number of prosecutions in the county as it was admitted that, 'in some cases the LEA (Local Education Authority) have refused to accept children for Industrial Schools, but in practically every case up to date satisfactory provision has, in some manner, been made for the children'.[16] In contrast to the flurry of newspaper reports of prosecutions, the longer-term national picture suggested a widespread apathy on the part of local authorities.

At the heart of this was that tension between the wider aim of society, encapsulated in national legislation, of universal education, and the day-to-day reality of life in the localities. Local authorities were primarily answerable to their ratepayers, who simply did not want Travellers in their area. It was easier for a council to evict a group of Travellers than it was to embrace them in a lengthy and expensive programme of settlement and education funded by the ratepayer. Given this attitude it is unsurprising that the legislation was as likely to be used to move on Travellers as to get them to stay. In 1926 Barnsley RDC discussed the best means of evicting a family of Travellers from private land. Dr Sadler, their medical officer of health stated, 'I am told that the best way is to press them to send their children to school (Laughter). I know one family who are about to leave the district rather than send their children to school'.[17]

Fundamentally, local authorities did not want to see Traveller children as their moral or financial responsibility. Councils felt Traveller children had 'no real connection' with the area, and as their parents had never been, nor were likely to be, ratepayers, it was easier all round to allow them to continue on their way.[18] An incident in 1939 was a case in point: a Traveller woman was arrested for allowing her children to beg in the streets, but neither Kent nor Surrey Education Committees 'were prepared to accept responsibility for the children. The Gypsy parents roamed from place to place and there was no evidence to show that they resided in either county'. The children were kept in care while the two Committees went to court to argue out who exactly should take responsibility for them.[19]

The parochial nature of England's local government encouraged a climate in which officials had little interest in enforcing legislation towards any individuals not seen as the specific responsibility of the locality. Yet, officials maintained that nomadism was the central reason for the poor educational state of the Traveller population.

Superficially, this appears a reasonable attitude: the law would work properly if only Travellers would stay still for adequate periods of time. The blame was put onto Travellers despite the fact that it was the duty of each LEA to ensure that children in their area received efficient full-time education, and local authorities, by and large, shirked this responsibility. The onus was apparently on the local authority to provide the education, but it was parents who were prosecuted and they, and therefore their lifestyle, implicitly blamed for non-attendance.

Further analysis confirms that blaming *nomadism* for the non-schooling of Traveller children is too simplistic. The importance of state intervention and changing social norms in shifting the attitudes and behaviour of parents has been demonstrated in research on the normalisation of school attendance among the settled working-class population in the late nineteenth century. Then it was not nomadism that was blamed but parents, who were accused of being 'too indifferent, or too ignorant, or too vicious or too little able to command their children' to use existing schools.[20] Work in this field has stressed the important role of school attendance officers, both the high profile nature of their prosecutions through the police force, and through low key, but persistent visiting of hostile parents: 'Attendance officers could be resisted and frequently were, but they did not go away. Time was on their side and they were tenacious. Their collective influence was like a steady drip on popular consciousness'.[21]

The task of enforcement officers, whose position was often strengthened by the fact that they were often from the community in which they were working, was made easier by changing attitudes among the labouring poor. Education increasingly and voluntarily had formed part of family expenditure well before 1870, at least among the skilled working classes. This meant that in some areas, at least, new legislation had little impact on attendance rates.[22] So, although compulsory education was an anathema to some parents, who ignored or fought its strictures,[23] in general it flowed with the grain of popular feeling. While it may have been a tool of social control it equally was true that it was seen as a channel for social mobility and working-class aspirations:[24] 'State schooling was thus at one and the same time imposed on working people, resisted by them, and fought for and used by them for their own individual and collective purposes'.[25]

Despite attendance officers and greater popular acceptance of schooling, the process of implementing compulsory education was slow, patchy, and by the early twentieth century, still a very recent phenomenon. As the 1909 Report on Irregular School Attendance made clear, huge numbers of children throughout the country commonly received nothing more than an intermittent education. Through working in cotton mills, on the land, in the holiday industry or in a whole host of miscellaneous jobs, children missed school. This was supported not only by the parents, but by the wider community including local elites, who might even be employing them.[26]

The extension of full-time, compulsory education to the labouring poor was only achieved through major commitment on the part of the state and aided by a certain level of support from among the working classes themselves. Not only did Travellers not experience concerted state interventions, but they themselves had little enthusiasm for schooling and met with considerable opposition from all levels in the school structure.

This is not to deny that nomadism presented bureaucrats and educationalists, whose lives were centred on creating structures to serve a settled population, with considerable challenges. Nor is it to assert that nomadism was not a primary factor in Traveller children receiving an intermittent education. But by stressing the continual nomadism of the 'true' Gypsies – who both made things more difficult for the enforcing agencies, and reduced the problem by confining it to only a very small percentage of those on the road – central and local government officials were consistently able to absolve themselves of any need to make a concerted effort to educate Travellers.

The issue of nomadism was tied up with the wider question of the relationship between central and local government, particularly the amount of independence given councils in their implementation of legislation. As with other measures involving Travellers, educational legislation was implemented as and when it suited the authority concerned, and not in any consistent manner. Local authority officials were conveniently able to latch on to the myth of the pure-bred itinerant Romany as an excuse for inaction and continual official avoidance of the roots of the situation.

Experiences of schooling

More than the working classes, some of whom might have some hope of progress,[27] Travellers were assumed by educationalists and teachers alike as incapable of a high level of achievement, being both socially and racially unsuited to academia. While it is true that the

children in question often suffered educationally from repeated absences and a lack of a literate home culture, there is little sense from
the available evidence that where possible they were 'pushed' aca-
demically. The general attitude was that while 'no great advance in
intellectual attainments could be looked for ... the children ... would
gain much from the influence of school order and discipline'.[28]

While not rejecting working-class children's experiences within
an education system that attempted more to socialise than educate,
the models promoted and perpetuated by that system were mani-
festly less alien to them than to Traveller children. For Travellers,
success was measured almost solely in terms of attendance and the
creation of 'normalised' behaviour, not in educational achievement.
Furthermore, as I show below, where Travellers were educated within
a conventional school setting, their needs and interests were typically sidelined in favour of settled pupils.

Travellers experienced discrimination and social conditioning,
either as individuals or as a tiny minority within a school, set apart
from other pupils and their parents. Thus, key to the reality of schooling for them was prejudice received from every level of education.
At the frontline of the school experience was the reaction of fellow
pupils and their parents to the presence of Travellers. While this was
not universally negative and hostile, it was overwhelmingly so. Belle
Stewart remembered how 'it was murder going to school. They
wouldn't sit behind you in the seats. They wouldn't play with you in
the playground, you was always being knocked about'.[29] Physical
aggression was a common occurrence:

> And of course the cock of the school had to have a battle with
> the Gypsy boys so we had to defend ourselves at all times. Not
> many days passed without a fight ... We seemed forever in
> trouble – all because we were Gypsies and looked different from
> the others ... at lunchtime our dinner was pinched and we had
> to go without. If we reported it – well, it meant another fight
> after school.[30]

The overwhelmingly negative reaction of settled pupils to the
presence of Traveller children echoed attitudes of parents and officials. Their prejudice was often articulated through stereotypes of
Traveller hygiene and behaviour. It was commonly believed that they
'so abounded in vermin' and anti-social habits that schools were right
to refuse admittance on the grounds of potential physical or social
contamination:

[Surrey Education Committee reported that many Traveller children had been presented to schools by their parents] in consequence of warning notices served by the police on all Gypsies and van dwellers, but the managers have felt bound to exclude them on the grounds that the presence of these malodorous, untidy children, who are also reported to be loose in speech, manners and morals, ought not in fairness to the other scholars to be allowed. The school medical officer has authorised the exclusion of these children.[31]

Negative experiences naturally had some impact on attendance levels. As one Traveller explained of her children's truancy: 'When I sent them to school they were clean and did not look like Gypsies, but the other children shouted 'Gypsies' after them, which hurt them'.[32]

Teachers and school managers also expressed their prejudices more subtly through the expectations they held about the children and their educational achievements:

We were not put on the register book. If the school master asked: 'What standard were you in last school?', and we answered: 'Standard Three', it was ; 'Put him in Standard Two teacher – they're not here for long ... it was always [me as a] big boy in a class of little ones.[33]

That brither o' mine was kept seven years in one class ... he knew absolutely naethin'. Well, my mither went to the schoolmaster and asked why my brither wasnae even able to sign his name ... and she [sic] says, 'Och! I would never dream o' learnin' that laddie onything, he's the best message-laddie I have in the school'.[34]

The combination of an apathetic central government, local authorities and rate payers who were more keen to see Travellers out of their district than educated, and ingrained prejudice at all levels of a school, meant that for most Travellers, in most areas of the country, mainstream education was a patchy and often painful experience.

Special provision

For the majority of Travellers, who moved around for much of the year, settling in a house in the winter months, the chances were that they would be in the minority in whatever school they attended. In some areas, however, the concentration of Traveller families meant that they became a particular target of attention for those providing education in the locality. In such instances some educators viewed segregated schooling as the best way to socialise Travellers. It entailed the least disruption to the rest of the population as the groundwork was done out of sight. Only when a certain level of acceptable behaviour was reached were Traveller children introduced into schools: 'as soon as the children's behaviour and morals improved and their bodies and clothes became clean, they might graduate in small numbers to local elementary schools'.[35]

The agenda of such special schools and classes was to educate the Gypsyness out of their pupils. While numerous schools created temporary classes for Travellers when they had a particular influx of the children, and thus educated them largely separately,[36] there were a few long-term cases of separate provision for Traveller children. Different examples of separate provision for Travellers demonstrate that while the structure schooling took was significant, the methods used were of equal importance.

The rationale behind Inverness's establishment of separate facilities for the Traveller children in Merkinch school shows that negative stereotyping was ingrained in the scheme. Staff believed 'in the interest of the vagrant children themselves as well as of the other children', and for public health reasons, 'segregation' should be 'insisted upon'.[37] Segregation may have been seen as the solution but scanty references to the scheme in the school records suggest that this was not easy to achieve. Infant children seem to have all been taught together as a matter of course, and although the older ones were given a separate teacher they were given their lessons in the same room as the other children.[38] However, over time a special department of the school was built and devoted solely to the project, and a two-and-a-half-acre field bought and used for teaching horticulture and agriculture:

> This segregation of the Tinker children enabled the teacher (a) to give more careful supervision, (b) to teach such practical subjects to both boys and girls as might induce them to acquire a desire for settled occupations, (c) to keep in touch with them during their journeyings in the country, and (d) to induce cleanliness among all.[39]

Such an emphasis on practical and supervisory elements of schooling shows how the scheme was designed to socialise and not educate:

'careful supervision' could have enabled closer attention for each individual to improve their literacy and wider academic education, but instead the focus was on 'practical' skills and personal hygiene to promote settlement and integration.

In its own terms the Merkinch scheme was a success. Rigid enforcement of the two hundred attendances rule was supported by vigilant checking of certificates by the local police force. Commentators believed the project caused parents to stay longer in town, and generated 'a noticeable wish that their children should get out of the special class and be drafted into the ordinary school'.[40] The scheme had a long-term impact: a report in the 1950s stated that 'in the course of time these families became *socially acceptable to the community* and the special school was abandoned' [emphasis added].[41] This highlights the one-way nature of the bargain imposed on Travellers through an enforcement of educational legislation, that assimilation was the duty of the minority and entailed no reciprocal change on the part of majority society.

The same themes are found in the story of the Gypsy school in Hurtwood, Surrey, but under a slightly more benign guise.[42] It is unclear why Justice Bray, who had showed such antipathy towards Travellers in the pre-war period, allowed a camp to become established on his land. Conditional to living on the site was attendance of children at the purpose-built Gypsy School, rented from Bray for 1 shilling per annum,[43] and abiding by a number of rules.[44]

From the outset it is clear that rather than attempting to shoehorn Travellers with no previous experience of education into a conventional school routine and curriculum, efforts were made to work within the constraints and opportunities presented by the children. Surrey Education Board advertised for a teacher who was required to be:

> sympathetic with the needs of nomad children, many of whom may not have previously attended school, and who will shew [sic] tact in dealing with them and their parents. The instruction to be given will have to be much modified from that usually given at a public Elementary School, especially at first, and the teacher will be free from many of the restrictions which govern ordinary public Elementary Schools.[45]

As in Merkinch, the board was concerned that it would not get a teacher at all, and so stressed the freedom from usual curricular restraints and opportunities for promotion. The teachers appointed,

Mr and Mrs Milner, stayed with the school from its inception until
it was closed and the camp residents resettled in East Walton in 1934.
Civil servants noted that it was the 'outstanding energy, ability and
devotion'[46] of teachers, and a willingness to adapt, that was the secret of the success of the enterprise: 'the students could not concentrate for long at one time on one subject', so craft subjects were
'worked in with the general education subjects' and on a daily basis
'the period of instruction is divided up between the various subjects
... as considered necessary'.[47]

As well as flexibility over when subjects were taught, the timetable also jettisoned certain subjects deemed inappropriate, such as
physical education, and instead the focus was on basic literacy and
numeracy and various practical skills including basketry, boot-
making and gardening. In addition, at the request of a number of the
Traveller women, adult evening classes were established, which were
often attended by up to fifty individuals.[48] Accounts of the progress
of the school stressed how successful it was in civilising its pupils:

> Many of the students have to be taught to read and write, and,
> in the case of the women students, how to use a needle. Men
> are being taught carpentry and boot repairing, and the younger
> ones drawing ... Citizenship has included the duties of police-
> men and an explanation of the special set of Regulations to be
> observed by the members of the Gypsy community to the satis-
> faction of a local Committee of Control.[49]

When the school closed in the early 1930s public comment makes it
plain that the experiment was judged solely in terms of the level of
settlement it produced. In fact, the scheme itself ended in order for
the camp inhabitants to be rehoused: 'The families in occupation [at
Hurtwood] are now given the opportunity to take their places as
ordinary citizens, and live in bungalows provided though the gener-
osity of friends ... With education has come a desire for a higher
standard of living and comfort'.[50]

It was not only outsiders who saw the school's main function
as promoting socialisation and settlement. Extracts from the teacher
Mr Milner's reports reveal that he was strongly committed to these
goals:

> We have steadily persevered with the Gospel of discontent and
> there is a keen desire on the part of several of the boys to im-
> prove their lot when they leave school. It is, however, very dif-
> ficult to combat the parents ... It is time they were made to live
> under conditions approaching decency ... made to treat their

children properly ... made to behave and obey the law like ordinary people and made to pay rent ... these children should,
for the latter part of their school life at any rate, attend an ordinary school ... the eventual solution to the problem lies in education, but by segregating them away from civilisation we are
defeating our object – *April 1932*

Milner made it clear that he saw this separate, more sensitive schooling provision as a bridge to mainstream education and employment.
He wrote with pride about the 'success' he had had in getting children to leave the camp – eight girls and eight boys since the camp
had been established. The girls largely were directed towards domestic service or a Church Army training home in Notting Hill,
while the boys tended to stay in the area and work with their fathers
although one had been apprenticed and another joined a training
ship.

In later decades the Department of Education felt that the initiative offered several lessons on the issue of assimilation:

(1) one camper in 1926 asked the Head Teacher to find him a
permanent job in the district so that his boy's attendance would
not be broken; (2) In 1927 the Campers asked that the school
holidays should be arranged for the times when they would
normally be away, e.g. hop-picking. This was done with excel-
lent results; (3) The Gypsy Nuisance Committee at first not
unfavourable to the school because they thought that it would
drive the families away became very hostile when it became
apparent that the school was a powerful attraction; (4) In the
first five years of the school's existence sixty families applied
for permits to camp on the site so that their children could go
to the school. Only two were allowed to do so; (5) Several families appear to have left the site because the school made them
dissatisfied with their own condition and they migrated to better quarters.

The minute further noted that attendance levels throughout the
school's existence remained consistently between 87 per cent and
100 per cent, and that the whole scheme was helped by the adult
evening classes.[51]

The initiative's ability to attract Travellers suggests that the
school reached beyond the assimilationist motivations of educationalists to touch the needs of Travellers themselves. The success of the
Hurtwood case would seem to lie in the sensitive nature of the educational provision, as well as the fact that it was linked to a secure camping ground, and tailored to meet the travelling patterns of Travellers.

Another scheme that met the needs of Travellers was a mobile school run by the mission of the Diocese of Salisbury from 1882 to 1916, and headed for most of the period by Revd Swinstead.[52] It followed van-dwellers around the fairs and sales of the West Country and took a flexible approach to schooling: '[If] you would guide those children, let them teach *you* one of *their* games with mud-pies and coconut-balls, and you will soon begin to think out a line of treatment suited to their tastes and ingenuity'.[53] Swinstead believed that most of the children were sharp and bright and 'well worth all the attention that can be given to them'. As a result of his observations, he started to run informal classes for the children when a fair was in progress. He tended to intersperse writing practice on slates with singing, 'woolwork, boxes of picture bricks and nursery rhymes' in order to fight boredom:[54]

> The plan of holding a special school, which is very elementary indeed, has taken root. Twenty-nine times in the tent, and by the help of incumbents twenty-six times in rooms, have children gladly worked at their slates and wool and bricks for hours … School lessons always include prayer, a hymn and the Creed … Of 184 pupils, none have attended more than 13 times.[55]

To try and encourage children to come regularly, Swinstead introduced an attendance card, with the holder receiving a prize upon achieving twenty attendances. However, he felt that the measures he was taking were merely palliatives in the face of a widespread absence of provision, and so suggested that a network of forty travelling schools should be established with the aim of providing this section of the community with an elementary education. He strongly believed that it was counterproductive to try and force Traveller children into the mainstream education system, feeling instead that a 'modified and elastic Code' was necessary:

> We cannot treat them as we treat residents, nor bind them round in the beautiful red tape which adorns our stereotyped regulations. Therefore we prefer to leave them alone, and refuse to manufacture any new tape or elastic … I cannot conceive that the ingenuity of any department would break down under the strain of attempting this most necessary of reforms.[56]

Segregated schooling could present Travellers with opportunities when compared to the typical experiences of Travellers within integrated education. By definition, non-Travellers were absent, and so the bullying and prejudice encountered from other pupils, their parents and the mainstream system did not occur. Rather than being isolated from other Travellers, they were educated together with normal friendship and kin networks intact. Perhaps most significantly, the relative success of these schemes indicates that where schooling was tailored to fit in with their lifestyle, it could prove to be an attractive option. This suggests that Travellers were often keen to receive a certain measure of schooling, if it did not impinge unduly into their lives and did not result in stressful contact with the settled population. That Travellers were able to glean something for themselves from such institutions does not change the assimilationist agenda of their founders.

The foregoing examples demonstrate the importance of Travellers' responses to education in the success of a project. It is too simplistic to hold government, at its various levels, responsible for the failure to educate Travellers, and in reworking the analysis of the failure of educational initiatives to embrace Travellers, it is important not to depict them purely as the victims. Instead, a richer understanding of the history is gained through acknowledging the significance of Traveller agency in rejecting socialisation. If the approval of working-class parents was an important factor in the acceptance of education among the masses, then the hostility of Traveller parents was equally vital in inhibiting the spread of regular schooling among their children. The dislike felt by local parents and school officials towards Travellers often combined with an equal level of antipathy felt by Travellers for mainstream society that could become crystallised over the issue of schooling.

Boswell's parents demonstrated a fairly typical attitude when they insisted he went to school to 'learn to read and write – and then [he] needn't go any more'.[57] Officials and mainstream society rarely accepted the idea that, rather than failing to attend school through chance or apathy, Travellers avoided it because they simply did not value it. Traveller parents had very different aspirations for their children than their working-class counterparts, and so saw formal schooling as an irrelevance. Traveller children from an early age accompanied parents in hawking, dealing and other activities in order to learn the necessary skills, and by their early teens to bring in money as well. Parents were also justified in being suspicious of formal education's role as the vanguard of dominant culture. It was not that they necessarily rejected schooling outright, but rather were suspicious of the package in which it was wrapped – the popularity of the Hurtwood and Diocese of Salisbury's schemes can be explained by their attempts to adapt to the needs of Travellers.

In summary, we can see that the failure to extend schooling to Travellers did not lie solely, or necessarily largely, in the nomadism of the community. Equally, the prejudice of school officials, parents and other pupils that combined to create an overridingly negative experience of education, was only part of the explanation for poor attendance and achievement levels among Travellers. Evidence from the extension of regular schooling to the children of the labouring poor demonstrated the level of sustained effort needed to produce longlasting results, and the importance of enthusiasm for education from parents. Therefore, of primary importance was the consistent failure of the state to make a concerted effort to reach out to Travellers in anything beyond a punitive way. This was reinforced by the fact that there was no unity of action between different levels of the state. Central government may have passed legislation, but it took no responsibility in enforcing it. Local authorities were required to educate Travellers, and while in theory they might have wished it to happen, were unwilling to dedicate resources towards people who did not seem to have any claims on the locality. Even where they had a general policy of enforcing attendance, they could rarely require an individual school to accept a child if they did not wish to, nor to ensure that once there, they stayed in school, or received a rounded education.

While commentators, therefore, were wrong in putting the onus on Travellers in their analysis, they were right to point to the importance of their agency in the matter. Travellers were able to take advantage of the contradictions inherent in the system and move on if they wished to avoid schooling, which they rightly saw as a threat to their cultural integrity. For a largely non-literate community, whose way of life revolved around extensive family networks, self-employment, and the necessity of children learning appropriate life and employment skills, a prolonged formal education was irrelevant for a nomadic way of life. The success of both the Hurtwood school and that of the Salisbury mission indicate that Travellers were relatively enthusiastic about education when it could fit in with their lifestyle and made no assumptions about long-term commitment.

In general, the experience of Travellers in mainstream education appears to have been negative, with bullying and institutionalised prejudice being the norm rather than the exception. There was little concern for the quality of the educational experience of the children, with the focus being on the mechanics of getting the children into school, and keeping them there long enough to become reasonable members of society. More remarkable than the fact that some Travellers became socialised through the combined process of education and settlement, was that so few were affected in this way. Education might have been a successful tool for the integration of the Travelling community, but it was too often a blunt instrument, and an infrequently wielded one at that, for it to achieve this goal.

Missionary efforts towards Travellers

Swinstead's work with travelling people in the south-west was a good example of how missions were able to provide services in a more flexible and targeted way than the state. Whereas the state, in general, before 1945 provided very little for Travellers, and then usually only as part of mainstream provision, from the late nineteenth century there were a number of British based missions working solely, or in part, with Travellers.

Attempts to evangelise Travellers can be set in the wider context of the new urban evangelism movement of the late nineteenth century, typified by such organisations as Methodist Central Missions, the Salvation Army, the London City Mission and the Church of England's Church Army. Schemes such as the Diocese of Salisbury's mission to its villages[58] suggest that the effect of this trend could also be felt in rural areas. Missions had emerged in response to fears that large sections of the population were either rejecting Christ, or had never heard of him in the first place. This new brand of home mission work was felt to be as important as oversees missions:

> [It is] absurd that the missionary societies should expend thousands and thousands of pounds for the purpose of instructing the blacks, and yet never for one moment to turn their attention towards the cultivation and conversion of the Gypsies – a people constantly before our eyes, and living in a state of total ignorance, either or moral responsibility or religious obligation ... [59]

The efforts of missionaries towards Travellers broadly fell into two categories: those whose attempts at converting them were aimed ultimately at settlement and 'civilisation', and others who were content that their congregation should continue to travel, and were primarily concerned with spreading the Gospel. Within these two groups was to be found the whole range of attitudes towards Travellers, from sympathy with their way of life and an anxiety to improve their living standards, to a very clear lack of empathy and a belief that it would be best for all if Travellers ceased to exist as soon as possible.

Mayall has suggested that by the close of the nineteenth century there was a shift from attempts to 'civilise' Travellers through the informal means of missions and other voluntary measures, to more formal state methods of intervention, most notably through legislation.[60] Yet the impact of educational legislation was patchy and unsustained and in the remainder of this chapter I explore how missionary efforts well into the twentieth century continued to fill gaps left by the absence of state services.

There is no link between chronology and cultural sensitivity towards a nomadic lifestyle, as the following comparison between the work of the New Forest Good Samaritan Charity and the mission of the Diocese of Salisbury demonstrates. Both were active at roughly the same time, but took completely different approaches. Swinstead was the first of the Diocesan itinerant missioners to live in a van for the course of his ministry, feeling that it was important to become identified with his congregation, rather than to set himself apart from them: 'I was soon convinced of the necessity of living with them, sharing their noises, buying from the same shops, drawing water from the same pump, and laying my coat on the same grass'.[61] He felt that it was important to understand their life, 'claiming first their sympathy, and next their respect'. Very quickly, the work of the mission expanded beyond simple preaching, visiting and the handing out of tracts, although this always remained the main focus of its work. From the beginning a small measure of material assistance was given to needy van-dwellers,[62] and as time went on a female missioner and nurse were added,[63] as well as the travelling school.

In contrast, work in the New Forest under the leadership of H. E. J. Gibbins, who persistently refused to acknowledge the validity of a Traveller lifestyle, promoted settlement and integration.[64] As one report stated, 'it is to the public advantage that the Gypsy life, only another name for Nomadic thievish tramps, should be made impossible'.[65] The main focus of its efforts was in giving material aid to individual Traveller families, as 'until they have been to school and learned a little, preaching is only idle talk. Practical work, such as getting them into cottages and their children to school, will do more real good for them than any amount of preaching'. In the course of his career Gibbins believed that he had 'placed some twenty families of these nomads in cottages, and putting eighty of their children in various schools, I have found good employment for many Gypsy lads and their fathers'.[66] It is clear that he experienced difficulties in battling against the preferences, attitudes and habits of Travellers: 'A Catholic woman who I placed in a cottage with her husband and family, whose rent I paid for some ten months, getting the kids clothed and kept at school, seemed to be doing well; but all at once they took a moonlight flight to Ascot, and have not been seen since'.[67]

In other cases in which he had tried to settle other families, he discovered that they had lied to him about their circumstances, or simply left 'the place worse than a pig sty' and had disappeared in a matter of hours. After twelve years of trying to settle and 'civilise' Travellers, his overall verdict seems to have been that one 'might as well try to bend an old forest oak as to convert them'.[68]

Other missions also aimed to extend support to itinerant Travellers while encouraging settlement. One of the largest schemes occurred in Scotland in the 1930s. Gaining their inspiration from the Gypsy school in Hurtwood, the Home Mission Committee of the Church of Scotland established a programme encouraging the settlement and rehabilitation of Travellers from Perthshire.[69] It was partly a reaction to a growing shortage of stopping places in the county, and the mission felt that 'grounds might be secured and set apart' for Travellers who would be 'under supervision'.[70] The scheme, supported both by the police and local education committee, aimed at 'regulating and restricting vagrancy and protecting the Tinkler families of the district', who were seen as being threatened by an influx of Irish Travellers and those who 'canna get a hoose'.[71] This latter phenomenon was a result of the Depression and the shortage of cheap housing, as poor settled families moved into sub-standard and condemned dwellings, usually the preserve of Travellers. The committee felt that these difficulties should not be allowed to affect the lives of Travellers who, whatever their unattractive points, typically 'supported themselves with ... little reliance on public assistance'.[72] Experimental camps were set up in 1934, which:

> Involved the co-operation of local landed proprietors on whose ground the camps were established, although these had been used as customary stopping places by generations of Travelling folk. The essential difference was that they would not be open to all comers, but restricted to tinker families with Perthshire connections. For the six months when their children attended

school, the permit holders would be afforded security of tenure. Indeed, it was a 'primary condition' of their residence that the children would attend school on a regular basis.[73]

Maitland's scheme was experienced by Sandy Stewart, a Perthshire Traveller who was in his early teens at the time the scheme was instigated:

> Thir wes naebuddie supposetae come in [to a permit camp] but wirsel. Ye see, ye hed a little book an it wes made like a motor licence, green covered ... Any police that come intae you when you wir in the camp, ye jest let them see that ... They got thae camps for hus ye see, from the lairds ... Miss Maitland got camps an then she wid hae ye mak baskets for her – skulls [a type of basket] and lots o things. She got big truck loads, taen them ower tae Edinburgh as she paid ye for them. An if ye couldnae get enough stuff growing fer tae mak them, she sent ye stuff ... tinwork or oniething – the lady Maitland wed buy it.[74]

As Leitch has observed, while the schemes were ostensibly concerned with the simple promotion of education, the underlying aim was to bring a religious influence to bear on the lives of the affected Travellers, and to 'reconcile them with a better mode of life'.[75] As an investigating committee, surveying the potential offered by the scheme stated:

> We do not contemplate that camping life should be perpetuated ... There should be no massing of Tinkers together, the aim of the permit system being to secure control over single families ... The supervision of these camps would include strict attention to sanitary matters and tidiness as well as the orderly conduct of Tinkers, regard always being had to the interests of the ordinary residents in the neighbourhood.[76]

A contrast to the work of this mission was the work of the London City Mission (LCM), the largest initiative in England specifically targeting the Traveller community.[77] More conventional than the Salisbury mission, but still one that followed its congregation around rather than trying to persuade them to stay in one place, the LCM was based in London and the home counties. Early on it was rather dismissively described by one commentator as a mission in which various 'ladies, young and old, endeavoured to wash away the Gypsies' sins with tea'.[78] In the early years there was undoubtedly more than an element of truth in this observation, but as with the Salisbury mission, efforts went much further than simply tea and pamphlet distribution.[79]

Initially the LCM's efforts towards Travellers were not distinguished by any particular understanding of their lifestyle and culture, with descriptions of them not rising above common stereotypes and preconceptions. The 'true Romany' was described as having 'flaunting air, the wizard look, the whimsical manner, the sense of wonder', and was 'familiar with life of heath and hedgerow, of dingle and dell': 'Their tawny skin and dark lustrous eyes, their tangled tresses and gaudy attire, their pleasant drawl and half-bewitching ways ... Begging and pilfering are the common means of subsistence ... like the Arabs they have no chairs or tables.'[80]

Despite such unpromising accounts of their congregation, from the outset the LCM made no attempt to try and change the travelling lifestyle of Gypsies, but rather brought the Gospel to their camps and firesides. Abraham West of the mission regularly visited the camps in Banstead, Eastwood and Wanstead, and was apparently 'affectionately regarded', and preached to the inhabitants in 'their own vernacular':

> I have to take things as they come, and crawling into huts and tents, and climbing into vans and wagons, more 'things' are seen than I can describe! My chief object is to adapt the Message to the different characters I meet, and clothe it in words they can understand.[81]

This approach did not mean that that the missioners were always able to view Travellers' lives with equanimity: West stated that those who converted tended to be 'hot-red for Christ', but that it was 'not easy to break loose at a bound from evil habits'.[82] Commenting on the words of a Traveller who described how they tended to get firewood or potatoes from a nearby hedgerow or field, one missioner observed how this sounded like 'correspondence with the environment; but at bottom it is a sin called by another name'.[83]

The LCM was able to score some measure of success in its efforts, most notably perhaps at Eastwood, just inland from the Essex coast. This site was established in 1908 after a number of Gypsies moved there having been expelled from Epping Forest. Its population of about one hundred and fifty people included Bartholomew Smith, who had experienced, along with his wife and daughter, 'a visitation of the grace of God'. As a group they bought a disused tramcar and used it as a place of worship:

There are no sermons. Testimony is the burden of those who speak, coupled with burning appeal ... For ourselves, to have heard these 'spoilt children of nature' tell how they became obedient children of grace was a real spiritual uplifting [sic]. For their simplicity and want of book learning does not detract one iota from the value of their experience.[84]

As well as visiting camps and speaking to Travellers, the other major strand of evangelical effort of the LCM was an annual hop-picking mission, as for many itinerants who were not concentrated on one of the larger, or better known sites, it was 'one of the few occasions when they can be reached with the Gospel ... we can go to them as they stand at their baskets picking or visit them at home'. Perhaps to soften the impact of being forced to listen while at work, the mission also gave out free food and clothing, and provided a first aid service on the sites.[85] The ambivalent reception they could receive from the pickers is revealed in this testimony from a man whose daughter had been helped by the mission:

I remember four years ago when we were on the common and you and your band of good workers tried to put into my heart nothing but good; but I scoffed at you, and would not accept the books which you offered me ... since you have shown me this kindness I cannot do no other than apologise.[86]

The LCM was not alone in their concern for the morals of hop-pickers. The Alton and District Hop-Picker's Mission, founded in 1868, paid similar attention to the annual influx of workers to their area at harvest time.[87] As with the LCM in this context, they came across 'Gypsies' simply as one group among the many other groups of pickers who engaged in this work, who would also include, 'a good many respectable villagers ... many tramps and a good many representatives of the "submerged tenth" from the slums of Plymouth, Southampton, Salisbury etc'. The missionaries distributed literature, talked to workers, and gave out tea – 'The capacity for tea shown by the average picker is extraordinary' – followed by meetings and lantern shows in the evenings.[88] From the outbreak of the First World War a Red Cross worker also joined the mission, usually dealing with burns, bruising and blood poisoning from infected cuts.[89]

As with so many mission attempts of the time, both among the working classes and abroad, the object was not simple conversion or reaffirmation of faith, instead it was the lifestyle that was seen as being as unacceptable as godlessness: 'Several of the missionaries speak of the social reformation of the Gypsies ... Their behaviour is distinctly improving; there is less bad language used, less quarrelling and less drinking. As one of them said, "We have found the best side of the Pub is the *outside*"'.[90]

This does not mean that mission efforts were automatically rejected by the pickers. Very often they were welcomed, both because of their material gifts, but also perhaps because people appreciated the fact that their lives were important to someone else. Frank Cuttriss, a gypsiologist writing at the beginning of the period, noted how the Church Army was welcomed for the 'tactful, considerate help rendered in times of distress',[91] and for the fact that its workers did not engage in 'button-holing' but instead organised lantern shows and tea distribution to which all were welcome.[92]

What do these missions show about the relationship between Travellers and settled society and the state? Missions continued well into the twentieth century and in no way were their efforts replaced by a formal legislative framework. Undoubtedly, with their more proactive approach, missions were able to reach certain marginal groups far better than the state was able or willing to. Consequently, when missions chose, they delivered schemes to Travellers that otherwise would not have existed. More broadly, the variety of attitudes and approaches of the missions reflected the contrary attitudes held in settled society towards Travellers. There was no agreement over whether settlement and 'civilisation' was a surer way to salvation for Travellers than allowing them to continue a nomadic life, with the additional support of Christ. Finally, the work of the missions demonstrates how Travellers, just as with education, were not passive recipients of schemes, but instead took what they liked from what was on offer, and rejected the rest. In doing this they were establishing a pattern that was to continue during the time of the more formalised welfare state.

Notes

1 Okely, *Traveller-Gypsies*, 160–2.
2 The terms of the 1921 Education Act and 1933 Young Person's Act did not substantially alter the 1908 Act. Section 61 of the 1933 Act intended a child 'in need of care and protection' to include one who was not receiving an education owing to the fact that they were being taken from place to place.

3   Symons, 'In praise of Gypsies', 295. See also E. Camm, 'Hurtwood school', *JGLS*, 13:3 (1934), 221–2.
4   'Gypsies at school', *Times Educational Supplement* (12 June 1945). See also 'Gypsies at school – Useful with their hands and good at sport', *Hampshire Advertiser* (27 February 1937).
5   *Report from the Departmental Committee on Habitual Offenders, Vagrants, Beggars and Juvenile Delinquents (Scotland)*, 1895, C7753, xxxii.
6   Evidence of Mr Atherley-Jones, *Select Committee on 1887 Temporary Dwellings Bill*, 357.
7   For cases of prosecution of Travellers see 'Woking Petty Sessions', *Surrey Times* (28 January 1911); 'Gypsies and their children', *Birmingham Daily Post* (2 March 1910); 'Gypsies and their children', *Dorset County Chronicle* (27 November 1911); 'Birmingham police court', *Birmingham Daily Post* (1 December 1911); 'Horsham police court', *Sussex Daily News* (30 March 1912); 'The condition of Gypsy children', *Yorkshire Post* (19 October 1910).
8   'New Forest Guardians and district council', *The Western Gazette* (25 December 1910).
9   'Gypsy children and school attendance', *Dorset County Chronicle* (10 October 1907).
10 Author's conversation with Roseanna MacPhee, 28 November 2006.
11 *Tinkers in Scotland*, 16–18.
12 See for example, 'A wandering Gypsy', *Western Daily Mercury* (24 August 1909); 'Gypsy children and school', *Western Daily Mercury* (22 November 1909); 'Gypsy children and school', *Sheffield Daily Telegraph* (10 August 1910).
13 'Education of Gypsy children', *Surrey Advertiser* (21 December 1912).
14 SHC, CC28/249A, West Riding County Council to Surrey, 10 March 1913 and East Riding County Council to Surrey, 20 January 1913.
15 *Ibid.*, Kent County Council to Surrey, 31 January 1913.
16 *Ibid.*, Berkshire County Council to Surrey, 17 January 1913.
17 'Van dwellers', *Barnsley Chronicle* (22 May 1926).
18 TNA, ED11/234, County Council Association, Education Committee, agenda item 8, 'Memorandum prepared by Mr T. S. Lamb with regard to children of school age passing through casual wards', 7 January 1937.
19 'Gypsy children problem', *Evening Standard* (27 November 1939). There is no indication of which county was eventually obliged to accept responsibility for them.
20 Form of Report for Her Majesty's Inspectors of Schools, 'Minutes of the Committee of Council on Education' (1845) i., 155.
21 P. Gardener, '"Our schools, their schools": The case of Eliza Duckworth and John Stevenson', in R. Lowe (ed.), *History of Education, major themes, vol. II: Education in its social context* (London and New York, 2000). The *Bristol Daily Post* (12 January 1874), gave an indication of the density of effort put in by attendance officers, stating that in the preceding two years seven officers made a total of 51,534 visits to homes of absent

children.
22 P. Miller, 'Historiography of compulsory schooling: What is the problem?', in R. Lowe (ed), *History of education, major themes, vol. II: Education in its social context* (London and New York, 2000), 178.
23 *Hansard,* 1 July 1875, col. 803.
24 P. Miller, 'Education and the state: The uses of Marxist and feminist approaches in the writings of histories of schooling', in Lowe (ed.), *History of education,* 261.
25 Miller, 'Historiography of compulsory schooling', 178.
26 *Ibid.*
27 See for example A. Davin, *Growing up poor: Home, school and street in London, 1870–1914* (London, 1996); Gardner, 'Our schools, their schools', pp. 184–215; R. Johnson, 'Educational policy and social control in early Victorian England', in Lowe (ed.), *History of education,* 9–31; J. Spring, 'Education as a form of social control', in Lowe (ed.), *History of education,* 52–60.
28 'Problem of the Gypsy child', *Westminster Gazette* (20 October 1910). Also *West Sussex Gazette* (17 November 1910), and J. W. R. Adams, 'Gypsies and other Travellers in Kent: Report of the survey carried out 1951–2 by Kent County Council Planning Department', unpublished Kent County Council, 1952, Appendix IV.
29 Quoted in Sandford, *Gypsies,* 88. For similar memories of bullying at school, see Whyte, *Yellow in the broom,* 16; E. MacColl and P. Seeger, *Till doomsday in the afternoon: The folklore of a family of Scots Travellers, the Stewarts of Blairgowrie* (Manchester, 1986), 18; and several accounts in Davies, *Tales.*
30 Seymour, *Book of Boswell,* 40. There is also rare evidence of a good relationship between Travellers and their class mates, see Leitch, *Book of Sandy Stewart,* 16.
31 'Gypsy children excluded from school', *Midland Evening News* (7 March 1910). See also *Select Committee on Temporary Dwellings Bill,* 544; and E. Hodder, *George Smith (of Coalville): The story of an enthusiast* (London, 1896), 174.
32 'Odiham police court', *Aldershot News* (4 August 1944).
33 Seymour, *Book of Boswell,* 25.
34 MacColl and Seeger, *Till doomsday,* 18. Also *Salisbury Diocesan Gazette,* (February, 1894), 25; and the interview with Nan Joyce in J. Keenan and D. Hines (eds), *In our own way: Tales from Belfast Travellers* (Belfast, 2000), 65.
35 *Report of the New Forest Committee,* 1947, Cmd 7245, 103.
36 See for example 'Schools for Gypsies', *Star* (18 October 1910).
37 Highland Council Archive, Inverness (hereafter HCA), CI/5/7/9, Staff Committee notes, 10 June 1914.
38 HCA, CI/5/3/1639, entry for 2 November 1914.
39 *Tinkers in Scotland,* 1918, 16.
40 *Ibid.*

41 TNA, AST7/1480, Edinburgh Unemployment Assistance Board central office to London office, 17 December 1955. A similar attempt to cater for Travellers occurred in Dull, Perthshire, where between 1930 and 1939 the school ran a special class for their children; L. Spence, 'The Scottish Tinkler-Gypsies', *Scotland's Magazine*, (February 1955), 20–4.

42 Debates over establishing the school may be found in TNA, ED 41/433, Application for Recognition by Board of Education (hereafter BoE), 25 January 1926, and a BoE minute, 19 May 1926; also SHC, CC767/40/1/9, 1925–6, Surrey education committee minute books, 68, 133 and 239.

43 SHC, G85/38/3/256, Surrey BoE to Bray, 12 November 1925.

44 There were debates over whether rules were kept, see TNA, ED 147/13, minute, 'The Gypsy School at Albury, Surrey', 5 October 1951.

45 SHC, 6246/4/1, 1925–32, Circular E.495, 22 October 1925.

46 TNA, ED147/13, minute 'The Gypsy school, Albury, Surrey', 5 October 1951.

47 TNA, ED41/433, BoE minute on HMI Mr Charles's visit to Hurtwood school, 24 March 1926.

48 *Ibid*. The timetable also contained general history, geography, needlework, citizenship, woodwork, handicrafts and rug-making.

49 *Ibid*.

50 'Successful Gypsy experiment', *Surrey Times* (8 December 1933). See also 'Exit the Gypsy: Civilisation extends its conquering sway', *West Lancashire Evening Gazette* (11 December 1933).

51 TNA, ED147/13, minute 'The Gypsy school, Albury, Surrey', 5 October 1951.

52 J. H. Swinstead, *A parish on wheels* (London, 1897), 9.

53 *Ibid.*, 61.

54 *Ibid.*, 92–3.

55 *Salisbury Diocesan Gazette* (1895), 35.

56 Swinstead, *Parish on wheels*, 97.

57 Seymour, *Book of Boswell*, 42. See also Margaret Lee, quoted in Sandford, *Gypsies*, 39.

58 See the *Salisbury Diocesan Gazette* 1900–10 for accounts of its 'Itinerant and parochial mission'.

59 Letter to editor from 'Free Trade', 'Foreign missions', *Liverpool Daily Post and Mercury* (19 February 1909).

60 Mayall, *Gypsy Travellers*, 184–5.

61 Swinstead, *Parish on wheels*, 121.

62 *Salisbury Diocesan Gazette* (1890), 31.

63 *Ibid.* (1892), 33.

64 H. E. J. Gibbins, *Gypsies of the New Forest and other tales* (Bournemouth, 1909), Preface.

65 Quoted in Symons, 'In praise of Gypsies', 294.

66 Gibbins, *Gypsies of the New Forest*, 41 and 43–5.

67 *Ibid.*, 31.
68 *Ibid.*, 29, 39 and 42.
69 D. Maitland, *An account of Gypsy camps in Surrey supervised by Hurtwood control committee, with a bearing on Tinker camps in Scotland* (North Berwick, East Lothian, 1932).
70 SHC, G85/38/10, Maitland to Bray, 28 April 1932.
71 A. McCormick, 'The Tinkler problem', *JGLS*, 12:3 (1933), 142.
72 Maitland, *An account of Gypsy camps*.
73 Leitch, *Book of Sandy Stewart*, 44, fn. 1.
74 *Ibid.*, 31–2. The baskets and other goods were sold though Highland Home Industries Ltd, based in Edinburgh.
75 *Ibid.*, 45, fn.1, and quoting 'Particulars of a scheme for the welfare of Tinkers in Perthshire', prepared on behalf of the Home Mission Committee, Edinburgh , 25 December 1932, 2.
76 *Report on Vagrancy in Scotland*, para. 96.
77 For an example of a smaller, local and personal mission see 'Youngest', *Sunday Mercury* (31 March 1946).
78 E. O. Winstedt, 'Gypsy civilisation', *JGLS*, 1 (1908), 336.
79 The Gypsy Mission was originally funded by dividends from a failed Gypsy school in Farnham, Dorset. TNA, ED 49/1729A.
80 'Glad tidings from Gypsydom', *London City Mission Magazine* (1911), 173–4.
81 *Ibid.*, 175.
82 'Good news from Gypsydom', *London City Mission Magazine* (1918), 119–21; 20.
83 'A day in Gypsydom', *London City Mission Magazine* (1925), 74.
84 *Ibid.*, 182.
85 'The harvest of the hops', *London City Mission Magazine* (1910), 233–4.
86 *Ibid.*, 236–7.
87 Hampshire Record Office, Winchester (hereafter HRO), Catalogue notes, 85M93/1. Evidence of Catholic efforts towards hop-pickers can be found in, 'Nuns in gum boots nurse sick in hop yards', *Universe* (14 September 1945).
88 'Alton and District Hop-Pickers' Mission, 'Annual Report' (1914), 5.
89 *Ibid.*, 6.
90 Alton and District Hop-Pickers' Mission, 'Annual Report' (1920), 4.
91 Cuttriss, *Romany life*, 10.
92 *Ibid.*, 217–22.

Part II

Post-war and the 1960s

4

Travellers' lives, 1945–68

Plastic flowers were appearing in house windows, competing with fresh or shredded wooden blooms; nylon garments were replacing the 'old woollens' that made trade; spin-driers in better-off homes dismissed clothes pegs ... horse-drawn transport seemed noticeably outmoded, receiving some crooked looks even amongst their own folk.[1]

As this description of Traveller life from the early 1960s suggests, the years after 1945 presented a number of challenges for Travellers. While attitudes of the settled population towards Travellers continued to revolve around engrained stereotypes, their lifestyles underwent some profound alterations. In this chapter I show how Travellers were affected by and responded to changes in society in the post-war era, including increasing motorisation and other technological developments. These caused Travellers to make some profound shifts in content of their livelihoods, while maintaining the central continuities of self-employment and an emphasis on nomadism. As with the settled population, this period also saw Travellers being touched by the expansion of the 'welfare state', but I deal with this separately in Chapter 6. In the second section of this chapter I move on to discuss the important phenomenon of the changing landscape of post-war Britain. Shanty and caravan sites, already a feature by the 1930s, expanded significantly as a result of war-time bombing and the profound housing shortage. Subsequent debates on the role of caravans in modern Britain, as well as the housing boom had significant and contradictory impacts on Travellers. The latter put pressure on land used by Travellers for decades, while the existence of large shanty sites allowed Travellers to find semi-secure spaces from which they could conduct a seasonally nomadic lifestyle. Over time, however, it became clear that there was a growing crisis in site provision for Travellers, and that there were disparities between the treatment of Travellers and other caravan-dwellers.

The changing economy

A common refrain among commentators by the middle of the twentieth century was that Gypsies were dying out. The crafts and rural employment, which were seen to sustain them, were increasingly superseded by plastics, motorisation and mechanisation:

> The twentieth century ... has dealt [Travellers] a series of crushing blows each one of which has made the possibility of survival more difficult. The automobile has usurped the horse, mass-produced kitchen-ware has made their skill with iron and tin superfluous, the invention and development of plastics has put them out of business as basket-makers, and machines are more and more taking over the human function in fields and orchards.[2]

As we have seen, this attitude was based on an assumption that Travellers' lifestyles were tied to a particular content – rural crafts, horses, seasonal farm work – rather than to the practice of flexible self-employment. However, an analysis based on the importance of form and not content of income generation leads to the hypothesis that the profound changes of the post-war era caused Travellers, along with the settled population, to adapt to face the challenges and opportunities presented to them.

As I suggested in Chapter 2, some changes experienced after 1945 had their roots in earlier decades. Already in the 1930s some Travellers had become motorised and had moved into scrap and vehicle dealing. The post-war period saw this trend gathering pace and becoming dominant, so that the 1965 census of Travellers found that only 6 per cent were horse-drawn.[3] Acton has noted how motorisation masked an increasing shortage of stopping places by allowing longer stays in one place, as Travellers could cover a wider area for work from a single base. This, he argues, economically 'propped up traditional Gypsy values and working methods', but changed its style.[4] For example, Tony Butler and his wife bought a pick-up truck in the early 1960s, as a way of coping with the decline in need for seasonal agricultural labour due to mechanisation. Opportunities for work were further apart, and they were unable to reach them if they were horse-drawn. While they were unhappy about the change, it enabled them to continue a nomadic lifestyle based for a large part on agricultural labour.[5]

Alongside motorisation came the spread of bottled gas and electric generators, allowing many Travellers by the end of the period to exchange cooking on open fires and sitting outside for the some of the luxuries of consumerism enjoyed by settled society, including refrigerated food, convenience cooking and watching television.

At the same time as bringing benefits to Travellers, these changes 'destroyed a potent range of symbols', notably horse-drawn travel,[6] as expressed by Dominic Reeve, who became motorised in the late 1950s:

> We had come to a decision to abandon the old ways for the new. The world of the horse and wagon Traveller is very small and insular ... The thought of obtaining a lorry and a trailer caravan, and the ensuing complications such as running costs, insurance, a driving licence and the various other necessities of an up-to-date way of life, had all required some deliberation ... The trailer-caravan however, was completely devoid of any charm whatsoever; its only attraction lay in its value as a stepping stone to a new mode of existence.[7]

Mechanisation affected numerous agricultural activities after 1945, with hop, sugar beet and potato harvesting being largely mechanised by the late 1950s:[8] 'We done tattie gaitherin an neep [beet] shawin an harvest tae. But that's oot o' the fashion. It's finished. They've aa machinery fer that'.[9] It did not, however, affect the need for large numbers of workers for certain fruit and vegetable harvesting: soft fruit picking in the Fens and Hampshire, for example, continued to act as important economic and social points in many Travellers' calendars.

Notwithstanding the continued availability of certain types of agricultural labour after 1945, it is clear that there was an overall decline in demand for labour in this sector. Similarly, better national transport networks improved distribution and undermined the importance of itinerant pedlars,[10] leading to Travellers moving away from hawking-based activities, which were largely the preserve of women. This is not to suggest, however, that there was a simple 'progression' from rural craft based activities and hawking, in which women played a central role, to male-dominated scrap dealing, larger-scale trading, building and garden work. As this account from the late 1950s suggests, while men were expected to conduct the larger deals it was women who still were seen as central to the family economy:

> [The Traveller woman] who keeps the family in 'bread and meat' throughout most of the year except for short periods when the family is engaged in some form of casual piece work farm employment, or, of course, for a short time after she has had a child. And as the family increases in size so the woman's earnings must increase accordingly – more articles have to be made to hawk, and more clothing has to be monged [begged].[11]

As with earlier periods, Travellers aimed to be flexible in their economic activities, and a family group might combine scrap dealing with hawking, fortune telling, seasonal fruit picking, construction jobs and work on the fairs in a fluid combination, depending on the time of year and opportunities available: 'I do other jobs in between [trading scrap] like farm work, farm labourer, painting, decorating. I never saw a job yet I couldn't do or try to do'.[12] Equally, it is too simplistic to assume that traditional craft activities disappeared completely during this period: for some Travellers they continued to be important sources of income throughout the 1960s and beyond. A sample of Travellers' occupations included in Hampshire's 1962 survey described 15 as 'labourer', 7 as 'general dealer', 2 as scrap dealers, 2 as 'shipyard labourer', 2 as agricultural workers, and one each as flower seller, gardener, forestry worker, rag and bone collector, 'self-employed', and plumber's mate, confirming while there was a tendency towards self-employment and flexible labour, in fact Travellers engaged in a range of occupations.[13] The census of Travellers in England and Wales in 1965 and in Scotland in 1969 found that, for men, general and scrap dealing predominated (52 per cent and 36 per cent respectively), with agriculture and horticulture being of next importance (15 and 19 per cent). There was a range of other occupations including labouring, roadwork/tarmacking, building, timber and factory work. The majority of women (just over 60 per cent in both surveys) were described as 'housewives'. This may be an indication of a shift away from an active economic role of women within the domestic economy, but may also be the result of the surveys being conducted outside the main travelling season. These figures do not take into account such shifts over the year, nor the fact that Travellers often engaged in a range of activities, with their relative importance fluctuating over the course of a year. Similarly, the relatively high return for 'no occupation/unemployed' for Scotland (23 per cent for men and 17 per cent for women) may have been increased by two factors: seasonality, and a desire to hide any subsidiary economic activities on the part of recipients of benefits.[14]

As a broad assessment of the way in which Travellers adapted to the challenges presented to them in the mid-twentieth century, evidence nevertheless points to a move towards scrap, salvage and construction work, in which there were fewer individual transactions, with each being worth more. This, as Acton observed, had the effects of reducing the economic independence of women, gradually making gender relations more 'conservative', as well as reducing the frequency of economic contact between Travellers and the settled population.[15] In addition, scrap and other materials increasingly kept for trade caused conflict with settled society, who saw it as rubbish not working capital.[16] While in the short term these trends were largely invisible, masked as they often were by the flexible nature of Travellers' economic strategies, over time they helped to lay the foundations for new forms of mistrust of Travellers from settled society, as the amount of actual contact between the communities reduced, and as Traveller family organisation and gender patterns were seen as increasingly out of step with those of late twentieth-century British society.

A further significant change in this period was the shift in the social make-up of Britain's travelling population, as Irish Travellers came to Britain in increasing numbers, either temporarily or on a more permanent basis. During the Second World War some English Travellers had moved over to Eire, creating or extending links with the Irish Traveller community. In 1963 the Irish government carried out a census of Travellers in Ireland, and on the back of this supported policies of the Irish Itinerant Settlement Committee, which aimed to settle Travellers into houses. This, in combination with the more limited economic opportunities available in the Republic, meant that in particular between 1963 and 1970 there was a large influx of Irish Travellers to Britain.[17] For these migrants, at least before the Troubles in Northern Ireland, being in England offered advantages beyond greater economic possibilities, as they might 'pass' in English society as working-class Irish, whereas their idiosyncratic speech would be immediately identifiable to an Irish listener as that of 'an itinerant'.[18]

There were, however, difficulties thrown up by this mass migration: 'they had to enter into economic competition with often resentful local Travellers and Gaujos, but with an inferior knowledge of the country and fewer business contacts. They therefore had to use the abrasive methods of price-cutting and quality variation' in sectors in which English Travellers were already active, such as tarmacking and scrap collection. Other sectors, such as the antiques trade, which was relatively neglected by English Travellers, tended not to see this fierce competition. In addition to creating resentment among some English Travellers, the new migrants attracted the attention of the authorities and settled society, as initially at least, there were 'large geographical and site concentrations, with a high proportion of fairly recent immigrants', such as in Balsall Heath, Birmingham in 1967–68:[19]

> They are reported to travel widely in large groups ... mainly dealing in scrap metal, not staying in one place very long and frequently leaving a trail of litter and police summonses. Local authorities regard them as undesirable because of their alleged tendency to defy the law and disturb local residents, while the indigenous travellers despise the low standards and dirty conditions of the tinkers which cause trouble for all groups of travellers.[20]

The post-war period was thus a time of considerable change: one of the ways in which this was explained by contemporaries, both from Traveller and settled communities, was to point to the influx of Irish Travellers. However, the reasons went far deeper than this. Increased pressure on land and shortage of stopping places was masked to an extent by motorisation, which allowed Travellers to stay in one place for longer and to travel further. For Travellers on the move, the introduction of the 1959 Highways Act made life more difficult as it made stopping on the edge of a highway 'without lawful authority or excuse' a criminal offence for any 'itinerant trader or gypsy'.[21] At the same time, remaining in one site for longer increased both the potential of hostility from surrounding residents and the likelihood they would come to the attention of school attendance officers and other officials.

Travellers were not uniformly affected by these changes, nor did they respond to them in the same way. In areas where there were large shanty/caravan sites as a result of the war, Travellers were often rendered relatively invisible, at least for a time, and where they were seen, they tended to be viewed as an insignificant part of the problem. Some, particularly those who tended to be based in more rural parts of the country, the south-west, central Wales and rural parts of Scotland, for example, were able to continue their lives much as they had in the 1930s. They lived in horse-drawn caravans and bow tents, as much as in newer motorised outfits; picking up seasonal work, hawking and attending the seasonal round of fairs through the 1950s and into the 1960s.

In other, typically urban, suburban and commuter areas, where there was greater pressure on land and where councils were more actively controlling its development, Travellers, often of necessity rather than free choice, tended towards an increasingly less nomadic lifestyle. This was often either through staying in a house for much of the year and only travelling in the summer, or through staying on what were becoming quite large sites. Very often these sites provoked the ire of local media and residents, as they were seen to typify all that was worst about Travellers in a settled, peri-urban context. A 1951 magazine report entitled 'The Unromantic Gypsies' featuring the long established site at Corke's Meadow, St Mary's Cray in Kent, was subtitled 'The Glamourised People of the Open Air and the Care-free Verse: This is How They Really Live'. Under a photograph of the site, angled to ensure that it maximised the squalor of the area, was the caption, '"The Pit" was once a piece of England's green and pleasant land', and, failing to mention that before the Travellers moved onto the site it had been a rubbish tip in an old brickworks, commented that the site was 'a piece of twentieth century urbanised squalor at its worst'. The report painted a picture of a people out of place in modern Britain. Without the little protection a 'picturesque' lifestyle in a bow-topped caravan offered them in the eyes of the public, resident Travellers were seen as nothing more than an unattractive anachronism, best dealt with through eviction and resettlement in houses: 'all Gypsies' have a 'horror of two things: officialdom and living in houses. At Corke's Meadow the first is already with them, and they are threatened by the second'.[22]

Contemporary accounts showed little or no understanding of the changes to which Travellers had to adapt in this period, nor did they accept that for some, a place like Corke's Meadow, unattractive as it may have appeared to outsiders, was the best option for Travellers aiming to maintain their lifestyles under a growing deluge of outside pressures.

The changing environment

Road widening schemes have obliterated many verges, whilst commons have been fenced off (sometimes illegally), and the

widespread building projects around all the large towns have
covered much of those long-used patches of wasteland which
have been temporary resting places for countless Travellers for
generations ... even when mechanised it is difficult to find any-
where to pull in for a night or two, though at least there is no
need to look for grazing for the horses![23]

As well as changes in the economic and social realities of Travellers' lives, the post- war period saw increasing pressure on land, as
local authorities simultaneously attempted to make good the housing shortage resulting from the Second World War and continued
programmes of slum clearance begun in the 1930s. Housing and re-
development were at the heart of post-war efforts at reconstruction.
The war had contributed to the housing crisis in two main ways: through
the destruction and damage of existing housing stock, and by preventing the building of any new houses for the duration of the conflict.[24]

After 1945, Travellers were not the only people who chose to
live in caravans, as the bombed-out homeless from the inner cities
had contributed to the growth of many shanty sites on the peripher-
ies of large urban centres.[25] Some moved out to places they had used
previously as holiday or weekend retreats, others simply arrived with
their remaining possessions and constructed homes on wasteground.
Norman Dodds MP wrote that of the people who settled in his constituency at Belvedere Marshes:

Some could not stand the bombing during the war and left
their rented homes to live in a caravan in the country. The war
over, they could not get back into a house having lost any living qualifications for consideration for Council accommodation, and, not being in a position to raise a mortgage such people
swelled the ranks of the so-called didikais.[26]

The spate of post-war squatting incidents indicated that
demobilisation only compounded existing housing difficulties. Travellers squatted along with other members of the population:

One can appreciate the stern necessity which drives normally
law-abiding people to take possession of Service huts and thus
become 'squatters'. When Gypsies do the same thing the reason is not so obvious. Yet, I have seen that some of these wanderers have invaded a camp and have brought their horses, dogs,
chickens and a goat with them. Apart from the inconvenience
caused to genuine squatters, this seems a sad reflection on the
Romanies. Surely they are not losing their old love for a roving
life and instead wish to settle comfortably?[27]

For the homeless who did not resort to squatting, and did not wish to carry on in cramped households with their wider family, caravans and other moveable dwellings were a viable alternative. In some cases, these were sited in older plotland developments such as Belvedere, but often they were on new sites, as the pressure for land increased.[28]

Official attitudes to caravans in the post-war era were intimately tied up with the house-building programme and new planning laws, both of which were at the heart of the wider debate over the nature of post-war Britain. Aiming to end the uncontrolled development of the old inner cities, with chaotic slum housing, polluting industry and no open spaces, the 1947 Town and Country Planning Act provided for the clear separation of working space and living space, and aimed to ensure that there was only planned development occurring in each designated area. Similarly, new housing was designed to fulfil certain minimum standards of size and persons per room, in order to ensure slumland overcrowding was a thing of the past.

Where in this environment was there room for caravans? In brief, while a minority believed caravans could make a valuable contribution to the process of rebuilding the country, most civil servants and planners saw them as perpetuating pre-war slum standards of accommodation.

The National Caravan Council, representing caravan manufacturers, argued that caravans were easily assembled and were ready for immediate occupation, making them 'an ideal form of housing where housing is urgently needed'. The organisation even made the claim that 'every time one such individual problem is overcome ... a moral and practical victory has been won, affecting the happiness, comfort and efficiency of a British citizen and his wife'.[29]

Despite strong arguments in their favour, caravans remained a deeply controversial subject. While the Ministry of Supply could see the value of caravans for those whose job involved short-term or long-term travel, the Ministry of Health 'aimed at having the population properly accommodated and viewed with disfavour any arrangement that tended to divert raw materials from permanent houses'.[30]

The Ministry of Health's refusal to allow a council to provide temporary caravan accommodation for homeless families was an indication of the depth of their prejudice towards caravans, which went far beyond simple fears that caravan production would jeopardise the supply of materials to house-building: 'The Department strongly deprecates the creation of any *sub-standard accommodation* of this nature and is not prepared to consent to the Council embarking upon such a scheme' (emphasis added).[31] Behind this was an assumption that after the housing crisis, caravans would not become a permanent feature of the landscape, except in a holiday context: '[Caravans might be] tolerated at the present time owing to the housing shortage, [but] must cease to be used for such purposes when conditions improve, and local authorities must take statutory action to ensure that such structures are not used permanently for human habitation when the housing shortage is overcome'.[32]

Central government concerns went wider than a desire to ensure high housing standards for the nation, to embrace issues of control:

> The problem [of caravan dwelling] had reached serious dimensions in the USA before the war. The floating population, paying no taxes (equivalent to our rates) was growing, and caravan parks were reaching the size of small towns ... The problem is not likely to reach such dimensions here partly because of our climate and also cars and petrol are much more expensive ... On the other hand this is a very much smaller and more crowded country and the war has uprooted a good many people.[33]

This voiced bureaucratic fears over the impossibility of controlling a nomadic population, both in simple planning terms and in making them accountable, taxable beings. The sum result was that central government, although suffering from an acute housing shortage and planning chaos, was not willing to accept the advantages that caravans might present.

This attitude was also strongly present among local planners.[34] One local authority official spoke for many when he asserted that even before 'town planning came into its own it was the view of most members and officers of local authorities ... that it would be a good thing to clear [caravans] off the landscape entirely'. He felt that it was 'fair to say that in the eyes of most planners caravans ... their presence should be regarded with at least disfavour'.[35]

A central consequence of official attitudes to caravans was that, except in specific instances, caravans were seen as having only a very limited place in the new planned environment of Britain, with caravan sites being almost entirely absent from local Development Plans. The impact of the 1947 Town and Country Planning Act on caravan-dwellers was felt both through the general ethos behind the legislation, and in the specific sections relating to moveable dwellings,[36] which together made it clear that if caravan sites were to exist they were to do so through private, and not state-sponsored initiative.[37] While this period saw intense debate over state involvement in development and planning,[38] from the outset caravan sites as a land use were seen as marginal to the process. In an era where both planning permission and state-generated development were often vital to the success of a project, the lack of engagement by local authorities in site provision was to have profound consequences.

The situation on the ground, however, ensured that despite an ideological dislike of caravans, the reality was that in many areas they formed an important part in local housing solutions. Hampshire, for example, took a relatively pragmatic attitude towards sites in its area, giving planning permission for a limited period and even turning a blind eye to unpopular long-term shanty sites:

> If legal proceedings are taken against these people they will merely move on to repeat similar conditions on some nearby spot … [We should therefore] try to eliminate the most objectionable sites, and, if possible, direct them on to less objectionable sites which must be found to fulfil this present social, or anti-social need.[39]

Surrey County Council similarly recognised that while for unauthorised sites 'powers exist for enforcement … it is impracticable to use them against an occupant with no other home unless he can be directed to a site where proper facilities exist'.[40]

Faced with the enormous housing shortage, and the sheer scale of the problem, even Whitehall was forced to accept unpalatable truths, with Hugh Dalton admitting privately, 'the experience of my Department has been that, even where shacks have been erected in contravention of planning control, the housing problem and the state of public feeling generally makes effective action impracticable'. This observation was passed on to local authorities but not made public, for fear it might result in 'an even greater degree than exists at present for the unauthorised parking of caravans on land for permanent or semi-permanent occupation'.[41]

For the first half of the 1950s central government asserted that it was not a deficiency in the legislation that caused the rash of unregulated caravan sites, but rather a failure of the housing programme to work fast enough to keep up with demand.[42] It saw live-in caravans as a temporary phenomenon, one that would disappear when enough houses had been provided. Over time, however, civil servants at the Ministry of Housing and Local Government were forced to accept that even when housing was provided, there would still be a substantial number of people living in moveable dwellings.[43] By late 1955 they admitted the problem would 'be with us for several years yet',[44] and that 'the time [had] come to review our policy on caravan sites'.[45] This resulted in a shift in emphasis in policy, with 'the decision to *encourage* the provision of local authority sites, whereas the policy hitherto has been rather *not to discourage*'.[46]

Initially, the change of attitude of central government towards caravans had included Travellers, as a result of questions having been asked in the Parliament and in the press over the 'serious hardship' caused 'when a traditional Gypsy camping ground is closed'.[47] In a meeting convened on the issue, civil servants in housing and local government suggested local authorities should 'provide an alternative site when traditional caravan sites are closed',[48] but the response of the various local authority associations was unanimous and negative. Specific provision of amenities, and particularly sites for Travellers, was not seen as appropriate, partly on the grounds that representatives 'did not think that Gypsies were likely to confine themselves to camps that might be provided for them'. A representative from Kent used the reason for not providing sites as being 'their deep distrust of all authority'. The County Councils' Association felt that there was no point trying to provide sites as 'sooner or later local residents were driven to take action against "Gypsies" because of their activities and general way of living'. Other speakers 'referred to activities of scrap metal dealers ... which were generally deplorable'. The meeting decided that 'it would be left for problems of this kind to be dealt with *ad hoc*. When these problems arose they were apt to be troublesome, but they did not arise in any large scale'.[49]

This illustrated the continuities in attitude towards Travellers held by the settled population: Travellers were depicted as inherently anti-authoritarian, untrustworthy and the cause of their own problems. As with earlier decades, although central government might have initially positioned itself as impartial – in suggesting that Travellers be dealt with alongside other caravan-dwellers – the absence of political will meant that this was not pursued, and the more illiberal stance of the localities held sway.

The separation of Travellers from other caravan-dwellers which was implied in this meeting, and an unwillingness to deal positively with the problems encountered by Travellers, were both characteristics of future government policy. Despite the attitude that the problem was not 'large scale' and therefore did not require state action, increasingly through the 1950s and into the 1960s a crisis developed as Travellers' ability to find suitable stopping places was greatly reduced.

The shortage of sites

> In the coming winter many of us will be faced with certain prosecution, followed by fines or imprisonment, because we can find nowhere to stay. So many of our traditional camping sites have been declared unsuitable and closed ... No alternative accommodation has been offered to us ... We have seasonal occupation with which we earn an honest living through the spring, summer and autumn months as long as we are mobile. Then comes the winter and we hope to settle in one place. What shall we do this winter? The Oxford camp is now a speedway track, the Forest of Dean camp was closed last year. Camps at Elmstone Hardwicke, Uckington and Swindon village, near Cheltenham, have been closed recently. A court order now prevents us from staying ... where many of us have stayed since the government's request to farmers to allow stranded people (during the war) to camp on their land. Those of us who have bought land have been refused licences to build and may only stay on our land for six weeks in a year ... We do not want to be crowded together in large camps ... the church has land and she has schools, some of which are now closed. We appeal this winter to be allowed to stand our vans ... in the yards of those village schools that have been closed.[50]

Problems experienced by Travellers in the 1950s were charted in national, rather than merely local press, and comment and concern over the eviction of Travellers became more widespread. In a number of highly public cases,[51] Travellers were moved off from apparently squalid sites. Some of these were located by the new council and private estates that were the symbol of post-war reconstruction, such as the ironically named Gypsy Lane Estate in Walsall.[52] The response of central government to these evictions are on one level consistent with the line taken by Whitehall from the beginning of the century, in that it argued for an impartial approach to the treatment of Travellers. But in the radically changed context of 1950s Britain, impartiality increasingly appeared as apathy and an abandonment of Travellers to local pressures:

> So far as Gypsies are concerned, the line taken is that if they want to live this way, nobody is going to stop them, but they must make their own arrangements for the use of camping sites.

> There is no call for action by the government, or for that mat-
> ter the local authorities except in the normal exercise of their
> planning and public health functions ... It seems beyond ques-
> tion that the Gypsies cannot be singled out for special treat-
> ment in the matter of sites and living accommodation when
> their whole way of living cuts right across any notion of settled
> community life.[53]

Where central government did feel action was appropriate was
in local authorities providing temporary sites or accommodation,
'say for ten years, during which time we should hope that the back of
the problem would be broken by *the building of permanent houses*' [em-
phasis added].[54] Significantly, the Ministry felt that the situation
might be solved by housing rather than by providing pitches for
caravans on official sites. Clearly, if any state support was to be forth-
coming, it was envisaged to be with the purpose of bringing Travellers into line with the settled community. This memo is revealing in
central government's attitude towards Travellers as a minority. Equality of treatment here meant making no allowance for difference, particularly when that difference undermined mainstream values of
'settled community life'. In this view, Travellers' welfare was not
defined as part of wider community needs, but rather set apart and
defined as primarily outside the realm of government action.

A newspaper article of the period gave an accurate summary of
the situation:

> There is no particular reason why the authorities should help
> the Gypsies preserve their way of life. It is foolish to claim that
> the Romanies are 'good citizens', they are not ... Most Gypsies
> ask for no more than to be left alone, but those few who are
> politically articulate seem to want two things: winter sites with
> water and sanitation provided at a reasonable rent, and some-
> where to camp on the outskirts of big towns.[55]

This call for designated stopping places gradually began to
emerge in the early 1950s, but went largely unheeded by central government, which was unwilling to accept the existence of any national
pattern or problem. However, following a particularly high-profile
eviction, it reluctantly initiated a survey of all Chief Constables in
the winter of 1950–51.[56] It explored the level of Traveller harassment, particularly whether they were being evicted from traditional
winter quarters in any great numbers. The report found that there
were 2,084 'Gypsy camping grounds' in the country, 480 of them
being permanent, and the rest temporary. It asserted that about 7,000

Travellers lived in the permanent camps, and that over 20,000 were on temporary sites. The report concluded that in 90 per cent of counties and just under 90 per cent of cities and boroughs there was 'no indication' of Travellers being moved from their winter quarters.[57] On these figures, and those provided in the 1952 Kent Survey, one civil servant felt confident enough to state that the 'only problem about winter sites is where these are close to towns … and have become unsuitable because residential development has taken over the area'.[58]

The detail of the report, however, painted a less optimistic picture. In Kent it was estimated that about one-fifth of Travellers were being driven from their usual winter quarters, roughly 750 individuals, as the large and long-term sites of Belvedere Marshes and St Paul's Cray were in the process of closing.[59] In Hampshire the local authorities were attempting to close established sites and to re-house the occupants in ex-RAF huts. As well as the closure of some long established and often infamous sites, there was also evidence of moves by local authorities to take action against more temporary camps. In Coventry and Warwick, for example, there had been 'certain instances' of Travellers 'being driven out of their usual winter quarters', while in Derby there was a case of a Traveller being moved by the local authority from a site owing to a lack of sanitary provision.

There is also some doubt over the accuracy of the survey. Manchester had only reported one case of a Traveller family being evicted from their usual winter quarters, suggesting a lack of a problem in its area.[60] Yet correspondence with the Ministry from concerned members of the public revealed a different picture. One letter detailed the case of an eviction of over 70 Travellers from a long-established site that had not been reported in the survey.[61] While civil servants corrected some of the assertions made by the correspondent, they did accept that 74 people had been moved on.[62] This suggests that if one police force could omit to mention such a large eviction, then it is possible that many smaller incidents that had not needed a police presence also went unrecorded.

The government response to the report displayed a fundamental lack of understanding of the repercussions that even one large eviction could have. The Ministry were apparently satisfied that '[apart] from the New Forest, Gloucester and Erith, which we have heard about, the problem does not appear to be an extensive one'.[63] Just taking the populations of Travellers living in the places mentioned in this memo meant accounting for a few thousand people,

who, once evicted compounded matters through putting pressure
on existing sites, or creating new ones. Even without a shortage of
sites and stopping places in the surrounding areas, the arrival of a
few hundred more Travellers put considerable pressure on a locality.
Beyond the flaws in the government's analysis lay a more sub-
stantive point. Though the bulk of the problem may have been concentrated in a few hotspots, throughout the country Travellers were
experiencing difficulties in finding long-term stopping places and
in gaining planning permission. This was not simply the result of
local factors, but was the product of embedded problems caused by
national legislation and the stereotyping of Gypsies.

An understanding of the deeper structural issues facing Travellers were set out in an enquiry initiated by the Bishop of Gloucester,
which aimed to determine the situation of Travellers in his diocese.
It found the police were rigorously enforcing the 1835 Highways
Act in order to move on Travellers.[64] There was less difficulty in
summer when Travellers worked 'on farms and in fruit and hop gardens ... [where] they are usually provided with camping grounds'.
The main problem was that Travellers increasingly had nowhere to
go during the winter, when the farmers employing them were 'unwilling' to give them any room or 'to have them settling in the vicinity'. The Bishop concluded:

> [The] problem must be dealt with; and I do not think it can be
> dealt with on a local level ... We cannot as a nation treat the
> Gypsies as though they did not exist ... They cannot be exter-
> minated and if they disappeared their loss would be severely
> felt as they provide a reservoir of labour ... on the other hand
> ... they are generally unpopular and no one wants them to settle
> for long periods in any given neighbourhood ... It seems obvi-
> ous that the problem must be dealt with on a national basis.[65]

His call for a national solution was based on the belief that throughout the country Travellers were facing a shortage of land on which to
stay, and that local prejudice prevented proper provision of sites.
Land shortages were not only the result of the post-war building
programme that had colonised space traditionally used by Travellers, but were also the product of the changed planning process (see
Chapter 5).

Central government took no action and over a decade later there
occurred possibly the highest profile eviction to date: the removal of
Travellers from Darenth Woods, a piece of woodland in Kent, in the
winter of 1961–62. This eviction was illustrative of the Travellers'

position in relation to the authorities when faced with removal from a site, and can be usefully contrasted with an eviction of caravan-dwellers from the settled community from a site in Egham in the winter of 1958–59. This provided a stark contrast as although both cases drew massive publicity and support involving local notables and drew in central government, their immediate treatment and ultimate fates were quite different.

Darenth Woods had been a Traveller site for several years, but the land had recently been sold to Dartford RDC. The Labour-run council not only wished to remove the Travellers to appease local opinion, but also to comply with green belt planning regulations.[66] Over the winter, plans were set in place to remove the growing number of inhabitants of the site. Through their constituency MP, Norman Dodds, a campaign was mounted with the Prime Minister and various government departments being lobbied. On the ground a tactic of passive resistance was offered, with families refusing to move on to other sites or to remove their trailers during the eviction. Ignoring appeals to wait until the worst of the winter was over, the camp was evicted in mid-January and, although having ample warning of their removal, no alternative site had been arranged by the local authority. The families then spent several months living on the side of the A2 while the council and central government argued over their fate.

In contrast to the Traveller evictions, the removal of caravan-dwellers from an unauthorised site in Egham drew in the Prime Minister, the Lord Chancellor and the Ministry of Supply, as well as the local authority and the courts. The plight of the residents of the site was similar to that experienced by thousands since the war. Individuals had bought a caravan and rented a pitch on the site, only to discover that there was no planning permission and that they were liable to be removed. The residents fought to be allowed to stay and conducted a high-profile campaign, which had included sending urgent telegrams to the Prime Minister.[67] As the case had gone to court it was theoretically no longer in the hands of government, either local or national.[68] However, this did not stop the Prime Minister from being moved by their plight and personally intervening in the matter:

> [The company] have obviously behaved very badly and ought to be punished, but I do not think their tenants should be punished. The council should find another site or else build them some houses to live in. If you want to give them an extra quota of houses I will see that this is made possible.[69]

The Lord Chancellor's office intervened and delayed the eviction until the end of the winter, while the Ministry of Housing and Local Government pressurised Surrey county council to provide accommodation for the caravan-dwellers.[70] Within three weeks of the first telegram being sent to Macmillan an alternative site had been found, to which the Egham residents could move within a fortnight.[71] In this case the government were clearly concerned about the outcry that would result from such an eviction:

> [The injunction must be obeyed.] But this must be brought about in a manner acceptable to public opinion, and the forcible simultaneous removal of sixty-one caravans with their occupants was in my view an impracticable task unless force was used on a scale that would shock public opinion.[72]

Tactics adopted by Egham residents were no different to those used by Travellers throughout the 1950s, but the results were very different, with the eviction delayed to miss the worst of the winter weather, and an alternative site provided. Residents, rather than being seen as the authors of their own problems, were depicted as victims of an unworkable system and an unscrupulous company.

A comparison of the Egham case with Darenth Wood suggests that the claim Travellers had on the state was not seen as strong as that of caravan dwellers from settled backgrounds. Travellers were seen as a nuisance and as responsible for their own misfortune. This contrast was emphasised in the aftermath of both cases. The Darenth eviction eventually resulted in the provision of a site for the Travellers in West Ashford. However, it was a private site funded by Norman Dodds himself, and only received planning permission for two years. In contrast, not only were the Egham residents provided with a permanent alternative site, but their case generated the impetus needed to change the tone of government statements on caravans and to discover the facts surrounding their existence and use.

The Egham caravan-dwellers' plight was seen to highlight the fact that 'the present powers to control caravans and the methods adopted by the local authorities are hopelessly inadequate'.[73] By the end of November 1958 a government survey, later published as *Caravans as homes*, was announced and set in motion.

The main function of the report was to confirm and justify the more positive approach to caravans adopted by central government, and to pass this attitude on to the localities. Significantly, Gypsies were specifically excluded from its terms of reference.[74] The main thrust of the study was that caravans were a permanent feature of the accommodation landscape, and that those living in them were largely respectable, ordinary, working members of the public, or those of retirement age.[75] The report confirmed that local authorities had generally taken a negative attitude towards caravan developments of all types.[76] It may have excluded Gypsies from its terms of reference, but this did not stop it from using them as a foil to stress the difference between them and caravan-dwellers:

> [Caravan dwellers should not be depicted as] belonging to the depressed or shiftless class ... If anything [they] are rather more endowed with self-respect, initiative and a keenness to get on and make a decent life for themselves ... the Gypsies or vagrant caravanners usually move frequently about the countryside; they often park their caravans without any permission from the landowner concerned; they are said by many local authorities to leave filth and litter where they have been, and to contain more than an ordinary share of law-breakers.[77]

The survey's main conclusion was that caravan sites should be viewed and 'dealt with positively rather than negatively', and that while more controls were needed, they should be based on the premise that they were to create and maintain better conditions.[78] Central government accepted the need for legislative action, and the fact that they also needed 'to see a change of heart on the part of some local authorities'. These changes were put into place in the 1960 Caravan Sites and Control of Development Act which required anyone occupying land with a caravan to have a site licence, and for all holders of site licences to first have received planning permission.[79] Not only did this make it difficult for Travellers who had bought a piece of land to use it to overwinter, but the legislation was also used against farmers who allowed Travellers to stay on their land before or after the period when they were actually working on the crops. The Act also gave district councils the powers to create sites, but as I show in Chapter 5, this was a little-used measure.[80]

Despite the potential negative impact on Travellers of the new legislation, central government depicted it as a move forward for those living in caravans. Henry Brooke MP felt it would 'do justice to caravanners, to get caravans on to the right sites and off the wrong ones, to give freedom to the single travelling caravan and to stop caravan slums ... [so that] all Local Authorities will feel able now to pursue a more positive and constructive policy towards caravans'.[81]

The end of the 1950s thus saw a move away from a negative view of both caravans and their inhabitants, but the new positive approach specifically excluded Travellers. Rather than creating more tolerance of Travellers, in the long run, the effect of the massive post-war expansion in caravan-dwelling was to confirm their status as outcasts with scant claim on the resources of the state. While 'caravan dwellers' were seen as respectable and integral members of the community eligible for the full protection offered by government, Travellers were viewed as twilight citizens, a deviant minority whose nomadism caused nothing but problems. This attitude was fuelled by the myth that 'true Gypsies' were disappearing, caused by the disappearance of Travellers' visible markers of ethnicity, notably bow-topped caravans and certain rural and craft occupations.

Notes

1 Strange, *Born on the straw*, 193–4.
2 E. MacColl and P. Seeger, *I'm a freeborn man, and other original radio ballads and songs of British workingmen, Gypsies, prize-fighters, teenagers – and contemporary songs of struggle and conscience* (New York, 1968), 15.
3 Ministry of Housing and Local Government (hereafter MHLG), *Gypsies and other Travellers* (London, 1967).
4 Acton, *Gypsy politics*, 47.
5 Strange, *Born on the straw*, 185.
6 Acton, *Gypsy politics*, 46–7.
7 D. Reeve, *Whichever way we turn* (London, 1964), 20–1.
8 There had been developmental work on hop, potato and sugar beet harvesting during the 1930s and the war, but widespread mechanisation mainly took place in the two decades after 1945. Thanks to Jonathan Brown, Museum for English Rural Life, Reading, for this information.
9 Leitch, *Book of Sandy Stewart*, 88.
10 Acton, *Gypsy politics*, 44.
11 D. Reeve, *Smoke in the lanes* (London, 1958), 85.
12 Jim Riley quoted in Sandford, *Gypsies*, 50.
13 HRO, H/WLF1/3, county welfare officer, 'Survey of Gypsies and Travellers', 1962.
14 MHLG, *Gypsies and other Travellers*, 34; and H. Gentleman and S. Swift (eds), *Scotland's Travelling People* (Edinburgh, 1971).
15 Acton, *Gypsy politics*, 44–5.
16 Sandford, *Gypsies*, 4.
17 Association of Chief Police Officers' Archive, The Open University Milton Keynes (hereafter ACPO), National Gypsy Council, 'Site provision in Britain: A short briefing paper' (July 1992).
18 ACPO, Department of the Environment (hereafter DoE), 'The

accommodation needs of long-distance and regional Travellers: A consultation paper' (February 1982).

19 Acton, *Gypsy politics*, 207.

20 MHLG, *Gypsies and other Travellers*, 3.

21 Section 127 of the 1959 Highways Act.

22 'The unromantic Gypsies', *Picture Post* (28 July 1951).

23 Reeve, *Whichever way we turn*, 30.

24 In 1939 Britain had 12.5 million houses. Nearly a third were destroyed or damaged during the war, and the majority of the remainder were not repaired during these years. Added to this was the baby boom – there were 33% more births in 1945–48 than in 1936–39. See M. Foot, *Aneurin Bevan, vol. I* (London, 1962), 65–6.

25 The raids of 1940–41 made 2.25 million people homeless; two-thirds of these were from the London area. Failures of local authorities in coping with the bombed-out homeless are dealt with in R. M. Titmuss, *Problems of social policy* (London and Nendeln, 1952), 251–8.

26 N. Dodds, *Gypsies, didikois and other Travellers* (London, 1966), 37.

27 'When Gypsies squat', *Ipswich Evening Star* (29 August 1946). See also 'Stay put Gypsies turfed out of Corston', *Bath Chronicle* (14 December 1946). For a general outline of the squatting movement see C. Ward, 'The hidden history of housing', *History and Policy* papers, www.historyandpolicy.org/archive/policy-paper-25.html, accessed April 2006. For central government's reaction to the squatting crisis see MoH Circular 174/46, 'Squatters', reported in *The Sanitarian*, 55 (1946), 119.

28 H. J. Heeley, 'The need for and control of moveable dwellings', *Journal of the Royal Sanitary Institute*, 70:5 (1950), 560.

29 TNA, HLG 52/1527, letter 'Caravans and emergency housing', National Caravan Council to MoH, 26 November 1946.

30 *Ibid.*, minutes of meeting between Ministry of Supply and the National Caravan Council, 21 December 1948.

31 HRO, 59M76/DDC207, MoH to Hartley-Wintney RDC, 14 June 1950.

32 Heeley, 'Moveable dwellings', 553–4. For further examples of official prejudice towards caravans see D. E. Tucker, 'Moveable dwellings', *The Sanitarian*, 54:11 (1946), 2831.

33 TNA, HLG 52/1527, memo on Caravan Club, 26 May 1943.

34 Some planners did accept the importance of caravans as part of a more flexible solution to the housing problem. For example, TNA, HLG 71/903, letter from Erith town clerk to MoH, 12 April 1951; and a paper given by H. J. Heeley, Chief Sanitary Inspector of Epping RDC to the Essex Branch of the Sanitary Inspector's Association, Chelmsford, 20 January 1949.

35 R. J. Roddis, *The law relating to caravans*, (London, 1960), v–vi.

36 For a summary of the major debates surrounding the 1947 Act and the creation of the controversial Central Land Board, see A. Land, R. Lowe and N. Whiteside, *The development of the welfare state, 1939–1951: A guide to documents in the Public Record Office* (London, 1992), 65–6. For

a discussion of attempts to promote public participation in the planning process see A. Beach and N. Tiratsoo, 'The planners and the public', in Daunton (ed.), *Cambridge urban history, vol. III.*

37   The Act defined land used for camping or moveable dwellings as 'development'. Where such development had 'taken place contrary to any planning schemes before the coming into force' of the 1947 Act, it was subject to enforcement notices. Under Section 75 a pre-existing unlicensed site could be closed down by a local authority if it served an enforcement notice within three years of 1 July 1948. The site owner was given the opportunity to regularise their position by applying for planning permission under Section 23. The 1st Schedule of the Development Order dealt with the temporary use of land for periods of time not exceeding 28 days in any calendar year. Moveable dwellings were allowed this period before they were required to apply for planning permission, and if they did not apply, were given a further 28 days following an enforcement notice. See F. G. Bradley, 'The control of moveable dwellings including the effect of the Town and Country Planning Act, 1947', *The Sanitarian*, 57:7 (1949), 204.

38   Land, Lowe and Whiteside, *Development of the welfare state*, 65–6.

39   HRO, 59M76/DDC207, County Planning Officer, 'Moveable dwellings', 5 July 1949, Appendix I, 8.

40   SHC, 6128/2/127, North-West Surrey Area Sub-Committee memo, 'Caravan sites – Use as emergency housing sites', n. d., probably 1950. The following councils had either implicitly or explicitly accepted the existence of, often unregulated, caravan sites until the housing situation improved: Highworth RDC, Bedfordshire county council, Coventry, Solihull UDC, Biggleswade RDC, Hull, Esher, Nuneaton, Amersham, Cheadle and Monmouthshire and Cambridgeshire. See TNA, HLG 71/1653, letter from Battle RDC to Minister of Local Government and Planning, 'Local authorities (additional information)', 18 July 1951.

41   TNA, HLG 52/1533, Hugh Dalton to H. Morrison, 25 May 1950, and letter from Surrey County Council to all clerks of district councils, 27 July 1950.

42   For example TNA, HLG 71/1653, statement by the Minister of Housing and Local Government to the Association of Municipal Corporations, 6 November 1954.

43   TNA, HLG 71/1653, minute by Youard to Jones, n.d., 1952.

44   TNA, HLG 71/2269, minute, 21 October 1955.

45   *Ibid.*, minute, 2 December 1955.

46   *Ibid.*, minute, 10 July 1956. Original emphasis.

47   TNA, HLG 71/2269, minute 'Caravans', 27 September 1956, and circular letter from MHLG to Local Authority Associations, 17 October 1956.

48   *Ibid.*, minute, 16 July 1956.

49   *Ibid.*, RDC Association to MHLG, 17 December 1956, and summary of meeting held between MHLG and local authority association

representatives, 'Caravans', 29 November 1956.

50 Quoted in A. M. Fraser, 'The Gypsy problem: A survey of post-war developments', *JGLS*, 3:3–4 (1953), 87–8.

51 TNA, HLG 71/1650, details a number of these cases, in Iver, Eton RDC, Brierley Hill, Staffordshire, and various sites in Essex and Kent.

52 *Walsall Observer* (4 January 1957), and B. Adams, J. Okely, D. Morgan and D. Smith, *Gypsies and government policy in Britain: A study of the Travellers' way of life in relation to the policies and practices of central and local government* (London, 1975), 192–6.

53 TNA, HLG 71/1650, internal memo, response to Kent Survey, 15 January 1953.

54 *Ibid.*

55 'The English Gypsies: maintaining a life apart in the modern world', *The Times* (7 December 1952).

56 This case, which involved a Miss Wilmot-Ware and Cheltenham RDC, is discussed at length in Acton, *Gypsy politics*, 140–7.

57 TNA, HLG 71/903, 'Camping places for Gypsies, findings from 1951 police questionnaire'.

58 TNA, HLG 71/1651, internal MHLG memo, 14 October 1952.

59 There were 1,150 people living on sites in Kent, with over half of them being concentrated in the larger sites of Belvedere, Corke's Meadow and Ruxley Chalk Pit. See Adams, 'Gypsies and other Travellers', 5–12.

60 TNA, HLG 71/903, Summary of findings of police questionnaire by region, 1951.

61 TNA, HLG 71/1650, Adams to Hugh Dalton, 4 April 1951.

62 *Ibid.*, Manchester town clerk to MoH, 11 April 1951, and TNA, HLG 71/1650, background notes for Adjournment debate, 17 April 1951.

63 *Ibid.*, MHLG minute on the Chief Constable's survey, 26 February 1951.

64 Section 72 prohibited camping on a highway and the lighting of a fire within 50 feet of the centre of a road.

65 TNA, HLG 71/903, letter from Bishop of Gloucester to Bevan, 16 October 1950.

66 Dodds, *Gypsies*, 60–1.

67 TNA, PREM 11/2725.

68 *Ibid.*, MHLG to Prime Minister's Office, 16 October 1958.

69 *Ibid.*, Macmillan to MHLG, 18 October 1958.

70 *Ibid.*, MHLG to Macmillan, 21 October 1958.

71 *Ibid.*, minute to Macmillan, 3 November 1958. The land belonged to the Ministry of Supply.

72 *Ibid.*, MHLG to Macmillan, 'Caravans', 27 October 1958.

73 TNA, PREM 11/3014, minute for Cabinet, 'Caravans and Planning Enforcement', 15 January 1960.

74 A. Wilson, *Caravans as homes*, 1959, Cmnd. 872, para. 1. As were vagrants and holiday caravanners.

75 *Ibid.*, 43 and 52. The investigation found that there were 150,000 people living in 60,000 caravans. The bulk of these were concentrated either

in holiday areas or parts of the country that had experienced significant post-war development and expansion in employment opportunities.

76 *Ibid.*, in the five years following 1954, local authorities had turned down about 6,000 planning proposals for 39,000 caravans, and had granted about 13,000 sites containing 42,000 dwellings. Over one hundred local authorities had refused absolutely all applications for caravan sites, and a further three hundred reported that refusal was their 'normal policy'.

77 *Ibid.*, 59 and 69.

78 *Ibid.*, 319–30.

79 Section 3 intended to ensure planning permission was given for extended or unlimited periods of time to ensure site owners invested in adequate facilities. In Section 4 the MHLG gained the power to create a model code of licence provisions to which all local authorities had to adhere. Section 5 allowed the closing of sites which are 'so offensive to the amenities', on the payment of compensation, even where it had planning permission.

80 D. Kenrick and C. Clark, *Moving on: The Gypsies and Travellers of Britain* (Hatfield, 1995), 87–8.

81 TNA, PREM 11/3014, Henry Brooke to Macmillan, 2 December 1959 and *Hansard*, 620 (84) cols 679 and 681.

5

The state and site provision

Chapter 4 showed how pressure on land and 'caravan dwellers' affected Travellers within the context of shifting Traveller populations, economic opportunities and motorisation. These developments did not occur in isolation, but rather were mediated through, and often intensified by, state attitudes, action and inaction.

This chapter opens by considering more closely how attitudes and biases within government culture and process affected Travellers in the context of the new formalised planning environment and shortage of stopping places. Through case studies of the Traveller survey of Kent, and an eviction in South Wales, I show how engrained governmental attitudes, and the balance of power and responsibility between central and local authorities, are again key to understanding the treatment of Travellers and the idea of official sites in this period.

Finally, I explore how, despite strong bureaucratic and political resistance to the idea of official sites, there emerged an increasing technocratic consensus that they were the only way forward. For some within settled society this was seen as a step towards permanent settlement; for Travellers it was often seen as the only viable means of maintaining a semi-nomadic existence in an increasingly regulated environment.

Governmental culture and planning

Central to the identity of the British state in the mid-twentieth century was how its impartiality and professionalism enabled its civil servants to deliver a reasonable technocratic solution to challenges posed to it. Yet Travellers were systematically failed by the post-war state at both central and local levels. The response of the Ministry of

Housing and Local Government to the shortage of stopping places was mediated through the bureaucratic vacuum that existed around the issue, particularly a persistent lack of specialist knowledge of Traveller communities. Lobbying revealed indifference and ignorance within government departments, along with an absence of any specific policy framework for Travellers.[1] At the root of this inertia was the firm belief held in Whitehall of the intrinsic fairness of the British system, leading to a position of general complacency on the part of civil servants:

> [In] times of peace Parliament is in the happy position of having to infringe liberty only to a relatively minor extent ... the British are instinctively a law-abiding people ... They respect the impartiality of the courts and the common-sense and fairness of the police ... Grievances are frequently ventilated, impartially investigated and frequently redressed. Where liberty is curtailed, the reason for its curtailment is widely understood and accepted ... because the liberal principles ... are deeply engrained in the British character.[2]

This belief in fairness may have caused the Home Office before the war to protect Travellers from deliberately repressive local bylaws, but it also perpetuated an attitude that the system was flawless. Such complacency inhibited any exploration by government of the difficulties experienced by marginal groups within the mainstream system and prevented national government questioning the depth of local authorities' commitment to equality.

The 'cult of the generalist' that was such a major part of the civil service's ethos led to officials making decisions on subjects about which they had no specific knowledge.[3] This was compounded by the persistent disinterest of the British state in systematically collecting information relating to its travelling population. As late as 1961, Dodds believed:

> Several comments made by [the Ministry of Housing and Local Government] show how little your advisers know about the problem and how out of date they are in what they do know ... your advisers are completely out of date when they stress the Gypsies 'value their independence and right to follow their own way of life ... I am sorry to know that your department is so ill-informed and so readily content to leave it to the local authorities.[4]

Even when a department had some insight into the Traveller situation, it tended to try and push the responsibility onto a different

ministry. For example, in 1950 the Home Office felt that police treatment of Travellers involved 'wider issues', and that 'whether the
police take action or not, there is a general picture of hardship which
perhaps *your Ministry can best deal with, through the local authorities
concerned*' (emphasis added).[5] To which the Ministry of Housing and
Local Government 'specialist' on Travellers replied that the 'general
prevention of hardship and care of the sick are not matters for me',
emphasising this point by returning all the correspondence on the
matter.[6]

Civil servants argued that the reason for their lack of involvement in Travellers' accommodation needs was based not on any bias
or incompetence on their part, but rather on the historical treatment
of Travellers. As shown in Chapter 3, moveable dwellings and their
inhabitants traditionally had been dealt with at the local level, a trend
confirmed by the 1936 Public Health Act. The role of the centre was
merely to provide a system of checks and balances:

> I hope you do not think the Department are complacent about
> it or are without sympathy for the Gypsies themselves. The
> Department try to persuade – they cannot compel – local au-
> thorities to arrange for the provision of alternative sites where
> traditional camping sites for one reason or another are lost,
> and we shall continue to do so. We shall also continue to hold
> the balance as best we can between public health and other
> planning considerations on the one hand, and the legitimate
> needs and desires of the Gypsies on the other.[7]

As well as the structural reasons for a lack of engagement by
central government in the Traveller question, the Home Office and
Ministry of Housing and Local Government believed that there was
'no evidence' that local authorities were using recent legislation 'as a
weapon against the Gypsies'. They argued that the provisions 'of
course apply to all sections of the community who use moveable
dwellings'. Their assertion, however, was based on an absence of 'separate records of summonses taken out against particular classes of
people',[8] not on any investigation into the claim.

The departments' argument that there was no national problem was boosted by their tendency to use racialised and spurious
definitions of 'Gypsies'. This allowed their civil servants to be seen
to engage with the issue of 'true' Gypsies, who did not want or need
official sites, and with racially impure 'didikais' and other Travellers
who did not deserve state provision of camps, but instead could be
subsumed under the wider 'caravan' problem and the housing

programme. Rather than examining the structural reasons behind repeated evictions, officials dismissed their importance by denying they involved true Gypsies:

> From time to time there are articles in the Press and questions in the house about Gypsies being evicted from their customary camping sites ... In all these cases the people are referred to as 'Gypsies', though the Romany element seems to have been diluted, with *Irish tinkers* in Cardiff, and with *scrap metal dealers* in Iver and Brierley Hill [emphasis added].[9]

Officials who worked on the Kent survey similarly agreed that 'the Gypsies proper' were 'a very small part of the itinerant population and that they generally remain in the country and are very little trouble to anyone'. In one case this led the official to ask:

> I would like to know whether Mrs Eastwood, her mother, and the rest of the family live in traditional Gypsy horse-drawn caravans ... whether the younger Eastwoods are Gypsies living a nomadic existence or are they too ... 'permanent residents' at Chalk Pit – if so, how do they earn their living?[10]

Concentrating on living style and economic occupation allowed government departments to suggest that those affected by the 1947 Town and Country Planning Act were 'not Gypsies at all', but rather 'people who without any special claim, choose to live in a way which does not harmonise to the local pattern':[11]

> The Town and Country Planning Act, 1947 leaves the Gypsies free to go on using all their old camping grounds – both the permanent ones and those which are used for part of the year only. They can also, like other campers, camp freely on any new site for a period of twenty-eight days in any one year. Only, if they want to stay longer on a new site, it is necessary for them to apply for planning permission ... there is nothing in the Planning Act to interfere substantially with the Gypsies' way of life.[12]

Such an attitude neither took into account Travellers' long held preference for remaining stationary for the winter, nor newer difficulties with the growing shortage of appropriate places to stop. It implied that 'real' Gypsies would not wish to be stationary, and that anyone wishing to have a long-term park-up was not a 'true Gypsy' and therefore could be dealt with through the provision of housing in the fullness of time.

Added to the Ministry of Housing and Local Government's belief that those affected were not Gypsies, was their idea that it was not a particular section of society but rather anti-social habits that were being targeted. It was, therefore, up to the wrongdoers to mend their ways, rather than for society to change its definition of nuisance, or to accept that it placed an unfair burden on a minority within society. While this attitude was consistent with central government's long-standing principle of not legislating against particular minority groups, but rather regulating certain behaviours, it was equally a product of the more general complacency existing within Whitehall over their administration's impartiality, and its tendency to assume it existed equally at the local level:

> Our information is that the local authorities and the police are not using their powers *against Gypsies as such but against the nuisances themselves*, whoever causes them … Local authority sites are out of the question; the local authorities would not provide them and there is, indeed, no reason why Gypsies should be given priority in this way over other people … we don't know where Gypsies want to go, and even if we did we can't make it an obligation on local authorities and land owners to accept them on these sites. Only Gypsies themselves know where they want sites and for how long, and now that they are getting organised I suggest that they should themselves select the sites they want to have … [then] go and get permission from the owners to go on the land, they should then, as a body, discuss with the local authority concerned, the question of planning permission and a public health licence. If this is done by Gypsies as an organised body, it should help them to get over what is, admittedly often a strong local prejudice. *But it must be done by the Gypsies themselves and it must be done locally* … if they are to avoid 'persecution' in the future, they must themselves get the thing on a proper footing with the local authorities, and convince them they are clean and respectable [emphasis added].[13]

The rationale behind Whitehall thinking was that 'true' Gypsies were not affected by the growing shortage of sites, instead continuing their isolated existence in inoffensive and picturesque rural locations. It was only 'tinkers' and 'drop-outs' who were suffering, and even then the problem was not widespread. Even if local authority sites were the solution, it was not acceptable for Travellers to take precedence over citizens. Instead, Travellers were to use the planning system to find support for their lifestyle. However, as they were not 'clean and respectable' (and implicitly different from caravan dwellers), it was up to them to forge some sort of link with local authorities: they could expect no help from central government.

Similar ingrained prejudice existed within the apparently impartial planning process at the local level. One result of Whitehall's avowed commitment to the impartial treatment of all citizens was that Travellers were dealt with as individuals and not as part of a minority group with special needs and interests.[14] Thus Travellers were subsumed into the larger mass of the populace. Yet within this framework of equality, Travellers were clearly discriminated on the basis of their identity. Part of this was the result of the unwillingness of a bureaucratic state to create channels appropriate for a non-literate, nomadic population. Along with other long-term caravan residents, Travellers were expected to make planning applications, but were often disadvantaged by illiteracy, the lack of a stable address and intimidated by local authority procedure.[15]

If Travellers surmounted these hurdles to place an application, evidence suggests that local authorities rejected a disproportionate number of their proposals. Records from Hartley-Wintney RDC are unusually unambiguous. Answering a questionnaire on its caravan policy, the council stated that in general it was 'very cautious of granting licences'. The council operated a sliding scale of prejudice against different sorts of moveable dwelling: holiday caravanning was 'encouraged where facilities were available'; and the council was 'generally opposed' to permanent caravan colonies, except as a 'temporary measure during [the] present housing shortage'. Travellers were the least desirable with Hartley-Wintney stating that they were 'strongly opposed' to any of their encampments receiving licences.[16] Insights into local government policy of this nature give lie to central government's belief of impartial planning regulation enforcement in the localities.

As with general council policies, Hartley-Wintney did not make this attitude specific or public. Owing to the housing shortage throughout the 1950s, it had adopted an unofficial policy of granting applications to those wanting to site caravans, with between 80 and 90 per cent of applications being accepted.[17] When a site application was specified as coming from a Traveller, the site was almost always described in negative terms. Accompanying an application from a Mr Lee and a Mr Brazil, was the comment:

> These families are of Gypsy type persons and have deposited themselves on land in Rosemary Lane, Blackwater … Several persons have made representations to the Council as to the living conditions of these two families … no water or sanitary accommodation is available, the site is very untidy and unsuitable.[18]

The application was turned down. The number of complaints about the site would suggest that it was not council prejudice alone that caused this outcome, but that pressure from the public was also a factor. Yet it is possible that even if the complaints had not been received, planning would still have been refused. The use of the phrases 'Gypsy-type persons' and 'deposited themselves' do not sit comfortably with bureaucratic claims of impartiality, and instead speak of an engrained official prejudice against Travellers.

In summary, government, supported by its own ignorance and racial stereotyping, refused to acknowledge either the existence of a national shortage of stopping places and longer-term sites, or a need for official sites. 'Real Gypsies' were seen as being unaffected by legislative developments, and other Travellers were to be dealt with through the housing programme. If long-term sites were to be a solution for Travellers, they were a matter for private individuals and not the state. At the same time, the tools to create sites were effectively withheld from Travellers, as the new planning system insisted both that they should be treated as equals and ensured that they were not.

The Kent Survey

Behind the unfaltering public stance of central government that there was no Traveller problem, privately there was a move towards accepting the situation as unsatisfactory. The winter and spring of 1951 saw increased agitation by supporters of Travellers, by Miss Wilmot-Ware who attempted to protect Travellers camped on her land in Gloucestershire, and by Norman Dodds MP, on behalf of his constituents at Belvedere Marshes in Kent. Aided by residents, Gypsy Williams and Mr Larmour from the London City Mission wrote and publicised a 'Gypsy Charter', and a Travellers' deputation to the House of Commons in May was organised in a fanfare of publicity.[19] By May 1951 the level of pressure was such that the Home Office decided not to confirm any more bylaws relating to the control of moveable dwellings until publicity had subsided, as otherwise 'it might be embarrassing'.[20] For a brief moment the Ministry of Housing and Local Government toyed with the idea of promoting the concept of 'a series of small sites, each one of six caravans or so'. Although this idea never developed beyond a short memo,[21] the department accepted that:

> Gypsies are finding it more and more difficult to carry on their
> traditional nomadic way of life. Food rationing, health insur-
> ance, pensions, allowances, registration and camping control
> under the Public Health and Planning Acts mean a regulation
> of life that is foreign to them ... Increasing difficulties of this
> sort in the modern planned society have led some of them to
> set out what they think must be done if the Gypsies are to adapt
> themselves to present day conditions.[22]

This statement assumed Travellers were still nomadic and untouched
by modernity, and that it was up to Travellers to 'adapt themselves'
rather than for society to change. Thus, although it was decided that
there was a problem, 'and that basically it is one of *sites*', any sites
created were not to be designed in order to facilitate nomadism. Instead, they were to act as agents of settlement, believing the 'questions of education and jobs will begin to solve themselves if and when
secure sites are obtained'.[23] From the outset then, official assumptions were based around the understanding that if official sites were
to be created they were to act as agents of assimilation.

A survey of Travellers in Kent was set in motion, partly because the local authority had already had some knowledge of the
issue and was possibly sympathetic to the provision of sites as a solution. It had been mainly forced into this position owing to the number of large established sites within its area – Belvedere Marshes, St
Paul and St Mary Cray – and due to the fact that it had experienced
difficulties with evictions and rehousing ex-residents.[24]

The importance of the survey[25] lay less in the information it
provided on the county's Travellers than in highlighting the conflicts that took place at the local level over the issue of site provision.
Initially there was some genuine commitment to the idea of creating
official sites, with talk of five permanent camps being provided
throughout Kent. At one meeting the county planning officer, Mr
Adams, was 'emphatic in pointing out that Corke's Meadow itself
was, in his opinion, a most suitable site for Gypsies and that he knew
of no better one in Metropolitan Kent. He considered that the existing deemed planning permission on Corke's Meadow could be revoked'.[26] At a meeting of Kent's local authorities in July 1952 he
tried to 'persuade them to agree in principle upon the need for improved accommodation for Gypsies in Kent, and municipal ownership of sites'. Adams particularly wanted the local council to accept
the importance of buying Corke's Meadow as soon as possible as the
situation in the area was 'urgent'.[27]

Despite these relatively auspicious beginnings, no progress was made. Acton blamed the disagreement of the various 'experts'.[28] But this underestimated the depth of resistance to change and positive policy formulation of any kind at the local level, and the degree of conflict between the various tiers of government. Whereas in the past, the main bureaucratic conflict had been between central and local government, developments in Kent activated a further layer of conflict. The county council, in this case represented by Adams, was enthusiastic about providing municipal sites, provided this was done at a *district* level. However:

> All the Councils refused to accept any responsibility for the Gypsies at all. Erith was very rude ... [Chislehurst] had in fact come up against a blank wall, and [Adams] is sure his Council who have no power to buy the land themselves unless the Minister gives it to them, will not ask the Minister to do so and are not going to be able to bring any successful pressure on the district councils.[29]

The fact that the county council was only enthusiastic insofar as it did not have to take action was made clearer in a statement made by Adams himself:

> The County Council is willing at any time to consider sympathetically a request from a County District Council for advice as to a suitable site ... in relation to acquisition, layout and administration of such a site, or for financial assistance in connection with any such project. The County Council *does not favour* the transfer of any of the relevant functions from County District Councils to the County Council [emphasis added].[30]

The possibility of the county council having to provide the sites was sufficient for Adams to retract his earlier statement on the importance of official sites. In discussion with the Ministry he later asserted that he felt the problem was 'essentially a short term one' and in fact centred on the 'provision of housing accommodation' for ex-site residents. That was 'principally a matter for the housing authorities and the Local Planning Authority'. One of the Ministry representatives suggested that 'there might well be a permanent irreducible minimum of people who for one reason or another preferred to live in caravans [rather] than accept the responsibilities of householders'. Adams accepted that 'this might be so but said that at this stage his Council were not prepared to accept the existence of anything more than the short term problem'.[31]

Kent was not unique in its response to suggestions for official site provision as a similar situation occurred in Staffordshire following its 1954 report. Despite recommendations for local authorities to provide sites, three years later no movement had been made, except for the county council 'trying to persuade' one local district council to carry out a 'pilot scheme' assessing the viability of local authority sites: 'we have not had much success, as each Authority is reluctant to be a guinea pig for the experiment'.[32]

These experiences show how district councils were implacably opposed to taking responsibility for site provision. While county councils might have been more enthusiastic in principle, they were no more willing than any other level of government to take control of matters. As central government believed site provision to be within the remit of local authorities, the overall effect was a continuation of the unsatisfactory status quo. Crucially, central government had no powers to coerce local authorities to act, even if it had the political will to do so. This was the legacy of its continual avowal of the localised nature of the Traveller problem.

The case of Leckwith Common

The weakness of central government was revealed in the repercussions of an eviction of a Traveller site at Leckwith common on the outskirts of Cardiff. Superficially the situation was nothing more than yet another series of complaints by local residents and the council against an encampment of Travellers on a piece of waste ground. However, the debates generated by the eviction over the winter of 1955–56 reveal how the events in Cardiff were indicative of wider trends in central and local government thinking and practice. Following on from events in Kent, they reinforced the reluctance of district councils to take responsibility for the provision of camps for Travellers, and highlighted the impotence of central government, through the medium of its Welsh Office, in the face of local authority intransigence.

Throughout 1954 and 1955 there were the complaints from locals of straying horses, insanitary behaviour, and the harassment of residents which resulted first in injunctions being placed on some of the Travellers, and then in eviction proceedings.[33] Events gathered momentum when one of the Travellers, Mrs Lydia Lee, wrote to the Queen, asking her to intervene:

My name is Lydia Lee, I am sixty-eight years old and with my family Gypsies have lived on Leckwith Common, Cardiff for fifty year. Now we are told we must leave here and we have nowhere to go. Can you find us, please, find us, some piece of land where we Gypsies can live. We are willing to pay rent to live in peace, all my family is being broking up because we have no place to live, please help us because we are loyal and honest people, many of my people fought in wars. (P.S. Mrs Lee is No Scholar so I, Sarah Hearne have written this as she talks)[34]

Over the following months Mrs Lee managed to gain the sympathy of the local press and some MPs, and the case developed a profile far beyond Cardiff. The image she presented of herself as a defenceless and respectable Romany, wanting to spend her last years in peace, was one that drew much sympathy.[35]

Against this background a debate developed between the local councils and the Welsh Office. There was a general recognition that given the level of publicity surrounding the case, it was important 'to show that all aspects of the Council's responsibility was recognised', towards the Travellers as well as towards the residents of the area. Councillors and bureaucrats also expressed some under-standing and sympathy for the situation of Mrs Lee and her fellow Travellers.[36]

As in Kent, initially there was a feeling that positive action would be appropriate but when this resulted in the suggestion of site provision for those involved, the local authorities started prevaricat-ing. There was the inevitable quibbling over the proportion of real Gypsies present – it was estimated that of the forty to fifty caravans on the Common, only 'Mrs Lee and possibly a few of the others were genuine Gypsies'.[37] This resulted in Cardiff Corporation, prompted by the Welsh Office, entering into direct negotiations with Mrs Lee. By dealing with her on an individual case basis, it could be seen to be solving the problem, without establishing the principle that the council was responsible for a wider 'Traveller' problem.

However, the Welsh Office used the Travellers' plight as an opportunity to highlight how the situation was 'part of a wider prob-lem' of the shortage of stopping places which, if dealt with, might pave the way for a more general solution. It felt that the city council should provide an official site for the Travellers, and if the council felt that there was nowhere suitable within Cardiff, then the Welsh Office felt that the authority was obliged to 'make sure that there

[was] some other place to which they [could] reasonably resort'.[38] The council immediately made it clear that they were not prepared to do this, emphasising how there were 'no sites in Cardiff suitable for Gypsy encampments',[39] a position they backed up by continually harrying the Travellers from one place to the next.[40]

At this point the impotence of the Welsh Office became clear. It felt Cardiff Council was 'cocking a snook at the Minister and more or less defying him to do anything about it'. The Welsh Office was concerned that if they did nothing they might, in the future, be accused of 'not having taken a sufficiently strong line'. However, it was conscious that if the council was pressed 'they may simply defy us to do anything about it, and bring discredit on us in that way. *We have no real status*' (emphasis added).[41] After the issuing of the injunctions, central government was forced to admit that: '*we have no real power* to prevent Cardiff from doing this and none to force them to provide a camping site. Our attempts to persuade them to be more reasonable have failed' [emphasis added].[42] This situation was the direct consequence of the central government position that Travellers were the responsibility of the localities.

In the face of continuing publicity the Welsh Office made an attempt to resolve matters by initiating a meeting between itself and the local district councils.[43] From this two themes emerged: one was a generally expressed prejudice towards Travellers for, during 'the general discussion ... it became evident that the feeling of the Councils' representatives was against Gypsies'. Mr Pyatt, from Cardiff Council, 'who had throughout the meeting not failed to display his strong antipathy, said that the best thing would be to keep them moving, to break them up and to make life so unbearable that they would be made to settle'.[44] Cardiff town clerk, Mr Tapper-Jones, said that if 'they are genuine Gypsies they should itinerate and should not stay in one place. If they do stay in one place they should have housing accommodation'.[45]

The second theme was that of shifting responsibility. The Welsh Office did not suggest that higher tiers of government would step into the breach and provide sites, merely that it was keen for the local authorities to do so. In response, each council gave a sound reason why they could not provide an official site. Cardiff stated how, on the grounds of equity, they had been obliged to evict the Travellers as they had 'refused permission of many people on their housing list to live in a caravan pending houses being built'. Llantrisant and Llantwit Fardre RDC felt that they were 'probably too far from large

centre[s] of population ... The Council would wish to see other remote neighbours of Cardiff brought in before they considered the
proposal'. Penarth UDC 'viewed the question sympathetically' but
felt they had 'no suitable sites'.[46] As in Kent, no local authority was
willing to solve their Traveller problem by actually providing a site,
preferring instead to keep them on the move.

Central government, over the years, had maintained that responsibility had sat with the councils, and now it found that 'with
the authorities unable or unwilling to find a site or sites on which
the "Gypsies" might settle, there is nothing further the Ministry can
do in the matter'.[47] The Welsh Office 'had no executive responsibilities in the matter', and was therefore 'unable to push [its] action
home',[48] despite feeling that the way forward was for all the local
authorities to work together to find a site. The Welsh Office felt that
the fact that there was no 'suitable' site was not the issue, the 'point
is where the *least unsuitable* area can be found'.[49]

Even if the Welsh Office, in this case, was relatively enlight-
ened in believing that local authorities should work together to find
a solution, as with the Home Office in the past, this did not mean
that it was acting out of the interests of the Travellers themselves:

> Each County Council has taken Local Act powers of a negative
> character, but the trouble is that negative action is no longer
> enough ... that is, from the point of view of the rest of the pub-
> lic. *A negative policy could be justified, perhaps, if it could be shown
> that this was the best way of gradually eliminating a wandering form
> of life* ... It was suggested at the last meeting, for example, that
> any attempt to provide controlled camps for the 'Gypsies' re-
> sulted in steadily increasing the numbers of people who took
> to a wandering life [emphasis added].[50]

The department's civil servants were preoccupied with how to remove a bureaucratically untidy mode of living, not with providing
safe sites for Travellers. Significantly, the lasting lesson that central
government took from the Leckwith case was not that local authorities were fundamentally unwilling to act unilaterally to provide sites
for Travellers, or that Whitehall had no powers to require them to do
so. Instead, it was the importance of using the welfare bodies of the
state to facilitate the integration of Travellers in British society. If
Travellers wanted to travel and have secure sites, then it was a matter for them as individuals, and not a concern of the state:

> By their housing, education and social policy the Government
> are making the greatest practical contribution they can to

persuade people to lead a settled life, but it is no part of their
policy to prevent people leading a roving life if they wish ... it
seems neither necessary nor desirable to provide at public expense a chain of camps for rovers. But such camps are legitimate use of land and roving families who wish to provide for
themselves are entitled to have their needs considered on their
merits by the planning and health authorities. The static families are part of the general housing problem and must be dealt
with *pari passu* with other families whose present living conditions are unsatisfactory ... Our conclusion is that the problem
... is not national but local.[51]

Sites and assimilation

Given the huge bureaucratic antipathy at both the national and local
level to sites, it is necessary to explain the trend of growing government acceptance for them during the late 1950s and through the
1960s.

The first observation to make is that official sites were never
overwhelmingly popular as they only ever found support among a
small proportion of Whitehall bureaucrats, and an even smaller percentage of local government officials. As Acton has shown in his
detailed depiction of the move towards official site provision,[52] acceptance in official circles was partly the result of pragmatism. Constant evictions and harrying of Travellers not only received bad
publicity, but also absorbed council finances and police time. For
example, a discussion over the provision of a site in Eton district
accepted that while there would be difficulties – primarily the objections of local residents – the problems would be 'small compared
with the social, health and welfare benefits to the Gypsies, and *the
saving of Police and Council Officer time*' (emphasis added).[53]

Beyond pragmatism was the belief that sites were a potential
tool to target the resources of the welfare state, and the means to
settle and eventually integrate Britain's nomads. In Scotland this
had been realised and discussed much earlier in the 1936 Vagrancy
Committee Report, which had concluded that education could not
be provided outside the context of secure sites. Over time such sites
could 'habituate' Travellers to a sedentary lifestyle, and were to be
followed by removal into permanent houses: '[Local authorities
should] gradually absorb Tinkers into ordinary society by housing
them and securing for their children a full time education'. This
would be realised by providing council houses in close proximity to

schools, but without concentrating the settlers into 'Tinker colonies', which would prevent them from breaking with old habits.[54]

Such arguments found resonance south of the border only in the 1950s and 1960s. The Winchester branch of the NSPCC in 1953 for example, found that Traveller children lacked access to education, even when they were stationary over the winter: 'It is then the children could go to school … It would therefore seem that what is required are some sites provided with tap water and sanitation to which Gypsies could come in winter months. These sites should be near to towns where there are adequate educational facilities'.[55]

By 1967 there were fourteen council sites spread throughout the country that had been provided by district councils under the provisions of the 1960 Caravan Sites Act. West Ashford rural district council in Kent, for example, created an official site after a group of Travellers were evicted from a common, had nowhere else to go and all 'expressed a wish for council housing'. An official site was opened the following year, where 'despite some initial problems about lorry parking and local residents' reaction, there was a reasonable success. Rents were paid, crime did not rise, and West Ashford was not invaded, as had been predicted, by thousands of Travellers all hoping to get on the one site'.[56]

Acton argues that the success of this site, in combination with the publicity surrounding the Darenth Woods eviction, prompted the Ministry of Housing and Local Government to issue circular 6/62, which represented 'a major shift in the tone of government policy statements'. It 'emphasised the gravity of the problem, instead of minimising it', and encouraged county councils to carry out surveys and to start sites, offering the case of West Ashford by way of encouragement.[57] While this circular, in principle, prompted Kent County Council to agree the provision of another ten sites in the county,[58] many of the district councils remained unconvinced. Other counties, while accepting the need for action, did not necessarily see official sites as the way forward. Hampshire, for example, following its 1962 survey, decided that 'simplified housing' as a step towards eventual council housing and assimilation, was the way forward (see Chapter 6).[59]

Although the circular did indeed acknowledge an increasing problem of traditional sites disappearing due to 'the spread of development and other causes', it also formalised and made clear two strands of Whitehall thinking: that there was a distinction between 'true gypsies' and other caravan-dwellers, and that sites were the first step in a project towards assimilation.

The circular referred to 'true gypsies, or romanies [who] have the right to follow their traditional mode of life, and they have a legitimate need for camping sites'. There was a second group, 'caravan dwellers': 'who are usually self-employed or dependent on casual work, and who for lack of regular sites put their caravans on unauthorised sites on commons, wasteland and roadside verges ... usually without sanitary facilities ... and then sometimes cause serious complaint on grounds of nuisance and unsightliness'. No explanation was given for how this second group differed from 'romanies'.

While making a distinction, apparently on the grounds of race, and accepting that Gypsies were entitled to sites, the circular also made it plain that in either case the solution was for these people to settle down. It observed that 'new occupations and new opportunities are making it less necessary for gypsies to move about in search of work and many are now more ready to settle down'. What they needed, therefore, was 'help and encouragement in their attempt to find a settled way of life'. For the second group, the problem of being moved from one unauthorised site to another 'can only be resolved by the provision of proper sites, in which the caravan families can settle down under decent conditions ... This is probably the only effective way of preventing the persistent use of unauthorised sites, continuing trouble, and hardship'.[60] Whatever the background of those on the road then, sites to facilitate long-term settlement were seen as the solution. Essentially a nomadic lifestyle was not seen by central government as having a place in modern Britain.

Observations by civil servants involved in the preparation of circular 6/62 make this attitude explicit: 'the problem is mainly one of sites, and that given adequate sites the other remedies will follow: the people will be able to settle down, take regular jobs and send their children to school'.[61] So, for example, the 'solution of the main educational problem [i.e. poor attendance] will follow fairly easily once the problem of permanent and tolerably decent quarters, at least for the winter, has been solved'.[62]

The role of sites in facilitating eventual assimilation was explicit, for example, in the way in which the function of West Ashford site was described. The circular noted how grateful the tenants of the site were, particularly the 'wives', all of whom 'are now hoping in the future to have the chance of a council house'.[63] This was picked up by the media: 'Twelve families of Kentish Gypsies will finally accept the embrace of the Welfare State. Under the benevolent eye of

West Ashford rural council, they will settle down, the council hopes, to a less raggle-taggle existence on the first permanent camping site of its kind in Britain'.[64]

An equation of official site provision with assimilation was the premise on which the recommendations of the 1956 Staffordshire report were based. This accepted that Gypsies were distinctive by their 'separateness, their traditional and continued exclusion from the settled life of the rest of the community', and the fact that they led 'a nomadic, persecuted and exclusive life'.[65] It identified constant eviction as one reason for Travellers' poor education and social isolation: 'they have little opportunity to become part of the community or to make full use of the social amenities which the community provides'.[66] The report concluded that some form of 'social rehabilitation' was desirable:

> [Travellers] become and remain detached from the apprecia-
> tion and responsibilities of normal existence and as the chil-
> dren increase so the problem increases ... adult nomads are in
> the main social misfits who have forsaken the ordinary ways of
> life ... The general object in dealing with the problem should
> be to gradually break down the sense of exclusion of these no-
> mads, and create conditions in which they may be enabled
> gradually to take a fuller share in the general life of the com-
> munity.[67]

This shows how authorities could see travelling as an indication of social failure, and a means of evading the responsibilities required of 'normal' citizens, rather than a legitimate expression of an ethnic identity. The solution proposed in the report was for local authorities to provide sites for Travellers that could be used as centres for the dissemination of welfare services and as a stable home from which children could go to school and so become gradually integrated into the rest of the community.

Many of the same themes were to be found in the considered report produced by Eton RDC, which was by 1961 making some attempt to deal with its Traveller population. It considered the time was ripe for the provision of a local authority site, not least because Travellers were becoming better off and having higher aspirations: '[The] wives are anxious to improve their standard of living, arrange for schooling for their children and enjoy more of the benefits of the Welfare State. Many Gypsy families are ripe for habilitation but never has it been more difficult to merge into the conventional way of living'. This report believed that if the local authority provided a site, then welfare and educational services could be made available and 'a start could be made in habilitation *with a view eventually to the housing of families in Council houses*' (emphasis added). The sites would also provide an opportunity to improve their health through the provision of clean water and sanitation:[68]

> The site would be very strictly controlled and a high standard of cleanliness maintained ... The children would be able to attend local schools and the Children's Officer and other interested parties would be in a position to exercise more control over them. For similar reasons the Police would doubtless find the arrangement of some convenience.[69]

Thus local authorities never saw sites as the means to allow Travellers to simultaneously exist within the framework of modern society and continue their nomadic lifestyles. Instead, the only redeeming and attractive feature of official sites in the eyes of the authorities was to give the authorities the opportunity for controlling the most persistent nomads, something that had so far been denied to them. These assimilationist aims continued a long tradition, the difference was in the state's ability to put them into effect. The expanded capacity of the welfare state allowed local authorities to believe that sites could be used as the focus for the activities of agents of the social services who would bring about Travellers' reformation (see Chapter 6).

In contrast, Travellers who felt that there was a need for official sites saw them as a way of allowing their nomadic lifestyle to continue despite the strictures of modern life: 'If there was a place in every town ... you [could] go and pay a week's rent if you wanted to and pull off somewhere else when you wanted to'.[70] A feeling gradually emerged among Travellers, as it became clear that life on the road was becoming more difficult to sustain: 'something should be done for travelling people. Constant harrying and badgering by officials does not solve anything'.[71]

The survey of Travellers in Hampshire in 1962 revealed how its respondents sought a range of solutions to their situation. It found that of 157 families, only 38 were 'fully' nomadic, with the remaining described as 'static', which included families who might travel during the summer.[72] Of the 70 families already on the council housing list, 34 did not want to change their circumstances, and 14 expressed a desire for an authorised permanent site. Only 9 families wanted to continue travelling and expressed no desire to settle. The report also revealed a generation split, with younger people being more willing to be housed and older people preferring 'to remain in their present surroundings'.[73]

In some parts of the country the call for sites from Travellers was prompted not simply by a general shortage of sites, but by targeted and increased harassment of Travellers by local authorities and the police. Local authorities argued that their actions were a response to larger and prolonged unauthorised Traveller sites from which stemmed anti-social behaviour and lawlessness, and which often contained high proportions of recent Irish Traveller immigrants. Such evictions usually, although by no means exclusively, occurred in and around the larger conurbations of Greater London, the West Midlands and West Yorkshire. Walsall, for example, developed a policy of concerted harassment of Travellers within its district:

> Twenty-eight times that day I produced my driving licence and insurance. The first day's summonses totalled sixty-two and the full total was three hundred. Every two minutes of the day we were summonsed for an offence ... where could we move to? All camping sites were banked up with piles of earth, and trenches dug across all open land to prevent us from camping on them ... A harmless child is blown to bits at the hands of the local authorities ... Walsall – during an eviction, three little girls burned to death.[74]

As this testimony by Jimmy Connors, an Irish Traveller, indicates, evictions could be violent and occasionally fatal. He was gaoled for beating a policeman who he stated, 'nearly kills my little son through prejudice and kicks my wife unconscious a few hours before her child is born, and breaks my caravan and beats me stupid'.[75]

Connors, in 1969, took his case to the European Court of Human Rights, and his action was part of a more assertive and overtly political approach by Travellers, which had been growing since the mid-1960s. Stimulated in part by the actions on non-Travellers, political activists emerged such as Gratton Puxon who facilitated active and physical resistance to evictions by Travellers and supporters when other means had failed. Some Travellers began to feel that formal organisation and challenging the political and legal apparatus of the country was imperative. The story of the formation of the Gypsy Council in 1966 and its attempts to secure greater rights for all Travellers through traditional lobbying and direct action has been detailed by Acton, who was himself involved in the movement, so it is unnecessary to repeat it here.[76] It is worth, however, exploring how

Traveller activists of the period came to support official sites, even when, as I have shown, government saw them as a route to assimilation.

Tommy Doherty, an Irish Traveller whose family had moved to England in order to escape severe harassment in Northern Ireland, became based around Leeds, where he was involved in resisting evictions. Aided by students from the university, Doherty coordinated the protest against countless evictions:

> We put children into the trailers and pointed out to the police that the council was breaking the law, as it is illegal to tow a trailer with people inside. We also put Travellers on the towbar and underneath the back axle to stop them towing the trailers onto the road ... . [After] two years, Leeds City Council realised they were losing the battle and invited us to a meeting to set up a site on a temporary basis ... at last our families had somewhere to stop without being shifted all the time.[77]

It was only in 1969, after the passing of the 1968 Act but before it was enforced, that the Leeds Cottingley Springs site was opened, providing 15 pitches for a city that held 225 Traveller caravans. While this was clearly an inadequate response to the scale of the problem, it was largely welcomed by the city's Travellers. For men like Doherty, the immediate problem they faced was preventing evictions, and finding somewhere for people on unauthorised camps to go. In this context the prospect of an authorised pitch on a secure site was a haven, a way of being able to continue a way of life, rather than a means for assimilation.By the late 1960s, a still suspicious but increasingly pragmatic approach to the necessity for official sites was adopted by both Travellers and elements of government for diametrically opposed reasons: the former saw it as a means of sustaining their lifestyle in an increasingly hostile environment, while the latter viewed sites as the best means of promoting settlement and ultimately integration:

> It was a sort of compromise between the authorities and gypsies. It stopped us moving around, but we didn't have to move into a house. These sites were clean, with brick-built communal showers and toilets, but many Travellers viewed them with suspicion and saw them as the beginning of the end of a centuries-old tradition of life on the road.[78]

Notes

1 Acton, *Gypsy politics*, 137–45.
2 Sir F. Newsam, *The Home Office* (London, 1954), 18. Newsam was the Permanent Under Secretary of State for the Home Department.
3 The problem of the 'cult of the generalist' was drawn out by the 1968 Fulton Commission and was seen to have far-reaching consequences, *The Civil Service (England). Departments of State and Official Bodies Civil Service Commission*, 1968, Cmnd 3638.
4 TNA, HLG 142/25, Dodds to H. Brooke, 9 October 1961. This was in reply to a departmental assertion that there was no 'Romany' problem, 'i.e., persecution of an ancient and picturesque race with a unique way of life', *ibid.*, minute 27 September 1961.
5 TNA, HLG 71/903, memo from Miss Wall, HO, to Mr Summers, MHLG, 11 October 1950.
6 *Ibid.*, memo from Summers to Wall, 12 October 1950.
7 TNA, HLG 71/1650, draft MHLG reply to Dodds, 17 July 1956.
8 *Ibid.*, letter from the Home Secretary to Norman Dodds, 19 April 1951.
9 *Ibid.*, background notes for Parliamentary Question, 19 June 1956. Note the automatic assumption that when Travellers adopted the seemingly urban, and definitely not picturesque scrap-metal dealing, they could not be pure-bred Gypsies.
10 TNA, HLG 71/2267, letter from MHLG to Chislehurst and Sidcup UDC, 8 October 1957.
11 *Ibid.*, internal MHLG memo, 10 October 1956.
12 TNA, HLG 71/903, Hugh Dalton to Somerset de Chair MP, 11 April 1951.
13 TNA, HLG 71/1650, notes by MHLG Parliamentary Secretary to prepare for Norman Dodds's question in the House of Commons, 7 May 1951.
14 Bauman sees this as a key feature of a liberal state's relationship with minority groups, Bauman, *Ambivalence*, 106–7.
15 Okely, *Traveller-Gypsies*, Chapter 7.
16 HRO, 59M76/DDC207, reply of Hartley-Wintney RDC to a questionnaire entitled 'Moveable dwellings' from the County Planning Officer, 8 June 1949.
17 This is based upon slips summarising planning applications found in file HRO, 59M76/DDC207.
18 HRO, 59M76/DDC207, application for site licence for moveable dwellings, 28 June 1951. The applicants' names have been anonymised.
19 For further details of this campaign see Dodds, *Gypsies*, 38–40.
20 TNA, HLG 71/1650, memo from HO to MHLG, 7 May 1951, and reply, 21 May 1951.
21 *Ibid.*, internal MHLG memo, 15 June 1951.
22 *Ibid.*, 'Gypsies', memo prepared by the Ministry of Local Government and Planning for the Nuffield Foundation, 19 July 1951.
23 *Ibid.*, J. D. Jones to Dame Evelyn Sharp, 29 August 1951.

24 TNA, HLG 71/903, Erith town clerk to MoH, 12 April 1951.
25 Adams, 'Gypsies and Other Travellers'. Adams was the County Planning Officer.
26 TNA, HLG 71/1651, minutes of meeting held at Caxton House, 2 November 1951.
27 *Ibid.*, report of meeting in Maidstone, 'Survey of Gypsies: Kent', 18 July 1952.
28 Acton, *Gypsy politics*, 148. The experts were Vesey-Fitzgerald, the missionary Mr Larmour, Will 'Dromengro' Smith and Gypsy Williams.
29 TNA, HLG 71/1651, internal MHLG memo, 1 August 1952.
30 *Ibid.*, Adams to MHLG, 11 October 1951.
31 *Ibid.*, minutes of meeting between Adams, Mrs Youard and others from MHLG, 17 October 1951.
32 TNA, HLG 71/2267, Staffordshire County Council planning officer to MHLG, 26 June 1957.
33 See for example TNA, BD11/ 3777, Cardiff town clerk, Mr Tapper-Jones, to Welsh Office, 10 September 1955.
34 TNA, BD 11/3777, Lydia Lee to Queen Elizabeth II (passed to Welsh Office), 31 August 1955.
35 Up until 1958 the *Western Mail*, *News Chronicle* and the *South Wales Echo* ran extensive stories and published correspondence on the case. See for example D. L. Evans, 'Romany problem', *Western Mail* (2 February 1956); and 'Fairplay', Cardiff, letter to the editor, *South Wales Echo* (22 September 1958).
36 TNA, BD11/3777, notes of discussion at Welsh Office on 'Gypsy encampment on Leckwith Common', 19 September 1955.
37 *Ibid.*
38 *Ibid.*, Welsh Office to Cardiff Health Committee, 25 October 1955.
39 *Ibid.*, Mr Tapper-Jones to Welsh Office, 22 December 1955.
40 In the winter of 1955 the Travellers were evicted and they moved to Corporation land in the Rumney area, 'arousing deep resentment in the neighbourhood', *ibid.*, Mr Tapper-Jones to Welsh Office, 22 December 1955. In January they were evicted again, and were served with injunctions barring them from all corporation land, *ibid.*, MHLG memo, 19 January 1956.
41 *Ibid.*, Welsh Office memo, 9 January 1956.
42 *Ibid.*, Welsh Office memo, 19 January 1956.
43 These were Penarth, Magor and St Mellons, Llantrisant and Llantwit Fardre, Cardiff rural district and borough councils, and Glamorgan and Monmouthshire county councils.
44 TNA, BD 11/3777, minutes of meeting, 6 February 1956.
45 'No Cardiff camp for the Gypsies', *South Wales Echo* (27 February 1956).
46 TNA, BD 11/3777, minutes of meeting, 6 February 1956.
47 TNA, BD 11/3777, answer prepared by Gillie in response to Parliamentary questions, 28 March 1956.
48 *Ibid.*, 'Gypsies', Welsh Office, 6 April 1956.

49 *Ibid.*
50 *Ibid.*
51 TNA, HLG 71/1650, memo on Leckwith Common, n.d.
52 Acton, *Gypsy politics*, 137–52. He provides a comprehensive account of the creation of the first official sites, and the lead-up to the 1968 Act.
53 TNA, HLG 142/25, Eton RDC, 'Report by the clerk and Chief Public Health Inspector concerning the need for a local authority owned caravan site to accommodate Gypsies', 19 October 1961.
54 *Report on Vagrancy in Scotland*, para. 94.
55 Winchester NSPCC, 'Annual Report, 1952–3', 10–11.
56 Acton, *Gypsy politics*, 149.
57 *Ibid.*
58 'Report of the County Planning Committee', 16 October 1962, in Acton, *Gypsy politics*, 150.
59 Other county councils that conducted surveys included Cheshire (1962), Gloucestershire (1964), Berkshire (1965), Oxfordshire (1966) and Essex (1968).
60 TNA, HLG 6/62, MHLG, circular 6/62, 8 February 1962, 1.
61 TNA, HLG 142/25, MHLG brief, n.d., probably January 1962.
62 TNA, ED147/567, Ministry of Education minute, 30 January 1962.
63 TNA, HLG 6/62, circular 6/62, 3.
64 'Gypsies will go no more a-roving', *Daily Telegraph* (30 May 1960).
65 *Report of the County Planning and Development Officer on Gypsies and Other Nomads* (Staffordshire County Council, 1954), 1.
66 *Ibid*, 2.
67 *Ibid.*, 4–6.
68 TNA, HLG 142/25, Eton RDC, 'Report by the clerk and Chief Public Health Inspector concerning the need for a local authority owned caravan site to accommodate Gypsies', 19 October 1961.
69 *Ibid.*, E. A. Canovan, 'Mobile slums: The Gypsy problem', 5 October 1955.
70 Geraldine Price, quoted in Sandford, *Gypsies*, 43.
71 Reeve, *Smoke in the Lanes*, 46.
72 The relatively high proportion of static Travellers can be explained in part by the existence of the New Forest compounds, in which a large number of Hampshire's Travellers had been concentrated since the 1920s.
73 HRO, H/WLF1/3, B. Long, County Welfare Officer, 'Survey of Gypsies and Travellers in Hampshire', 10 April 1962.
74 J. Connors, 'Seven weeks in childhood: An autobiography', in Sandford, *Gypsies*, 166–7.
75 *Ibid.*, 159.
76 Acton, *Gypsy politics*, 155–241.
77 Tommy Doherty, in P. Saunders, J. Clarke, S. Kendall et al. (eds): *Gypsies and Travellers in their own words: Words and pictures of travelling life* (Leeds, 2000), 116 and 232.
78 Stockins, *On the cobbles*, 56.

6

Travellers and the welfare state

In this chapter I explore how the post-war welfare state changed the ideological context in which Travellers existed. I consider how the ethos of citizenship was deployed in relation to the idea of a modern, reconstructing Britain, and how this fed into the establishment of the welfare state.[1]

While Travellers saw participation in the war effort as the 'qualifier' for full inclusion in the new benefits, bureaucrats saw citizenship as consisting of a wider set of responsibilities. This attitude combined with old prejudices against Travellers to affect their interaction with welfare provision. In the remainder of the chapter I focus on the deployment of education and housing policies towards Travellers, and show how, when they existed at all, they were based on an assimilationist agenda.

Citizenship and welfare

There is an assumption that the establishment of social welfare necessarily and inevitably contributes to the spread of humanism and the resolution of social injustice. The reverse can be true ... A multitude of sins may be committed in its appalling name ... Welfare may be used to serve military or racial ends ... to narrow allegiances and not to diffuse them ... What matters then ... is the objective to which its face is set: to universalise humanistic ethics and the social rights of citizenship or to divide, discriminate and compete.[2]

The existence of nomadic Travellers throughout the twentieth century had posed a problem for a state and society that viewed itself as modern and 'civilised'. Earlier missionaries had tended to express this in a specifically Christian context: Gypsies were being left behind by the march of progress and were being allowed to 'flounder struggle and die in the mud of sin'.[3] Local government officials, giving evidence to the two inter-war reports on the matter in Scotland, instead drew on a mixture of environmentalist and racialised theories to explain how a travelling lifestyle was largely the result of poverty and social failure.[4] Through close supervision and targeting of resources, they believed that Travellers should be brought up to the standards of the rest of the population.[5] Such ambitions were largely theoretical in the inter-war period as government did not look upon Travellers as a priority, and instead left matters to the piecemeal efforts of private individuals and missions. In addition, government views were not particularly out of step with more general attitudes towards welfare of the period, which still worked within a framework of the deserving and undeserving poor and tried to tie receipt of benefits to some form of moral, as well as material, improvement.

This attitude continued to exist in the post-war period and provided a strong sense of continuity, but after 1945 both the physical and ideological contexts through which Travellers interacted with the state altered significantly. The creation and extension of the welfare state changed the nature of social inclusion and exclusion and added a new layer of significance to citizen status. The legal rights that came with citizenship were enhanced by entitlements to new and extensive health, educational and housing benefits. This created a tension, as this extension of state services intensified the debate over who exactly was entitled to these benefits, while at the same time supposing that everyone should enjoy the same standard of living.

Based primarily on work-based insurance contributions, inherent in the creation of universal benefits was the marginalisation of those who were unable to make such contributions, primarily the wageless and those who operated within the informal economy. People were encouraged to view benefits based on national insurance contributions as their right, yet means-tested benefits provided to those who had not made full contributions, which were funded through general taxation had a certain, and increasing, stigma attached to them. Through the passing of the 1948 National Assistance Act, Travellers were structurally disadvantaged along with the majority of women, the civilian disabled and anyone else who did not engage in full-time, long-term employment. They were 'effectively ... denied full and equal citizenship ... social citizenship (the automatic right to social security) had to be earned through insurance contributions'. Therefore, Lowe argues, there was a 'permanent emphasis on the danger of scrounging', and that once on 'supplementary benefit the unemployed were treated with suspicion'.[6]

Such attitudes could lead local national assistance board officials to assume, for example, that Travellers were inherently untrustworthy and less eligible for relief. Local officials not only questioned their right to receive public money, but also made deductions, either assuming that they were not declaring their full income or that they did not need to maintain the same standard of living as settled people:

> There can be no doubt that there are undisclosed resources in most cases. A number of them have ancient cars in which they move around while our allowances are largely disposed of in the nearest bar that sells 'wine' ... no injustice would be done if allowances were withheld from all but the oldest and exceptionally, those with large families of young children.[7]

> Regulation III deductions are applied in almost all cases either because of suspected activities or purely because of the mode of life. It is felt generally that increased income does not improve a Tinker's standard of living but merely provides means to purchase more drink, which results in added trouble for the community in general.[8]

While regulations clearly allowed for deductions to be made on the judgement of local officers, particularly in relation to rent allowances, evidence from other sources suggests that this practice was most common in relation to outsider groups seen as 'undeserving', notably immigrants and unmarried mothers.[9] In this, the experience of Travellers can be put in the wider context of the experience of other stigmatised groups.

In addition to the practical effects of changes in welfare entitlement was the wider issue of social responsibility, as ideas of citizenship increasingly revolved not only around entitlement, but also the contractual nature implicit in the system. Gone was the thinking behind the poor law that relief was provided at the expense of one's wider rights as a citizen, as new benefits were in fact integral to citizen status.[10] Much of the basis for the new thinking was derived from the idea that the welfare state was founded on the notion of reciprocity:

> Citizenship is a status bestowed on those who are full members of a community. All who possess the status are equal with respect to the rights *and duties* with which the status is endowed ... If citizenship is invoked in defence of rights, the corresponding

duties of citizenship cannot be ignored ... Rights have been multiplied, and they are precise ... [Duties include] the duty to pay taxes and insurance contributions ... Education and military service are also compulsory. The other duties are vague, and are included in the general obligation to live the life of a good citizen ... of paramount importance is the duty to work.[11]

This idea of citizenship implied a contract in which, in return for the guarantee of equal status and access to now considerable benefits and services, the citizen was expected to participate fully in the economic and civic life of the community. For the majority of the settled population this may have had profoundly democratic overtones. For Travellers, whose commitment to and relationship with settled society was ambiguous, the welfare state, with this assumption of social citizenship, contained threats as much as promises.[12]

Not all of the population subscribed to this definition of citizenship, yet there emerged a popular sense that along with the war, the welfare state had been won through the active participation of the people. Groups not seen as having participated, such as Travellers or newly arriving migrants, were consequently seen to have less claim on the benefits of the new welfare state.[13] Travellers engaging in this debate disputed the idea that they had not participated in the war effort, emphasising in fact the depth of their involvement in the conflict, as well as mobilising the rhetoric of liberty so often deployed to justify the conflict:

Dear Fellow Briton – You don't like inhumanity, persecution or harsh treatment. You fought a War against the Principle of Unjust Power. So I am sure I can appeal to you for sympathy and help for some of your fellow countrymen who are slowly but surely being broken ... Despite prejudiced beliefs, Gypsies are hardworking people ... They also gave their sons willingly in defence of this country. Now the Public Health and Town and Country Planning Acts are being used as weapons to destroy them completely.[14]

However, for those engaged in the task of reconstruction, participation in the war effort was only one small part of the new wider definition of 'citizen'. As Marshall stated, duties to which the citizen should subscribe included generalised exhortations to good conduct and promoting the wider welfare of the community.

One way in which Traveller lifestyles could conflict with this was in the area of planning and environmental control. Behind the creation of the green belts, the national parks and stricter planning regulations, embodied in the 1947 Town and Country Planning Act, was the idea that the nation had the right to a clean and regulated urban environment and access to unspoilt countryside:

> While particular types of conduct in the country were held to promote good citizenship via mental, moral, physical and spiritual health, others signified a lack of citizenship. Citizenship became defined in relation to 'anti-citizenship', represented by those members of the public, whose behaviour did not live up to environmental standards ... [it] depended upon the identification of a unworthy, degenerate residuum for its self-definition. The creation of an inclusive nation therefore rested, in the short term at least, upon exclusion.[15]

The new environmental residuum did not merely include the 'urban minded' tourists who dropped litter and played loud music, but also those who threatened the landscape with their 'hideous settlements' in the form of plotland shacks, bungalows, and inappropriately placed caravans.[16] Beyond the dislike of badly sited caravans discussed in Chapter 4, planners and bureaucrats believed that the very existence of moveable dwellings perpetuated sub-standard housing and therefore undermined their efforts to create an orderly environment.

Travellers not only failed to become tidy, regulated citizens, but they also undermined the notion of 'participatory citizen' which demanded 'education in all aspects of good citizenship as an essential for its success':

> [Civil] rights are designed for use by reasonable and intelligent persons, who have learned to read and write ... political democracy [needs] an educated electorate ... [and] scientific manufacture [needs] educated workers and technicians. The duty to improve and civilise oneself is therefore a social duty, and not merely a personal one.[17]

Schooling of Travellers under the 1944 Education Act must therefore be seen not only in the light of extending schooling to all, but also as the means to create good citizens: it was not sufficient for government to lead, but the individual, through participation in civil society, must also actively follow.[18]

Given the failure of Travellers to match up to the new and exacting standards required of citizens of a new Britain, their relationship with the welfare state in all its forms was clearly problematic. While the ideals espoused by Marshall and others, concerning the notions of reciprocity and duty, were largely just ideals and ones which many settled members of society also did not meet,[19] they did form important guiding principles for those conceiving and implementing the new services.

The emerging relationship between citizenship and welfare rights contained an inherent tension: whatever people's feeling over the right of Travellers to services, it was both difficult and counterproductive to withhold them from these less-than-perfect citizens, as such services were the best weapons at the disposal of the state for civilising anti-social elements. The compromise position produced for Travellers a practice that was very little changed from the interwar conception of welfare provision: services were bestowed with discretion, based on a concept of social, rather than moral, improvement. For Travellers, the result of this ethos of welfare was not a new era of universal benefits wedded to a notion of citizenship and rights. Instead, Travellers were seen to have less right to services than the settled population, and that where those services were provided they were with a view to promoting assimilation. The remainder of the chapter discusses the practical implications of new welfare policies and thinking on Travellers in two particular areas – education and housing.

Education

A conference on Traveller education in 1971 revealed that, over one hundred years after Forster's Act, the 'outstanding feature of the [formal] education of Travelling children today is still its paucity'. It was estimated that of the six to eight thousand children of school age on the road, only about 2,500 attended school in 1970. This was the highest level ever recorded, and did not take into account the possibility of some children having been counted two or three times, as they registered with different schools. It also hid the fact that the attendance levels for those registered at school tended to be in the region of 40 to 60 per cent, and the widespread problem of 'an extremely low level of attainment'.[20]

The long-term and national picture showed that educating Travellers alongside the rest of the population was an unmitigated failure. For most Traveller children at the end of the 1960s, their experience of schooling was little different to that of their parents – short-lived, patchy, and dominated by bullying from other pupils and disdain from the teachers. Jimmy Stockins, who left school after two years, aged seven, in the mid-1960s, wrote:

> What did I want to go to school for? School was for gorgers.
> Why should I learn to read and write? No other person I mixed
> with could ... Don't ask me the name of the school ... I hated
> it. Sit still. Sit up straight. Single file. Fold your arms. It was
> like being in a fucking cage. All silly rules and saying prayers
> ... I couldn't understand why them calling 'Gypsy' or 'Gypo'
> across the playground was meant to annoy me. After all, that's
> what I was ... Gorger kids seemed to think we didn't like being
> Travellers for some reason.[21]

Generally, blame for low attendance figures was continued to
be directed towards two linked factors – the nomadism of the Travellers and the attitudes of the parents – articulated here by an attendance officer in Kent:

> When they return [in October from potato picking], to a great
> extent, I have to rely on my memory in getting the children
> back into school ... [Children are absent through being] kept
> to look after younger children, [having] insufficient footwear,
> and (mainly in the case of the boys) the taking of odd days for
> no reason whatever.[22]

It was this irregularity of attendance that officials saw as causing them to form 'an appreciable quota in the several retarded classes
in these schools'. One head teacher believed:

> A habit which might appear as a harmless and picturesque cus-
> tom has in fact thrown an unwarranted and unfair burden on
> the schools, retarded directly the educational development of
> the children concerned, affected the whole balance of school
> organisation, and set an evil example, in defiance of regula-
> tion, low standard of attainment and a failure to respond to
> social training.[23]

These concerns were reflected in the attitude of education authorities and the inspectorate. In cases where Travellers were relatively numerous, they recommended a policy of 'dispersal of small
groups over several schools' to prevent a 'concentration of the problem' and an 'undue preponderance in one school'.[24] In Kent, one
inspector believed 'a consistent policy of rehousing should be pursued to reduce the number of nomadic families'. He further felt that
where sites were provided they should be kept small to prevent Traveller children from 'swamping' local schools, and smaller sites would
have the additional benefit of allowing them to learn 'a more con-

ventional way of living'.[25]

While it is important to acknowledge the specificity of Traveller experiences of education, they can be fruitfully understood as part of a continuum of poor educational experiences, rather than a complete aberration. McCulloch had argued convincingly that, particularly after the age of eleven, most children's education was determined by their class rather than their ability, with the consequence that working-class children were concentrated in the poorest schools, with limited facilities, curriculum and exam opportunities. The 3,500 secondary modern schools in England and Wales catered for approximately three-quarters of children aged eleven to fifteen, yet in 1956 the secondary modern inspectorate were only able to identify 140 that were 'worth a second glance'.[26]

The majority of schools which Travellers and other ethnic minority children attended, therefore, existed in a world of scarce resources and limited educational horizons. If there was a pyramid of privilege that saw the mass of working class children near the base, then children from minority backgrounds were at the very bottom. Ian Grosvenor's work has demonstrated how educational policy 'complemented the state's construction of black people "as problem"',[27] with black pupils consistently being represented as taking resources away from white pupils, and threatening their educational opportunities.

Central to official thinking in the 1950s and 1960s was the presumption that migrant success in Britain would be determined by 'abandonment of their culture, traditions and values, and acceptance of the British "way of life"'. There were concerns about large concentrations of immigrant children in particular schools or classes. Circular 7/65 asserted that the 'task of education' was the 'successful assimilation of immigrant children', but warned the chances of assimilation were 'more remote' as the 'proportion of immigrant children in a school or class' increased: 'up to a fifth of immigrant children in any group fit in with reasonable ease, but ... if that proportion goes over about one third either in the school as a whole or in any one class, serious strains arise'.[28] Where it was impossible to redraw catchment areas, due to a school's location in an inner city area where there was a high proportion of immigrant children, 'every effort should be made to disperse the immigrant children round a greater number of schools', primarily through what became known as 'bussing' pupils out to other schools.

Grosvenor notes that local authorities reassured non-immigrant parents that the progress of their children would not be 'restricted by undue preoccupation of the teaching staff with the linguistic and other difficulties of immigrant children', but the circular was 'deafeningly silent on any benefits that would accrue to black parents where the policy of dispersal was adopted'.[29] The policy was not conducted on the grounds of 'educational need', as children were dispersed 'irrespective of whether they were immigrants or not, irrespective of whether they had language difficulties or not ... the children were dispersed solely on the basis of colour'.[30] Black students were perceived both as being intrinsically a problem, and a problem owing to their expected negative impact on the performance of white children. The same concerns can be found in relation to the presence of Traveller children in schools:

> The parents of children attending the elementary schools resent the fact that their children have to be in close contact with the Gypsy children. Their influence is bad, even when their numbers are small in comparison to other children, and in one school the number of Gypsy children roughly equals or exceeds the number of other children attending that school.[31]

In addition to the tension between a desire for assimilation and a concern over negative impact on the education of white pupils, studies have revealed an inclination to blame minority cultures for any failure to perform adequately, viewing their experience as a result of 'cultural pathology' rather than any limitations within the state system. For example, pupils were seen to fail either because their Asian mothers were too passive and stayed at home, or because their Afro-Caribbean mothers were too assertive and went out to work.[32] Hence 'African –Caribbean children were labelled from the outset as "underachievers" and segregated within schools into lower "streams" or teaching "bands" ... [or] were declared "educationally sub-normal" and placed in special classes or separate schools on this basis'.[33]

The experiences of Traveller children, therefore, fits into a more general pattern of marginalisation of minority children, for they, too, were depicted as a problem and underachievers, seen as a threat when too numerous in a class, and their parents and family background were blamed for their failure to assimilate into a classroom setting.

The educational experience of most Traveller children in this period, as in earlier decades, consisted of patchy and prematurely curtailed schooling, with attendance dependent as much on the willingness of a school to allow them entry, as the attitude of the parents and length of stay in a particular place. Children may have spent more time at school in the winter than the rest of the year, but they tended to finish their schooling early, often by the end of primary school, when they had mastered basic literacy and numeracy. In such a context, the use of education as a tool for assimilation was unworkable. However, the picture was complex as, in certain cases, typically owing to a greater density of contact between schools and Travellers, it was possible for education to have an impact on the children, even if it was more about socialisation than academic attainment.

Travellers in Hampshire were concentrated in the New Forest, where the establishment of the forest compounds in the 1920s had the effect of increasing the school attendance of the children. Instead of separate schooling, they were enrolled in the local schools where, by the 1940s, most compound children of school age were registered. Despite calls for segregation, the councils consistently rejected this as a possibility:

> I do not advocate Gypsy schools since to segregate the children is to make them more likely to stay Gypsies. More and smaller compounds should be made out of the three larger ones, preferably nearer schools ... so that the Gypsies do not loom so large amongst the other children. With an introduction to proper washing facilities and other amenities these Gypsy children may be weaned from the vagrant life in a tent.[34]

The reality of regular attendance served to resign the children to the classroom and to mainstream values. At Minstead School it was said that it was 'difficult to mark out the Gypsy children from the others. The older Gypsies you can smell in a moment ... but this is not noticeable with the children'.[35] It is clear that over the next fifteen years or so, despite the irregular attendance of some, the compound children became assimilated to a certain extent. This was seen as acting both as the foundation for, and result of, settlement into 'normal' housing. The county education officer in 1961 noted that the school attendance of static families had 'improved considerably over the last ten years':

> At two of the primary schools attended by a large proportion of these children the parents have been encouraged to take an interest in the school and in one case the children are wearing the school uniform ... when families are rehoused they show a tremendous improvement in all ways and constitute far less of a problem over attendance and behaviour than the children of

many other poor families.[36]

Even on a short-term basis, schooling could result in increased socialisation of Traveller children, as in the case of children from the ill-fated encampment at Darenth Woods in the winter of 1961–62. For Mr Poole, the headmaster of the local school which had 29 Traveller children on its books, segregation was initially seen as necessary, in order to socialise the children sufficiently before they made their entry into normal classes.[37] For the first week they were completely segregated as they were:

> [Foul]-mouthed, ill-mannered, uncooperative in the extreme, and generally showing suspicion and resentment towards all forms of authority. They were unable (or unwilling) to give their correct names, birthdays etc., and clearly had no intention of responding to the normal discipline of school ... [In terms of] general behaviour and conduct ... they may now be classified as normal children ... though at times they are inclined to revert to 'jungle habits' (and language!).[38]

For the Darenth children, as for those in the New Forest, there was an assumption that it was the responsibility of Travellers to 'normalise' and not for society to bend.

After 1945, as before, central to the state's relationship with Travellers and education was an assertion that nomadism and Traveller culture was the central problem. This allowed the state to blame Travellers and their culture, rather than acting on the fact that it was the duty of each education authority to ensure that children in their area received 'efficient full-time education'.[39] In common with local authority dilemmas over housing allocation, local education authorities were responsible for the allocation of scarce resources, and in this context Travellers' needs were sidelined. The 1944 Education Act[40] has been described as a national system locally administered, and created a tripartite partnership between central and local government and the individual schools and colleges. Its strength was seen to lie in its fluid structure: 'Power over the distribution of resources, over the organisation and over the content of education was to be diffused amongst the different elements and no one of them was to be given a controlling voice'.[41]

For Travellers, however, this system simply perpetuated the ability of all three levels of organisation to refuse to take responsibility for their education. As with other policy areas concerning Travellers, the Board of Education believed local authorities were responsible for enacting the legislation. Even where the Board accepted a need for action, it absolved itself of the need to take the initiative:

> The blatant truth of the matter is that both the Home Office and the Ministry of Health are afraid of facing the issue and until they make up their minds whether they want to dragoon the Gypsies into being tolerably respectable members of the community or whether they are going to leave them as a curious survival of the past, it is pretty well useless for the Board and the LEAs to get over excited about the educational aspect of the question.[42]

While the Minister for Education acknowledged that the paucity of Traveller education was a 'considerable social issue', he argued that 'the administration of the country is so fully extended ... [it is] reasonable not to undertake its settlement at present'.[43] Essentially the Ministry preferred to 'leave it to LEAs to deal with problems which arise in the different circumstances of their own areas'.[44]

Although the 1944 Education Act and the new climate of the post-war era might have resulted in a change of policy on Traveller education, on the ground very little movement was felt. Central government took heart from a retrospective analysis of the provision of Traveller education in Kent in the 1950s[45] that gave the impression that the only thing wrong with Traveller education was the attitude and lifestyle of the Travellers themselves. It was their 'widespread and traditional apathy' towards literacy and education, and negative parental attitudes, combined with a tendency towards irregular attendance that were the main causes for concern. In contrast, the education authority was seen as doing 'all they can be reasonably expected to do ... we have no reason to suppose that [other] authorities are not also doing what they can under existing conditions'.[46]

Much was made by officials throughout the period of the uncooperative attitude of parents towards formal education. In the New Forest, where parents were blamed for not being committed to the education of their children, it was said that they 'frequently state their children are ill as a reason for absence and they are very plausible in their excuses and lie without compunction'. This antipathy could spill over into active hostility and violence, with school attendance officers experiencing physical attacks.[47] The 1952 Kent report gave the main reason for the failure of the children to operate successfully as 'widespread and traditional apathy, if not positive antipathy to any form of literate education which exists among the adult Gypsies'.[48]

This must not be read simply as 'ignorance', but also as a positive assertion of Traveller identity in the face of assaults by majority society. Okely's fieldwork confirmed that parents tended to see prolonged education as a threat rather than something to be welcomed. She cited a woman who, while stating her keenness to see her children in school, did her best to hide them when the school bus, or attendance officer, came round: 'I don't want my child going [to school] any more. I don't want her to have one of those jobs pushing a pen in an office, what's the good of that to my girl?'[49] Sibley similarly identified the tendency of parents to assert a desire for education that was not backed up by action, believing that, 'such comment appears to be for *gauje* consumption and is not a consistent attitude'.[50]

If Travellers' agency often meant that children were kept out of school, by the 1960s it could also result in actively seeking education. As part of a wider campaign for Travellers' rights in Leeds, after approaching all the schools in the city and being told, 'they were full, there was no room ... we went down to the Education Offices by the town hall with all the children'. In a meeting, at which the press were present, Tommy Doherty challenged the local authority, 'According to the 1944 Education Act, you're not doing your job. These children need education'. Doherty believes that it was only this action that embarrassed the council into finding ten school places within twenty-four hours.[51]

In other cases Travellers and activists went down a different route to mainstream education, and instead sought to provide buses and other mobile classrooms that could be taken onto sites to reach children. In 1965, after discovering that none of the children of 650 Traveller families in the West Midlands were attending school and the local authorities were not attempting to reach them, a voluntary scheme was launched. Made up of about fifty members, half of whom were teachers, the West Midlands' Travellers school operated from a bus that visited five unauthorised sites during evenings and weekends.[52] Such schemes operated in other parts of the country, but they did not always meet with the desired response:

> There was a man, a gorger ... a good man who wanted to give the gypsy children the chance on an education. If they wouldn't come to the schools, he brought the schools to them. He sent double-decker buses in with teacher aboard, and they'd wait for the kids to come and learn. I felt sorry for the well-meaning teachers ... because the only people I ever saw on them buses

were the teachers.[53]

The period up to 1968 saw a strong degree of continuity with the pre-1939 era, despite the passing of new legislation, with central government passing responsibility for education to local authorities, who in turn looked to Traveller parents and nomadism to explain poor attendance and achievement levels of Traveller children. However, the arrival in Britain of significant numbers of migrants from Commonwealth nations and the entry of their children into schools allows Travellers' experiences to be put in a wider context. The state maintained that Travellers and their nomadism were an exception, yet the rhetoric deployed and solutions proposed to the challenges presented by greater ethnic diversity in schools shows that Traveller experiences often paralleled that of other minority groups. The later part of the 1960s saw a new trend, which again might be seen to mirror the growing assertiveness of new migrant communities, as Travellers used their emerging political action to fight for access to education, rather than simply resisting it.

Housing

> It seems incredible in the twentieth century that families live in the British Isles in such conditions ... These Scottish Tinkers are remnants of a persecuted race of outcasts ... Like relics of a primitive civilisation, three of the Townsley family's tents crouch on the bleak encampment near Campbeltown ... Two years ago this mother and her children were living in an old quarry. Now they are comfortably housed in Wick ... The main problem is to get people to realise that the Tinker who had gone to school and been conscripted in to the Services is quite different from his father. He wants to be done with the wandering life. He wants a house and a settled job.[54]

Behind the upbeat messages in the press – of the housing and 'civilisation' of Traveller families by the various agencies of the welfare state – lay a very different story. In the eyes of both officials and a large proportion of the public, nomadism was viewed as anachronistic and unacceptable. In post-war Britain, Travellers were less seen in a romantic light, except to bemoan the loss of an old way of life. Instead, they were termed a social problem, to be dealt with through housing, education and welfare channels, something that was compounded by the separation made between 'civilised' caravan-dwellers and anti-social Travellers. Housing of Travellers has to be understood not as providing accommodation for the homeless, but rather as a tool for solving a long-standing social embarrassment. Whereas the excuse often used for not providing sites for Travellers was that Travellers did not really want them, this reason was rarely used in the housing debate. Generally, the reluctance of Travellers to be settled in houses was seen as further confirmation of their need to relinquish their nomadic lifestyle, and become more fully socialised. This did not mean that central and local government were consistent in their attempts to house Travellers, but rather only instigated schemes when it proved possible or convenient. The post-war period was littered with contradictions: for every statement to the effect that 'steps should be taken to compel the Gypsies to settle in permanent dwellings and share in the responsibilities of modern civilisation',[55] there was one that assumed Travellers to continue to exist beyond the remit of local authorities.[56]

Where councils did instigate schemes, behind inevitable differences in detail between localities, lay consistent themes and patterns based on a presumption that Travellers should become integrated into society. At the same time these policies displayed unwillingness to either extend to Travellers the full benefits of the welfare state, or to allow them full and equal contact with settled society. As in education, the ultimate aim was to render Travellers invisible through assimilation, but without contaminating or disadvantaging the rest of the population.

A pressure on resources, especially building materials and housing, brought into focus the competing priorities of local authorities. For example, although New Forest council had a concerted Traveller rehousing policy, it still believed that housing Travellers must be put in the context of 'housing demand. All local authorities are under *constant and severe pressure* from substantial and growing waiting lists' (emphasis in original).[57] Councils felt that Travellers did not have the same claims on them as the rest of their population, either because they were not 'local' and did not pay rates, or owing to the more general sense that they did not perform the duties expected of a full citizen. These attitudes made their impact in one of two ways. The first, and most common response, was that Travellers were completely undeserving of the limited resources of the council and were therefore ignored or moved on as quickly as possible. The second response was to accept that, in the interests of removing the blot which Travellers left on society, services should be provided but to a lower standard. In many cases this was manifested through the medium of 'simplified housing'. Such accommodation was designed to act as a stepping stone from which Travellers could graduate into council accommodation and ultimately merge with the rest of the community. These lower-quality services were expected to result in the full and equal socialisation of Travellers, with blame for any failure being placed at the door of Travellers themselves.

Again, there are parallels with other groups in settled society. Designated 'problem families' in many districts could find themselves placed in condemned houses or other accommodation seen as unsuitable for ordinary tenants, where under guidance they could learn to raise their standard of housekeeping.[58] New Commonwealth migrants also found that such tenancies might be their only option. Through the 1950s and into the 1960s it was common for local authorities to refuse to house 'black' immigrants. Sheila Patterson's work found that there were 'few' black families with council tenancies, with the Mayor of Lambeth boasting that 'only six West Indian families have been rehoused', and this was 'in the worse type of requisitioned property – because no-one else would take it'.[59] Bourke notes that 'such discrimination was effective' for in the 1960s only 6 per cent of the black overseas-born population were accommodated in the state sector, compared with approximately one-third of the English and Irish-born population.[60]

The settlement and housing policies of local authorities raises a number of issues regarding the relationship between Travellers and the state, particularly over their perceived status as citizens and their claims on the benefits provided by society. Often, statements by officials implied that it was the very process of contact with the state and regulation that was important, rather than the quality of the service rendered. Local authorities enacting schemes felt it was better for Travellers to be allocated council-run 'simplified housing' than for them to live in similar, but unregulated, hut accommodation: the former received funding and official time, while the latter were hounded by the planning authorities. Given the low quality of the services provided and the often coercive ways they were implemented, their importance lay not in raising the quality of living for Travellers. Instead, the significance of these schemes was in the way in which they enacted the priorities and preconceptions of a growing state system. Settlement schemes were to be a process by which Travellers were forced to interact with the mainstream and gradually assimilated.

From the 1930s, some local authorities in Scotland had put

into place various housing schemes aimed at permanently settling Travellers, often specially buying or constructing houses.[61] Unlike in England, where councils rarely defied ratepayers,[62] across the border settlement was often carried out in the face of local opposition. Following the allocation of a house to a Traveller in Wick in which 25 tenants and householders in the street protested, the council ignored their calls, stating that the woman had been given it due to her medical condition.[63] In some cases the protests proved to be more obstructive, especially when they came from more influential members of the community. Ross and Cromarty County Council found that a number of large landowners refused to sell them land for Traveller housing experiments. This was despite the local authority's goal being to 'take them off the road and make them settled members of society' and placing the Travellers 'under strict supervision by county welfare officers'.[64]

It was not simply the local population who objected to settlement schemes; officials involved were often as guilty of prejudice as the rest of the population. At one local authority conference on the subject, 'the trend of the speeches was undoubtedly towards a condemnation of the Travellers as a class', with one speaker feeling that the whole issue of housing Travellers was a 'menace'.[65]

Even where objections were overcome and a scheme instigated, prejudice often appeared to be built into the fabric of the dwellings produced for Travellers. Opinions were divided over the quality of the housing to be provided and while the aim was to bring Travellers up to the same standards of living as the rest of the community, it was generally agreed that they were not ready for it, and would therefore simply ruin accommodation unless it was of a 'suitable' standard. This standard was inevitably deemed to be much lower than that allowed by planning regulations, and thus partly defeated the reason for settlement in the first place.

A scheme at Bobbin Mill, Perthshire initiated by the Church of Scotland but taken over by Pitlochry Council, was such a case. Two families had been hand-picked for the scheme, on the grounds that they showed the most potential for assimilation.[66] Inhabitants were 'subject to fairly close supervision', living in houses euphemistically described as not 'of a completely modern standard'.[67] Started in 1947, ten years later it was reviewed to assess its success. An internal memo from this time described the dwellings as 'old hut[s] ... constructed of weather boarding only, with internal walls formed of a very soft boarding', noting that they had not been painted or otherwise treated, and were in imminent danger of collapsing.[68] The constructions were 'not in conformity with the Building Bylaws' having been given special dispensation by the town council.[69] In the review of 1957 the council acknowledged that the initiative had only been partly successful: 'tenancy of these houses has meant a more settled way of life for the small number of families concerned, but ... there have been constant difficulties with additional members of the clan overcrowding the houses for longer or shorter periods, with an increase in the number of encampments in the vicinity'. People were still living in 'unsuitable bivouacs' and women preferred to stay in them rather than 'go into hospital for confinement'.[70] The buildings were condemned in 1962 but no action was taken, resulting in the inhabitants remaining on the site but the council refusing to extend facilities or to allow residents to conduct building work or improvements.[71] Bobbin Mill demonstrated that, contrary to expectations, being settled did not result necessarily result in the socialisation of Travellers into the mainstream of the community, but could rather provide a base for their distinctive lifestyle.

South of the border, the area most concerned with settlement was the New Forest. It too struggled over the quality and location of dwellings provided for its Travellers. Most areas were not faced with such a large and relatively stable Traveller population, merely providing housing for a limited number of 'local' Travellers while making the rest 'move on'. The local authorities of the New Forest, however, devised a two-stage programme of moving compound dwellers first into hutted camps and then into council houses. In this sense their concerted programme of resettlement was exceptional, yet it also epitomised mainstream and official attitudes towards Travellers and their place in modern society.

An emphasis on assimilation – the 'removal of a stain on the Welfare State'[72] – ran through the entire project. In part, concern centred around the possibility that Travellers might be evading the duties, as well as the benefits, associated with the welfare state:

> Whilst it cannot be denied that a large number of them are extremely poor, a certain percentage seem to be rather more affluent. By their present mode of living the more affluent ones can more easily evade such matters as National Health Insurance contributions, income tax etc., and some at least chose their present way of life for this reason ... [which] may deter them from accepting housing should it be offered.[73]

There is no evidence from the New Forest scheme, nor elsewhere, that settlement was driven by the demands of Travellers. Instead, the impetus came from local authorities concerned with dealing with what they saw as an anachronism in their midst.

In the 1920s the traditional right of Travellers to camp in the Forest was removed and they were gradually concentrated into a number of 'compounds' in which they were allowed to reside, on receipt of a licence from the Forestry Commission.[74] By the end of the Second World War it was clear that this policy had failed either to remove Travellers from the Forest or to improve their living conditions. Official reports concerning the compounds stressed the squalid conditions and the need to remove the inhabitants as quickly as possible.[75] Observers noted the ban on their dwellings having windows, floors or doors meant interiors were 'dark and cold and without privacy. The bare earth makes any attempt at cleanliness impossible'. Poor hygiene was compounded by the fact that residents had to carry water from standpipes, often some distance from the site. Given the abject standard of living in the compounds, it is unsurprising that most inhabitants wanted to move, although they wished to remain as a community and in the Forest.[76]

Save the Children proposed providing a designated social centre with nursery for the compound dwellers, but this was rejected as the councils were 'opposed to the further segregation of the Gypsies'. The local authorities made a counter-suggestion of locating the centre in a local village believing, 'if they want to make use of community centre facilities *they should to that extent share in the life of the general community* (emphasis added).[77]

Contrary to stated government policy in the 1950s, that government was not forcibly trying to settle Travellers but was giving them the opportunity to become integrated, should they so wish,[78] the New Forest local authorities were coercive in their methods and single-minded in their aims. Through both restricting the issuing of permits for those moving onto a compound[79] and actively resettling families already on the sites, they intended to clear the compounds. A policy of, if not forced settlement, then at least vigorous 'rehabilitation' was the logical extension of the aim to restrict the growth of the camp population. Between 1951 and 1957 Travellers from the compounds were transferred to hutted camps located on old Army bases in the area. These were unpopular with Travellers who resented being moved from their local area,[80] as well as with sanitary inspectors who felt the Nissen huts were 'very damp' and 'inadequate'.[81]

Welfare officials experienced difficulty in persuading compound dwellers to move into the huts and of those who did move, a 'number ... decided to go back to the compounds'.[82]

Not all those working with Travellers were inherently unsympathetic or wanted to pursue such a vigorous policy of integration. Some well-respected doctors raised their voices against council policy, with one stating that settling Travellers in houses would cause 'very real human suffering'. Another believed that:

> In a very real sense the 'Travellers' are our Native problem ... although only a small minority, they have as much right as the large majority to lead the sort of life they wish ... and they have the same right to security ... unimaginative pressure and repressive measures and making things as difficult as possible should *not* be used by local authorities in order to force them to conform to ordinary standards ... Local authorities should make as much provision for their *special* needs as they do now for the needs of the majority.[83]

In 1959 New Forest RDC decided to close all the compounds within five years and transfer the residents directly to council houses. But the policy of ending the use of intermediate camps was contradicted by the recommendations of the countywide report of 1960–61. This suggested that integration could best be achieved through 'offering graduated accommodation suited to the needs of each stage of progress towards a settled life'.[84] The report suggested establishing four hutted camps 'as intermediate accommodation', under the supervision of a resident warden with access to the services of a social worker. Each camp was to be 'separated into two sections, one for those families genuinely seeking a better way of life who can be taught the basic requirements of living in decent surroundings, and the other section for those who live by their wits'. Part of the aim of the camps was to provide 'proper training in the care and management of a council house', and to this end each hut was to have 'a water supply, sanitation, a WC and a bath, proper cooking facilities and separate sleeping quarters for the parents and both sexes of children'. The accommodation was to be post-war prefabricated huts that were being dismantled elsewhere, which would also have the advantage of being the most 'economical solution'.[85]

These recommendations were rejected by local authorities unwilling to spend money on more hutted camps. Councils preferred instead to concentrate resources on 'providing housing of the normal type'[86] and on social services. Close supervision of 'the most

difficult families' was still envisaged, however, 'in order to raise their
standard of cleanliness to the point where they are acceptable as council tenants'. To this end, council welfare workers were heavily involved in moving Travellers into their new council tenancies:

> *Family C* – eight children. Formerly compound dwellers.
> Housed from caravans ... Mrs C received four months reha-
> bilitation training at a Home in Surrey – cost of maintenance
> met by County Welfare Committee. Home completely furnished
> by County Welfare Department with the exception of curtain-
> ing, linoleum provided through grant obtained by Welfare
> Department from National Assistance Board. Family being
> supervised regularly by Officers of County Welfare Depart-
> ment.[87]

The resettlement scheme housed 51 families directly from the
compounds between 1959 and 1965, 'in spite of serious misgivings
about the ability of some of the hard-core to adapt to settled life'.
Despite the worries, only one family was evicted and although some
continued to 'need supervision' the 'problem has been no greater
than with other problem families'. The local authorities considered
by 1965 that 'in quite a high proportion of the cases' the families
were 'now indistinguishable from the other tenants'.[88] They felt that
one of the main reasons for the success of the scheme was the dispersal of Travellers throughout a number of estates, so that they had
been 'reasonably well accepted' by the other residents. This had broken through the problem of Bobbin Mill, where settlement had not
resulted in assimilation. This was only possible if Travellers were
isolated from their social networks that formed such a strong part of
their identity.

It is difficult to reconstruct the differing reactions of Travellers to
being settled on sites or housed on council estates – rarely did anyone canvas their opinions, and reminiscences of older people can be
overlaid with memories of 'the good old days' on the road. Despite
this, comments by exasperated social workers who found their Traveller clients not as malleable as hoped, as well as direct statements
from Travellers themselves, do help to give a picture of how they
responded to the challenges faced by their experiences.

This is not to argue that no Traveller wanted to settle down,
and that all found the offer of a council house unwelcome. Indeed,
given the difficulties of living on the road by the late 1950s many
were only too happy to be given a base. Pressures over constant

evictions from unauthorised sites, illness or death, particularly of a male spouse, and a desire from some Travellers to have their children educated, might lead some families to choose to move into a house. Houses could bring material comforts as well as security. One Traveller remembered how in an ex-Army hut they had 'electricity for the first time in our lives, and an indoor toilet – that was nice'.[89]

Moving into a house did not mean a family would never live on the road again, nor that they cut ties with the wider Traveller society. However, maintaining links with other Travellers when there was no room for trailers to be parked for visits was difficult, and often Travellers were shunned by neighbours, leading to isolation:

> The middle-aged and older ones, especially, were forced to go and live into houses all the time and were given money for doing nothing ... [It] was too much for them. They would nag and plead with their husbands, 'Take me out of here ... Am I going to waste my life polishing and cleaning inside a rookery of stones? Never seeing my friends, nor a soul belonging to me?.. So often they would take off and go and search the country for a place to camp or put a caravan. Then perhaps some other welfare people would take over and the whole thing would start all over again.[90]

Often a family might remain until a crisis had passed, or until they could bear it no longer, and then move back into a trailer:

> Kennas [houses] were not for us, but there was a lot of pressure at the time to stop gypsies travelling and promises of a better life. Maybe Dad thought it best for us kids ... [But being in a] house wasn't doing us any good at all. Dad's health was suffering from being all cooped up, and none of us could get used to having this strange thing called an 'upstairs' or going into a little cupboard to have a shit ... neighbours didn't take too kindly to us cooking our food over an open fire in the back garden each night either, and the horses upset the local dog and cat population. Finally, Dad said 'That's enough'. He bought a new trailer and we were off travelling again.[91]

Unlike settled society, Travellers did not automatically equate living in a house with abandoning their birth culture and become 'normal' members of society. Many simply wanted a safe haven and did not see this as being incompatible with maintaining their Traveller identity. In fact, the absolute stress placed on nomadism as being the primary indicator of 'Gypsyness' by wider society not only reflected a lack of understanding of Traveller culture, but also made the mistake of equating settlement with integration. Consequently, when Travellers left council or other housing, they were seen to have 'failed': failed to have learnt to live in a house, failed to assimilate and failed to take advantage of the benefits of the welfare state. It is significant that the Traveller activist movement of the 1960s did not call for houses for Travellers, but for secure sites. Housing was a solution of settled society and local authorities attempting to assimilate Travellers, not of Travellers themselves. Housing was rarely sought by Travellers except as a last resort, under direct compulsion or through life circumstances.

Specific settlement schemes directed at Travellers reveal how they were viewed simultaneously as less deserving of the fruits of the welfare state, and yet were seen as in greater need of its benefits, in order to end their anachronistic existence. Houses were more desirable than any other form of accommodation, as they were both in keeping with standards of living expected for the time, and provided the best vehicle for settlement. However, a desire not to divert scarce resources towards this group, and fixed attitudes about their standard of living meant that councils accepted that a lower form of accommodation might be necessary, either sites or simplified housing, in order to gradually bring Travellers up to an acceptable level of existence. This often brought out the inherent tension between the desire to settle and an ingrained prejudice that prevented the full allocation of resources to a perceived deviant minority.

Travellers' experiences of education and housing in the post-war period thus resonate with Bauman's questions over the true nature of the promise of assimilation[92] – the implicit bargain was that if Travellers gave up their lifestyle and settled down, they would in turn be treated like other citizens. But this claim has a hollow ring to it. That Travellers were seen as second-class citizens, combined with traditional prejudices against their community, meant that 'benefits' were commonly metered out grudgingly or as punitive sanctions. And, where Travellers failed to measure up to expectations they, and not the shortcomings of the state, were blamed for their failures.

Notes

1   There is debate over the precise definition of 'welfare state', and whether Britain ever enjoyed one. While acknowledging it is not an unproblematic term (for an introduction to this discussion see R. Lowe, 'The

second world war, consensus and the foundation of the welfare state', *Twentieth Century British History*, 1:2 (1990), 152–82) for the purposes of this work it is taken to mean the provision of the five 'core' services (social security, health care, housing, education and the personal social services) and the fact that these were widely seen as a universal right and free at the point of delivery, subject to the exceptions I discuss in this chapter.

2 R. Titmuss, 'The limits of the welfare state', *New Left Review*, 27 (1964), 28–37.

3 Smith, *I've been a' Gypsying or rambles among Gypsies and their children in their tents and vans* (London, 1883), 36.

4 For example, *Tinkers in Scotland*, 8–9.

5 *Report on Vagrancy*, 94.

6 Lowe, *The welfare state*, 138–9 and 159. For a feminist perspective on citizenship and welfare see R. Voet, *Feminism and citizenship* (London, 1998); and C. Pateman, 'The patriarchal welfare state', in A. Gutmann (ed.), *Democracy and the welfare state* (Princeton, 1988), 231–60.

7 TNA, AST 7/1480, Arbroath Area Officer, 'Tinkers', n.d.

8 *Ibid.*, Edinburgh central office to Whitehall, 17 December 1955.

9 M. J. Hill, 'The exercise of discretion in the National Assistance Board', *Public Administration*, 47 (1969), 75–60.

10 See M. Thomson, *The Problem of mental deficiency, eugenics, democracy and social policy, c.1870–1959* (Oxford, 1998), for an account of how mental defectives failed in this new construction of citizenship. In fact Jose Harris has argued that the poor law granted stronger citizenship rights, at least at the parochial level, than those tied to national insurance contributions of a male breadwinner, as right to receipt was based solely on belonging to a parish rather than on any contributory principle. See J. Harris, 'Contract and citizenship in social welfare, 1934–48', conference paper, Comparing Social Welfare Systems in Europe, Oxford, May 1994.

11 Marshall, *Citizenship and social class*, 28–9, 40 and 78–80.

12 This is not to deny that social control was absent from the welfare state's relationship with the wider population. Squires, for example, has argued how socialisation was its main goal. P. Squires, *Anti-social policy: Welfare, ideology and the disciplinary state* (Hemel Hempstead, 1990), 36.

13 G. Dench, K. Gavron and M. Young, *The New East End: Kinship, race and conflict* (London, 2006) discuss this in relation to the Bangladeshi community of the East End. Not understanding or valuing the contribution made by Britain's empire to the war, East Enders have consistently portrayed the new migrants as less deserving of welfare, and of housing in particular. I am grateful to Ben Rogaly for this observation.

14 TNA, HLG 71/1650, letter and enclosure from W. Smith, Traveller rights campaigner, to Hugh Dalton, 17 April 1951.

15 D. Matless, 'Taking pleasure in England: Landscape and citizenship in the 1940s', in Weight and Beach (eds), *The right to belong*, 182–3 and 185.

16 *Ibid.*, 192.
17 Marshall, *Citizenship and social class*, 25–6.
18 S. Taylor, 'Socialism, the British way', quoted in Weight and Beach (eds), *The right to belong*, 101.
19 Lowe asserts that, in general, people's support of the welfare state was 'both selective and selfish', typified by a 'lack of altruism' that accepted the taxes for services they benefited from as individuals, while questioning the funding of benefits servicing the unemployed, minorities and single-parent families. This was 'matched by a popular reluctance to accept the duties ... implied by welfare policy', Lowe, *The welfare state*, 98.
20 C. Reiss, 'Current trends in the education of travelling children', in T. Acton (ed.), *Current changes among British Gypsies and their place in international patterns of development*, Proceedings of the Research and Policy Conference of the National Gypsy Education Council, St Peter's College, Oxford, 26–28 March 1971, 26–7.
21 Stockins, *On the cobbles*, 46–7.
22 TNA, ED147/13, north-west Kent division report, 'School attendance – Gypsy children', 7 July 1947.
23 *Ibid.*, north-west Kent division memo to County Education Officer, 'Gypsy children', 4 March 1949.
24 Adams, 'Gypsies and other Travellers', 17.
25 TNA, ED147/567, HMI Mr Mundy, 'Education of Gypsies and other Travellers in Kent', 17 January 1962.
26 G. McCulloch, *Failing the ordinary child? The theory and practice of working class secondary education* (Buckingham and Philadelphia, 1998), 101.
27 I. Grosvenor, *Assimilating identities: Racism and educational policy in post-1945 Britain* (London, 1997), 49.
28 Quoted in *ibid.*, 53–4.
29 *Ibid.*, 50–4.
30 I. Grosvenor, 'A different reality: Education and the racialisation of the Black child', in Lowe (ed.), *History of education, major themes, vol. IV*, 108.
31 *Report of the New Forest Commission*, 101–2. See also evidence by Mr Andrew McCormick, Newton Stewart town clerk, *Report on Vagrancy*, Appendix IV.
32 H. Carby, 'Schooling in Babylon', in Centre for Contemporary Cultural Studies, *The empire strikes back* (London, 1982).
33 L. Bridges, 'Tory education: Exclusion and the Black child', *Race and Class*, 36:1 (1994), 34–5. For an analysis of the extent to which racism was engrained in the teaching materials of British state schools see W. E. Marsden, 'Rooting racism into the educational experience of childhood and youth in the nineteenth and twentieth centuries', in Lowe (ed.), *History of education, vol. IV*, 481–510.
34 TNA, ED11/234, HMI Mr Smith to Board of Education, 6 November 1944.

35 TNA, ED147/13, minute by HMI Mr Ritchie, 29 March 1949.
36 HRO, H/WLF3/1, County Education Officer to Hampshire Association of Parish Councils, 14 November 1961.
37 TNA, ED147/567, report of meeting at House of Commons on Traveller education, presided over by Dodds, 13 December 1961.
38 *Ibid.*, report by Mr Poole, 'The Gypsies at school', n.d., 1962.
39 PRONI, CAB/9B/224/1, 4.
40 Travellers were included in Sections 37 and 39 of the 1944 Education
   Act, which reiterated the power of the LEAs to instigate legal proceedings against those parents failing to send their children to school.
41 V. Bognador, 'Power and participation', *Oxford Review of Education*, 5:2
   (1979), 157–8.
42 TNA, ED11/234, Board of Education minute, 6 July 1944.
43 *Ibid.*, minute from Butler following meeting with Jeffreys MP, 9 November 1944.
44 TNA, HLG71/1651, Ministry of Education to MoH, 9 December 1952.
45 TNA, ED147/567. This was bound up with the question of site provision, and the lessons to be learnt from the provision of the Traveller
   site in West Ashford.
46 *Ibid.*, Ministry of Education minute, 30 January 1962.
47 TNA, ED11/234, Hampshire County Education Officer, 'Gypsy children', 14 July 1944.
48 Adams, 'Gypsies and other Travellers', 17.
49 Okely, *Traveller-Gypsies*, 162.
50 Sibley, 'Persistence or change?', 68.
51 Saunders *et al*, *Gypsies and Travellers in their own words*, 10–11.
52 Reiss, 'Current trends', 31.
53 Stockin, *On the cobbles*, 55–6.
54 J. Buchan, 'Tinker problem', *Scottish Field*, 690 (1960), 37–9.
55 'New law for Gypsies', *Sunday Chronicle*, (10 November 1946).
56 TNA, HLG 71/1650, 'Notes on Gypsies', n.d., probably February 1956.
57 HRO, H/WLF1/3, Hampshire Parish Council Association, 'Observations made on behalf of RDCs', 1961.
58 TNA, HLG 37/39, Central Housing Advisory Committee, House management sub-committee, draft report on housing of problem families,
   'Unsatisfactory tenants', 1955, 2.
59 S. Patterson, *Dark strangers: A sociological study of the absorption of a
   recent West Indian migrant group in Brixton, South London* (London, 1963).
60 J. Bourke, *Working class cultures in Britain* (London and New York, 1993),
   207–8.
61 Caithness bought four houses for the use of Travellers, 'Caithness buys
   houses for Tinkers', *The Scotsman* (30 November 1956).
62 For an exception see TNA, HLG 142/25, memo, 'West Ashford: Gypsy
   caravan site at Great Chart', 23 February 1961.
63 'Protest but Tinker gets that house', *The Scottish Daily Express* (29 June
   1955). For a similar case see 'Tinker family protest', *The Scotsman* (21

May 1956).

64 'Lairds' protest: Ban the Tinkers', *Empire News* (29 December 1957).

65 'Integration of Tinkers in society', *The Scotsman* (11 October 1958).

66 Travellers had been employed at the mill up to the 1920s, and continued to use to the land as a camping ground after this date. It was leased from the owner on a 99-year lease. Author's conversation with Roseanna MacPhee, 28 November 2006.

67 Perth and Kinross Council Archive, Perth, BM, county clerk to Mr Rushworth Fogg, 13 June 1956.

68 *Ibid.*, county factor to the county clerk, 24 August 1956.

69 *Ibid.*, county architect to county clerk, 15 September 1956. See also 'Integration of Tinkers in society'.

70 *Ibid.*, county medical officer to county clerk, 11 June 1956.

71 To this day there is no hot water or electricity on site. Conversation with Roseanna MacPhee, 28 November 2006.

72 Howard, Dr, 'Report on the Gypsies and other Travellers in Hampshire' (unpublished, Hampshire Association of Parish Councils, 1960), 7.

73 HRO, H/WLF3/1, senior area welfare officer to county welfare officer, 11 September 1961.

74 The licences were granted under a number of conditions that included forbidding Travellers to have doors, windows or floors on their dwellings. The right of unrestricted camping in the rest of the Forest was not removed from non-Travellers until 1948.

75 *New Forest Report*, 79–186, and Save the Children Fund, 'Report on tent dwellers in the New Forest', 1 March 1949.

76 Save the Children, 'Tent dwellers'.

77 TNA, ED147/13, Ministry of Education minute, opinions of HMI Mr Ritchie, 29 March 1949.

78 TNA, BD11/3777, background notes 'Gypsy situation', MHLG, n. d., probably February 1956.

79 HRO, H/WLF1/3, Forestry Commission to Mr H.G. Dixon, 5 February 1962.

80 HRO, H/WLF1/3, Christchurch welfare officer to Mr Long, 30 May 1962.

81 Grant E. D., 'Some problems concerning hutted camps and temporary dwellings', *The Sanitarian*, 57:10 (1949), 339–40.

82 Fraser, 'The Gypsy problem', 86.

83 Dr. Howard, 'Report on the Gypsies and other Travellers in Hampshire', unpublished Hampshire Association of Parish Councils, 1960, 12–13.

84 *Ibid.*, 1–2.

85 HRO, H/WLF1/3, 'Supplement to ten year plan for development of welfare services: rehabilitation of Gypsies in Hampshire', n.d.

86 *Ibid.*, county welfare officer to clerk of the county council, 10 November 1961.

87 *Ibid.*, lists of Travellers rehoused, county welfare officer, 4 November

1961.
88 TNA, ED147/567, MHLG 'Gypsies', Appendix II, result of 1965 Survey, June 1966.
89 Stanley, *Memories of the marsh*, 49.
90 Whyte, *Yellow in the broom*, 174–5.
91 Stockins, *On the cobbles*, 46 and 48.
92 Bauman, *Ambivalence*, 102, 106–7.

Part III

The later years

7

State developments and Travellers' responses, 1968–2000

Part II showed how the 1960s was a time of crisis and change for Travellers. The shortage of stopping places was no longer masked by increased mobility through motorisation, while tighter controls on the siting of caravans after 1960 restricted Travellers' access to privately owned permanent sites. Added to the changed spatial environment was settled society's perception of Travellers as social failures, and that their lifestyle was inappropriate in late twentieth-century Britain. At the same time, there was a continued belief that somewhere there existed 'true Gypsies' who continued to live unobtrusively in bow-topped caravans, with whom the rest of the travelling population was unfavourably compared. This led to situations such as in Walsall where local residents 'drew up a petition *to allow a wagon-dweller to stay on*, because it was decided that this man ... was not a Tinker at all, but was a "true Romani" ... at the same time some caravan dwelling "Tinkers" amongst whom were the close relatives of this man, were being evicted less than a mile away'.[1]

In this chapter I begin by considering the importance of legal definitions of 'Gypsy', before moving to consider the impact of the 1968 Caravan Sites Act and subsequent government policy, including the planning system. In the final part of the chapter I explore Travellers' responses to the impact of policy changes, the hardening attitudes in mainstream society, and the expansion of the 'multicultural' state through considering new approaches to Travellers' schooling.

Who is a Gypsy?

With the appearance of local authority site provision for Travellers, the issue of who exactly qualified for this resource became of importance. Section 16 of the 1968 Act defined Gypsies as 'persons of nomadic habit of life, whatever their race or origin', with show and circus people being specifically exempted from this definition. This de-racialisation of the term 'Gypsy' confirmed a government attitude that had been prevalent throughout the twentieth century, which saw 'true Gypsies' as nomadic. Liegeois has argued this was part of a wider trend throughout European governmental discourse and policy, which deliberately eschewed the use of either 'Gypsy' or 'Traveller'. Instead these terms were replaced by 'neologisms or paraphrases bereft of cultural connotations', such as 'persons of nomadic origin' used by the French government, or 'itinerants', as used by the Irish.[2] In the context of modern states where definitions of citizen or ethnic status were increasingly tied to rights and access to certain services, such semantics were important.

The practical result of the 1968 definition of Gypsies was that individuals became stripped of their ethnic identity on becoming stationary – either in a house, or through long-term settlement on a private or official site. Over time, the law was refined to indicate that a 'Gypsy' had to have a tradition of travelling, generally as a group, and travelled for economic purposes. Court judgments clarified that a Traveller could be sedentary over the winter, but still retain 'Gypsy status' if they travelled for work during the summer. Remaining stationary through illness or caring for relatives did not disqualify an individual from being a Gypsy, if there remained an intention to travel. However, the shortage of transit sites and the increasing difficulty of maintaining a nomadic lifestyle, and of travelling in groups in modern Britain was not considered relevant. In a case, for example, where an applicant had lived on one site for over fifteen years, the individual was deemed by a judge to be 'no longer a Gypsy for the purposes of the Act'. His submission that his family were all Gypsies, some of whom travelled a great deal, was not accepted. In another case, where a family only travelled occasionally in search of a permanent pitch, they too were seen as no longer being Gypsies:[3]

> At many enquiries where Gypsies are trying to get permission to station a caravan on their own land much time is spent debating whether the applicant has lost his Gypsy status. It comes as a surprise to the applicant that, even though all his life he has been treated as a Gypsy both by his family and the local pub, he is no longer one when it comes to trying to get sympathetic consideration for trying to find a place to legally stop.[4]

Conversely, the wording of the 1968 Act allowed other individuals not of a Traveller heritage, but who had adopted a nomadic lifestyle, to 'become' Gypsies. Cases involving New Travellers decided they came within the definition of the Act, and therefore were Gypsies, although they had to have travelled for at least two years in order to qualify.[5]

A further consequence of the legislation was the uncertain positioning of Travellers under the Race Relations Act, 1976 and anti-discrimination and multicultural policies more generally. While the Act initially was not held to apply to Travellers, the Commission of Racial Equality (CRE) in 1981 felt that Travellers did 'constitute an ethnic minority and as such are protected against the discrimination under the Race Relations Act 1976'.[6] Its pronouncement leant weight to attempts by the Gypsy Council and others, for example, to have the specific reference to 'Gypsy' removed from the 1959 Highways Act.[7] A 1989 test case brought by the CRE identified Romany Gypsies as an ethnic minority (*CRE v Dutton*) and an independent case in 2000 achieved the same for Irish Travellers (*O'Leary v Allied Domecq*). Scots Travellers, however, had failed to have their ethnic status confirmed in law by the end of the century.

Clarification of the ethnic status of Travellers meant that as the function of the state expanded to protect minorities from certain behaviours and attitudes, in law at least, Travellers gained specific protection. This meant, for example, that under the Race Relations Act 2000 they were included in the new requirement on public bodies not just to prevent racial discrimination, but to positively promote good race relations. Equally, under the 2004 Housing and Planning Acts local authorities became obliged to assess the accommodation needs of Gypsies and Travellers in their area and bring forward sites through the planning system, as they would do for 'bricks and mortar' housing.

Despite legal moves to confirm the ethnicity of Travellers, there was continued and 'considerable ignorance and confusion ... amongst local authorities, the police and government departments' over their status. Ignoring, or ignorant of, the policies of the CRE and a number of legal judgments, 'the majority of central and local government officials refuse to acknowledge the position of Gypsies and Travellers as coming within the definition of an ethnic group'.[8] In some areas, this led to a division in policy between different local authority departments, with specialist education, liaison and health staff working closely with identified Gypsy and Traveller families on the one hand, and planning departments in particular refusing to acknowledge the ethnic status of appellants on the other. As in the past, what may be seen as more liberal developments at the national level could not be assumed to filter down to the localities, where most policy was delivered.

The mismatch between attitudes to the status of Travellers in different sections of government could be seen in reactions to a Traveller site at Dale Farm, Basildon. Between 1993 and 2001 the district council licensed the land, located in a designated green belt area, for use as a scrap yard. Half the site, including a farmhouse, had been occupied by Travellers for a number of years, and from 2001 the other half was sold as plots to Travellers. Two planning applications for residential caravan development were refused – partly on the grounds that the road access to the site was inadequate – and the council decided to evict the forty to sixty families, at a potential cost of £1.3 million.[9]

The council accepted that any eviction would cause hardship and homeless applications from evictees – including adverse health effects and the removal of the children from their local schools identified by health visitors and the education services – and would result in an increased council tax bill. Despite the Office of the Deputy Prime Minister and English Partnerships proposing an alternative site in Pitsea, and Dale Farm residents agreeing to form a housing association to buy the land, Basildon refused to take this course of action.

The council argued the necessity of distinguishing between demand and need. They maintained they had provided sufficient pitches on official sites, and it was only due to the reluctance of neighbouring councils that they faced problems. However, the CRE stated, along with the Dale Farm legal representatives, that the council's policy was tantamount to racism, as the council essentially argued they had accommodated a *quota* of Travellers, and should not have to tolerate any more. In fact, Basildon's attitude can be seen as an informal version of official strategies adopted in Northern Ireland and Scotland in the 1980s and 1990s. There, policies of 'toleration' and 'designation' were introduced and maintained in order to keep numbers of Travellers in a district below a certain level. This was subsequently identified as 'institutional racism', on the grounds that the 'mere existence' of such policies 'enshrines and legitimises the harassment of Travellers once the 'government quota' has been reached':[10]

> Travellers are the last bastion of respectable racism ... change
> the words Gypsy and Traveller for 'blacks' or Pakistanis and
> ask yourself, would anybody stand up and say: 'We have taken
> our share of Pakistanis, we aren't having any more, it's not fair'
> ... The notion that Bradford, for example, could turn around
> to a Pakistani family and say, 'We're not housing you, we've
> got far more Pakistanis than the rest of West Yorkshire. We're
> not having any more Pakis here, go home'. Nobody would even
> think of saying it, but just change the words to Gypsies and
> Travellers and it's a respectable submission [to court].[11]

By the end of the twentieth century the function of the state may
have expanded to include the active protection of minority rights,
but as with central government assertions of impartiality earlier in
the century, its delivery at the local level remained a far more contested phenomenon.

State and sites

> The Bill is an attempt to break the present deadlock in which
> the gypsies create increasing trouble because they have nowhere
> to go and the local authorities refuse to provide sites for them.
> The policy pursued by many local authorities of moving the
> gypsies on has led to unpleasant scenes in which the police
> have had to intervene to preserve the peace.[12]

The 1968 Caravan Sites Act can be seen as the Labour government's response to the problems faced by and growing political
activism of Britain's travelling communities. The 1967 report on
Travellers admitted that legislation passed in the previous decades –
the 1936 Public Health Act, the Town and Country Planning Acts,
the 1959 Highways Act and the 1960 Caravan Sites Act – amounted
to the 'virtual outlawing' of the Traveller way of life.[13] For Travellers
who were unwilling or unable to live in houses or make their own
legal arrangements and were consequently living on unauthorised
camps, providing official local authority sites was seen as the answer. While this was accepted, sometimes grudgingly, by Travellers
and local authorities alike, both the structure of the Act and the way
in which it was implemented ensured that it succeeded in satisfying
neither group.

The legislation contained a paradox: for the first time the right
of Travellers to have legal places to stop, and hence theoretically also
to have a nomadic lifestyle, was enshrined in British law. Yet local
authorities had largely been sold the idea of official sites on the

grounds that they would offer a greater chance to control Travellers, target welfare services, and eventually to assimilate them. A review of the legislation by John Cripps in 1976 observed that while there was nothing in the Act to indicate the creation of sites 'was to be a stage in enforced settlement or assimilation ... Many local authorities, however, seem to have acted on the assumption that eventual assimilation is desirable'.[14] This tension continued at the heart of debates over site provision through the following decades. Travellers saw sites as a base for their nomadism and became frustrated that provision was inappropriate, while settled society resented providing and paying for facilities for an alien group who are seen to contribute nothing and refuse to become 'normal' citizens.

There is some debate over whether the Labour government of the late 1960s was prompted into action by the growing violence of evictions and the consequent militancy of the Gypsy Council, or whether 'twenty years of appeals to their ideas of social justice finally took effect', or a combination of the two.[15] Certainly the police and Home Office at this time became increasingly sensitive to the high-profile nature of the Gypsy Council.[16]

Despite the amount of Traveller evictions and action by the late 1960s, the government as a body did not see site provision as a priority, as the Caravan Sites Act originated as a Private Members' Bill, sponsored by Eric Lubbock MP (later Lord Avebury). It was drafted with two purposes: to protect the rights of all those living on official caravan sites from eviction without a court order; and to oblige local authorities to provide sites for Gypsies 'residing in or resorting to their areas'. This was to ensure that both relatively locally based Travellers and highly transitory ones were to have access to secure stopping places.

Under the Act county councils and London boroughs were given a duty to provide sufficient accommodation for Travellers in their area, although the latter were only required to create a maximum of fifteen pitches. The number of spaces for caravans other authorities were obliged to provide was based on caravan counts done for the 1967 report, and after 1979 on bi-annual counts.[17] While it was the duty of county councils to create the sites, there was no deadline by which time sufficient provision was to be made, and in all cases a district council had the right to object to any particular site.[18] The relevant provisions of the Act came into force on 1 April 1970.

In districts where sufficient permanent council sites were established, or where there were no Travellers, it became a criminal offence for Travellers to camp elsewhere in that district, through a local authority being 'designated' as providing adequate pitches. The Home Office described these new powers of designation 'as a reward' given to a local authority which had 'done its duty in providing sites'.[19] In this carrot and stick approach the Act mirrored the observations of Justice Bray to the 1910 Select Committee in which he stated that it was 'impossible to prohibit persons camping generally' unless local authority-run sites were also created.[20]

The years up to 1973 saw between one-fifth and one-quarter of the estimated needed number of sites being built, although this did not stop evictions from occurring. The Gypsy Council in fact contended that the years 1968–70 in particular saw evictions being pursued 'with great vigour' as councils tried to remove Travellers from their areas in order to avoid having to provide a site. Dudley and Luton, for example, had a 'sustained campaign' of harassment, while other areas with well-established Traveller populations, such as Southampton and Blackpool, tried to claim Traveller-free status.[21] Even after 1970 the Gypsy Council received 'at least' one phone call a day about an eviction or threatened eviction. However, the larger, more violent evictions and resistances became rarer.[22]

After 1973 the pace of provision slowed, leading to Cripps's appointment to investigate the implementation of the 1968 Act. His subsequent report, with its 'perceptive analysis',[23] demonstrated that while there had been significant progress in some areas there were a number of structural problems with the legislation.

Six years after the relevant sections of the 1968 Act came into force, 133 local authority sites had been created in England and Wales, containing 2,131 pitches. This only provided accommodation for an estimated 25 per cent of the Traveller caravans, wheras the majority of 'probably' 6,000:

> still have no where they can legally go and are usually within the law only when moving along the highway. So, the unauthorised encampments, which the Act was designed to eradicate, are as numerous and widespread as ever, not only causing serious worry and offence to the settled population but often offering barely tolerable living conditions for the Gypsies themselves.[24]

Cripps's research found that not only was there an absolute shortage of official sites, but when they were created they tended to have room only for locally-based Travellers, leaving little or no space either for visiting relatives or transitory families. There was consequently a mismatch between provision of sites for Travellers 'residing in' and for those 'resorting to' a district. This underlined the tension between local authority's continued desire to use official sites to settle Travellers, and Travellers' own desire to use them as a basis for their nomadism. Cripps believed that costly sites for the majority of Travellers were neither useful nor necessary, particularly as 'those who still travel frequently and over long distances regard them as too elaborate'.[25]

An ensuing government circular accepted that earlier advice had 'concentrated on the provision of residential sites for long-stay and permanent use', and that this needed to change, with the greatest need being for 'authorised stopping places, even if not ideally located and if suitable for only temporary use'. Local authorities were directed to concentrate on creating 'a substantial number of sites with a minimum of facilities'.[26]

An overemphasis on sites for permanent residents designed to model standards was confirmed in Okely's fieldwork conducted throughout the 1970s. She found that local authorities stated that they were 'against sites with "low level" provision because local residents (i.e. the dominant population of housedwellers and potential voters) objected'. Yet, her study of local papers from several regions indicated that local residents 'also objected to the high cost of the permanent sites, as well as to the existence of *any* type of sites'. Travellers themselves expressed a preference for temporary sites with lower levels of facilities, where the rents were much lower and the services provided were in keeping with their needs. Residents of official sites, where rents were up to 70 per cent of council house rents, particularly resented the chalets provided on each pitch: 'Obliged to furnish and decorate their chalets themselves, some complained this wasn't worth doing if they were only staying a while, and when the buildings did not belong to them'. A Traveller summed up the 'unhappy compromise' represented by the chalets: 'Having one of these huts you'd be better off in a house, but I'd rather travel'.[27]

The debate over many sites with more limited facilities versus fewer, more costly sites built to model standards reflected the dilemma of welfare provision more generally. Was providing Travellers with, what were in the eyes of the majority, substandard facilities a means of allowing them the independence to continue a nomadic lifestyle, or simply yet another way of treating them as second-class citizens?

Part of the answer to this lay in the third shortcoming of the 1968 Act identified by Cripps. This was the siting and quality of the sites themselves, located as many were in places unsuitable for any other development. He noted that they were commonly, 'excessively close to sewage plants, refuse destructors, traffic laden motorways, intersections of these and other busy highways, main railway tracks and other features contaminating the environment by odour, noise and so on. No non-Gypsy family would be expected to live in such places'.[28] In one case a site for twenty families, supplied by two London boroughs in exchange for them both acquiring designation, was built under two raised motorway access roads and bordered a railway. It therefore suffered excessively from noise pollution and dangers of lead poisoning, as well as a lack of privacy.[29] A survey of 65 sites conducted in 1974 found that only 3 per cent were located in residential areas, 28 per cent were next to industry and 12 per cent adjacent to land used for waste disposal.[30]

That such places were the only ones councils and local residents would countenance for Traveller sites sent a very strong message that Travellers were unwelcome, marginal and deserving of the bare minimum. The location of official sites in marginal areas, in the context of the post-war move towards single-use zoning in planning that made the built environment more homogeneous, had the effect of 'accentuating the deviancy of Gypsy culture'. This process of Travellers being 'extruded, bounded, confined',[31] also isolated Travellers from basic services such as shops, schools, surgeries and recreation facilities and from the rest of the population.

Cripps identified local opposition to every proposal made to establish a Traveller site as being the primary reason for the failure of proper functioning of the 1968 Act. Residents of Glais in West Glamorgan, for example, 'resorted to acts of vandalism' in order to prevent the building of an official site: 'They tore up parts of the public road across the farm, felling trees across it and putting up concrete barricades … [they] seriously damaged a bridge across the railway line'.[32]

Cripps's report represented in many ways the high point of central government sensitivity to the Traveller situation. He articulated a need for plentiful transit sites, 100 per cent central government funding and direction in the provision of sites nationally, as well as voicing concern over the damaging effect of vociferous local opposition. However, as Sibley observed, 'the government response to Cripps was less liberal then Cripps, who was not notably liberal himself'.[33]

Aside from the introduction of 100 per cent central grant aid towards capital costs of sites, made law in 1980, little came from Cripps' work. The Department of the Environment circular,[34] issued following the report, avoided any central government responsibility in creating official sites, keeping this firmly the duty of local authorities. It pointed to the fact that under the 1960 Act district councils had powers to provide sites for Travellers, and so need not wait for county councils to take the initiative,[35] but ignored Cripps' recommendation that central government should be actively involved in creating a national plan specifying the number and location of sites.

Even availability of one hundred per cent central government grant towards capital costs of sites, while helpful, was structured in such a way as to work against Traveller interests. As with the original intention of the 1968 Act, it was a double-edged sword, as more sites, funded through the new grant system, would 'extend the number of areas which may become designated', effectively excluding Travellers from stopping in these districts.[36] In addition, the grant disappeared into the total block grant allocated to councils for all capital projects, thus placing 'the cost of dealing with the most unpopular statutory task of Gypsy site provision in direct competition with all other demands ... More popular projects are bound to be given precedence especially by local councillors'.[37]

Despite the limitations of the 1968 Act and the structure of the central government grants, the 1980s did see a gradual increase in the number of official sites, and consequently areas that were also designated. By the beginning of 1985 it was estimated that were 9,900 Traveller caravans in England, of which 4,600 were positioned on 232 local authority sites, 1,900 on authorised private sites and the remaining 3,400 on unauthorised camps. The 100 per cent grant had facilitated a 'steady' 200 to 300 authorised pitches a year. Even so, over one-third of caravans had no authorised place to stop.[38]

These developments also meant that designation – a 'real spur' to providing sites – covered three entire counties, 22 London boroughs, 36 districts and ten former county boroughs. However, the 'vexed problem of designation' continued to be a controversial policy for Traveller support groups, which saw it as 'offensive' and a form of 'apartheid', as it applied only to Travellers and to no other caravan-dwellers. Furthermore, they argued that designation was granted in cases where an inadequate number of pitches had been provided by the council, partly based on the disputed bi-annual caravan count figures. A central government investigation found that there was 'unfairness, inefficiency and even dishonesty' engrained in the process, and that 'deliberate undercounting ... quickly erodes confidence in the overall fairness of the ... procedure'. The report recommended that designation be made more transparent, and that government needed to 'improve and increase the pressure on recalcitrant local authorities who refuse to provide any or too few caravan sites', and if necessary to withdraw designation from authorities who fail to comply. Only if Travellers saw 'manifest fairness' in the system would they 'probably accept the degree of discrimination inherent in the concept'. Otherwise their discontent would be 'greatly increased and this will show itself in more aggravation and vandalism, especially in areas ... where local authorities are know to be "bloody minded" and thought to be dishonest'.[39]

The 1980s thus saw the consolidation of official site provision with council sites becoming an established, if problematic, part of Traveller culture. The original ambitions of local authorities to use sites as tools for assimilation, 'to provide a means whereby gypsies could avail themselves of other public services, particularly health care and education for their children',[40] were in part borne out. Research by Save the Children showed that the increase in official sites resulted in a 'generally higher standard of care for the children', and had 'facilitated regular attendance at school, registration with a GP and regular arrangements for income support without the need for constant re-registration because of changing residence'.[41]

Initial research suggested that Travellers, where it was possible, tended to use official sites in a similar manner to houses, where families in crisis or at a particular stage in their lifecycle sought to retreat from nomadism. Okely's work found that the majority of families on official sites were 'the aged, the widowed and sick, some of their close kin, wealthier families with local contracts, and those least dependent on car breaking'. Other families, if there were sufficient pitches, used council sites as a regular base as part of a circuit of travel.[42]

A tendency of families to adopt a more sedentary lifestyle, even temporarily, was reinforced by the general scarcity of sites. Families were reluctant to move away in case they lost their pitch, as few places allowed residents to pay a reduced rent to cover absences. Sedentarism, however, must not be equated with assimilation. Sites provided a space where Travellers were able to maintain their separate identity, and this was often reinforced by the provision of site-based separate welfare and other services, and by their geographical isolation from other residential areas.

The growing tendency of Travellers to be static combined with inappropriately large sites to create difficulties. Official sites tended to contain fifteen or more pitches, owing to efficiencies of scale, problems of gaining planning permission for sites and a desire by councils to be able to target welfare and other services easily. This was a larger number of families than Travellers traditionally chose to live with, and could result in conflicts between feuding families allocated to the same site. As well as causing problems for other residents, such behaviour reinforced settled society's image of Travellers' sites as ghettos containing unpredictable, violent and anti-social individuals.

While in one context sites were too large, in another they were too small, in that they rarely provided the space to accommodate either visiting relatives, or to conduct activities relating to certain types of work, most typically scrap collection. Some sites specifically banned residents from car-breaking and related work, leading to people conducting it in the local area, causing conflict with surrounding residents. In other cases a communal area for scrap collection and breaking was provided, leading to potential arguments and conflict over allegations of theft.[43]

Okely revealed how these and other issues generated conflict between council wardens and the expectations of residents. She demonstrated how there was 'little or no awareness that individual families prefer to be surrounded by allies in the competition for work and camping places', as clusters of kin and allies help with care of the elderly and others in times of crisis. Kinship links, 'fundamental to the Gypsies' political and social organisation were commonly "rejected by Gorgio wardens as mere nepotism". Wardens were likely to pick families on the basis of whether they had school-aged children, or whether a family would be "good" tenants,[44] and rejected individuals who were part of, or allied to, perceived "problem" families'.[45]

Conflict with wardens over who was an appropriate tenant, or how a site might be run was almost inevitable in the context of an absolute shortage of sites, with pitches being a limited resource. One Traveller who became the informal 'guv'nor' of his site described the role he played: 'People came to me to settle disputes and ask advice, and I'd help them out if I could. There's normally a guv'nor on most sites: someone who is respected and can keep the peace. I decided who came on and when. Didn't allow any riff-raff on the site. We had a good bunch of families and I was determined to keep it that way'. However, this brought him into conflict with the council warden, and he was evicted, which failed to resolved the warden's problem: 'He couldn't control the residents and even though he was taking a few quid in backhanders for prime pitches, his life was made a misery'.[46]

Despite official sites being council-run, residents on those sites did not have the same rights as council house tenants, and the 1983 Mobile Homes Act, which gave security of tenure to tenants living on caravan sites specifically exempted Travellers on the grounds of their nomadism.[47] Not only did this situation continue post-war government practice to distinguish between Travellers and other caravan-dwellers, but it also discriminated between council tenants in houses and 'licensees' in caravans. Until a 2004 European court judgment, the practical effect of this was that Travellers had very little security of tenure. They could, for example, be evicted on an allegation of anti-social behaviour without the local authority either having to prove that the behaviour took place, or prove that eviction was a reasonable response to the situation. In contrast, for council house tenants both the behaviour and the reasonableness of the response had to be proven.[48]

Council sites may have provided Travellers with a degree of security and an opportunity to continue living in a trailer, but they could also be places of harassment, isolation and uncertainty. For up to a third of Travellers, however, the problems and cultures of official site living were only experienced occasionally, or indeed never. The slow rate of site creation in tandem with a growing Traveller population meant that unofficial sites, far from disappearing, continued as a central part of Traveller life. Wibberley's review of site provision in 1985 found that at a conservative estimate, there was a shortfall of between 3,000 and 4,000 caravan pitches.[49] Beyond the simple figures was the fact that as official sites were located in places that minimised interaction with the settled community, unofficial camps were the most visible way in which the majority population and the media experienced Travellers.

Research conducted by David Smith on the lifestyles of an estimated 500 highly mobile Traveller families in 1982, who centred their travel in an area bounded by the M4, M5, M6, M62 and M1 motorways found: 'Conurbations within this motorway "sleeve" consistently report problems caused by incursions of long-distance travellers while areas beyond report periodic incursions but on a much reduced scale'. At the time of the research roughly half of these Travellers were selling carpets door-to-door. The 'high value of stock carried' meant they travelled in groups of up to thirty and sometimes as many as one hundred families 'for their own protection'. Each group normally stayed from six weeks to two months in any one location. Other Travellers identified in the research moved in much smaller groups of three to six families, concentrating on tarmacking, and located themselves near new housing developments which were the focus for their trade. Given the highly mobile nature of their work, neither group expressed any particular interest in permanent site provision.[50]

Their arrival in any location, especially of the larger groups, caused considerable tensions, but although an element of criminality was identified by the police, it was the more pervasive disorder that was most problematic. The larger groups simultaneously brought 'the waste disposal problems of a small residential estate with the trade waste of a carpet supermarket'. Meanwhile, displays of 'conspicuous consumption' through expensive vehicles and trailers were a 'source of grievance for people living in an area which is besieged by such travellers who they suspect pay no taxes, rates, etc, and are generally taking advantage of society'.[51] Unusually, this research provided evidence both from a local resident who had been living near an unauthorised site, and a Traveller, to give both perspectives on the situation:

> They pay no rates – taxes – car tax or insurance and get away with it. They run £12,000 Volvos and have caravans worth thousands and when the Court Order is served, they are going to appeal it. It is now Friday – the site is looking like a dump. They have no sanitation. The dogs bark all night, the children are screaming all day and the generators are going until well past midnight. Our peace is shattered. The elderly around here are very nervous and unhappy – one old lady has had her fence broken down by the children and they throw rubbish over our back gardens ... Why can't the law be changed to protect the private landowners? Why do we pay rates?[52]

> It's a terrible business just finding a space to stay ... We go round in a convoy and sometimes we get ten to fifteen of us on the bit of land and the police come and stop the rest of us getting on. There's a lot of argument then and sometimes we all get on but it's bad if we don't, as the others have to go onto the

roadside. Then when we get onto the land the police will be onto us. Sometimes they dig a trench all round with JCB diggers and say we can't get off unless we take our caravans with us. Well, we're trapped then. Can't take out cars to get food even and we can't get out to get to work. Then they will come into our trailers and ask for receipts for all the stuff there. Might have to go a hundred miles back to the shop to get a receipt for the television, for example, and what do you do about the Crown Derby you've been given for the wedding? And there was one morning at six o'clock when they had warrants to search for firearms and we were all out of the trailers standing in a row while they searched. Tore the carpet up as well. It's all a kind of bluff to get us off as quickly as possible ... Sometimes people are ill: one time they hitched up a trailer and the midwife looked out and said that a baby was going to be born ... The local people we don't see directly but a few have waved sticks at us when we try to get on to a piece of land but that's not important. The worst is what the papers say about us. People panic automatically when we first arrive and too much is written in the papers to frighten people against us.[53]

The foregoing account highlights the role of the media in propagating images of Travellers, particularly as contact was rarely made directly with local residents.

Smith's research came to the conclusion that the current situation was unsatisfactory for all sides, and suggested a network of transit sites within the 'motorway sleeve', providing rubbish skips, access to water and toilet facilities for up to forty trailers, as well as a national network of small stopping places for the 'regional' families', with room for between five and six caravans, with basic facilities.[54] These proposals were received positively by police representatives at a national level,[55] but locally more acerbic views were voiced:

Frankly I have never read so much unadulterated bilge on a matter ... I can see no need at all for the general well-being of this country nor its solvency in these times of economic stringency to have facilities for gypsies and tinkers to be able to hove to at suitable locations as they move about selling their second-rate made-up lengths of carpet and indulging in dealing in scrap metal.[56]

As in earlier decades Travellers perceived lack of citizen status meant that they could be seen as undeserving of (scarce) public resources. By the mid-1980s the spectre of the unauthorised site had gained such prominence that it succeeded in distorting the debate on Travellers and site provision. Wibberley noted the 'severe, even phrenetic, opposition, by local people to site suggestions'.[57]

Yet, high profile sites and conflict made up only one part of a much more mixed picture. The south-west of England and the east coast experienced 'few problems', whereas particular parts of Wales had experienced difficulties in coping with large numbers of 'itinerant families arriving in the region from the Republic of Ireland'. The north-west of England provided a variable picture, 'where suitable facilities have been provided the problems arising from unauthorised encampments have tended to reduce. The lack of authorised sites has undoubtedly led to greater police involvement with the gipsy families'. The most serious problems reported by the police were in the south-east of England:

> Two sites in Surrey have appalling records of violence, damage and public order problems. Even where authorised sites are provided, unauthorised sites continue to be set up and can cause major problems ... Police are often pressed to adopt a high profile, almost to the extent of persecuting those on the unauthorised site in the hope that such action will cause them to move.[58]

Added to opposition to Traveller sites, official or otherwise, was the rise in what has been variously described as the 'peace convoy', 'hippies', 'New Age' or 'New Travellers'. Lurid media reports caused further publicity and opposition to what was seen as a chaotic and free-loading lifestyle. High profile incidents, such as the 'Battle of the Beanfield' in 1985, and free parties and festivals, culminating in Castle Morton in 1992, led to sections of the press and the government believing that nomadism was running out of control.[59]

Travellers generally distanced themselves from New Travellers, both socially and politically, and expressed concern that in some areas – notably Avon – where there had been confrontations over stopping places: 'this situation is likely to escalate where Authorities attempt to make provision for 'hippies' at the expense of providing sites for members of the *bona fide* Gypsy community'.[60] However, this did not prevent both groups from being dealt with under new legislation, notably the 1986 Public Order Act[61] and the 1994 Criminal Justice and Public Order Act.

The Conservative government claimed the number of Gypsy caravans had grown by 30 per cent since 1981 and, despite a 67 per cent increase in official pitches, there were 4,000 Gypsies and Travellers and 2,000 to 5,000 New Age Travellers camping illegally in England and Wales. The 1968 Act was blamed for failing to solve the problem and placing an 'open-ended' commitment on local authorities to fund sites.[62]

In the heightened atmosphere of the early 1990s, the Gypsy Council attempted to bring perspective to the debate, placing responsibility for the failure of site creation at the door of local authorities:

> we see our situation less in terms of a 'Gypsy problem', and more a local authority problem; Gypsies are not required under the 1968 Act to provide their own accommodation (although many have done so, and continue to do so), whereas local authorities are. A large number of local authorities have, in the past twenty-two years, deliberately flouted the law by not providing sites, or by opposing all plans for site provision in their area, and yet in the eyes of the general public it is the Gypsy who is to blame for camping illegally, even though he is forced to do so by the shortage of official sites.[63]

In fact central government's response, rather than to encourage the pace of local authority provision, was the 1994 Criminal Justice and Public Order Act. This was retrogressive in a number of ways. The legislation made it harder for Travellers, and New Travellers, to create and stay on unauthorised sites, as travelling or stopping in groups of larger than six vehicles became a criminal offence and evictions from unauthorised sites became much easier to conduct. Crucially, the legislation also affected official sites, as it removed the obligation placed on local authorities in 1968 to adequately provide for Travellers 'residing in or resorting to' their area, and removed the automatic granting of 100 per cent funding of sites by central government.[64]

The government's rationale behind removing the requirement to provide sites was based on the argument that there was a hard core of some 4,000 caravans on unauthorised sites, a number that had remained roughly static since the early 1980s, despite increased provision of authorised sites. It believed that this demonstrated 'that the more sites that are provided, the more people are attracted to the itinerant life'.[65] In line with an ideology of privatisation and the shortcomings of public services, central government believed that local authority provision could not make up the shortfall:

> We do not believe that it is in the public interest to continue to maintain what has become an open-ended commitment to provide sites for all gypsies seeking accommodation at the public's expense. It is our view that the right approach now is to encourage more gypsies to establish their own sites through the planning system. We know that many gypsy families would prefer to establish their own sites rather than reside on council sites. The National Gypsy Council has for a long time supported the case for private provision.[66]

Subsequent information on the consultation process surrounding the legislation revealed that the 'overwhelming reaction' of the approximately one thousand responses was negative. Even the Department of the Environment's own unpublished analysis of responses 'referred to the common perception that "the proposals present an attack on basic human rights and are designed to stop [Travellers] travelling for good … the phrase 'ethnic cleansing' was used by several respondents"'.[67]

Having failed over a 24-year period to encourage councils and local residents to overcome their prejudices in order to provide sufficient sites, the proposed solution was nevertheless to advise Travellers to buy their own land, and to work through the planning system alone to establish legal, private sites.[68] Yet, the policy also effectively reduced the opportunities for Travellers to obtain planning permission by explicitly excluding green belt as an area which might be considered as suitable for sites. While the government clearly had some legitimate motivations behind the decision to protect green belt, the advice ignored the long-standing practice of Travellers to locate themselves in peri-urban areas, where plots of marginal and wasteland were available both for unauthorised sites and for purchase.

The immediate effects of the 1994 Act on official site provision were not felt, as some sites which were already under construction came on stream after 1994. However, ten years after the passing of the legislation one of the most noticeable trends was a number of high-profile evictions of Travellers, not from unauthorised sites as was the case in the 1960s, but from land they owned which had failed to receive planning consent. By 2006 there were 1,200 such sites subject to council enforcement action.[69]

This was a direct result of government failing to tackle the 'disproportionate difficulty' faced by Travellers in the planning system,[70] and the passing of the 1990 Town and Country Planning Act

that had tightened councils' enforcement powers against unauthorised development. In 1994, two planning circulars[71] were introduced setting out the criteria for Travellers developing sites on
their own land and calling on local authorities to tolerate
unauthorised Gypsy and Traveller encampments where they 'cause
no nuisance', but this 'was frequently ignored or wilfully misinter-
preted'.[72]

A DoE report of 1990 revealed the success rate of initial planning applications by Travellers was about 10 per cent, while 50 cases
monitored in 1995 indicated a success rate for new applications as
low as 4 per cent. As a rule, therefore, Travellers had to use the appeal system, where they were also unsuccessful. Figures from the
planning inspectorate showed the success rate at appeal falling from
43.5 per cent in 1990–91 to 37.5 per cent in 1995–96. An analysis of
107 appeals involving Travellers between late 1995 and mid-1997
showed that the overall success rate at appeal was 34 per cent, with
half of these receiving only temporary permission.[73] This was against
a background level of success of all planning applications (including
appeals) of around 80 per cent.[74]

Engrained in the limitations of both official site provision
and an expectation that councils would approve private Traveller-
owned sites, was the fact that locally-made decisions were mediated
through the prejudices of the electorate. This had been a consistent
theme throughout the twentieth century, and one that may have increased from the 1980s, as more of settled society became home-own-
ers and felt that a Traveller site of any description would reduce the
value of their property.

Despite the manifest failings of the 1968 Act – most notably the slow
pace of provision, an imbalance between provision of permanent and
transit sites, and the issue of designation – the legislation did provide some Travellers with a degree of security. And while promoting
a more sedentary lifestyle, official sites did not lead to assimilation,
and instead created a space for the maintenance of a distinctive Traveller identity. The retreat of central government after 1994 from a
position of, admittedly weak, leadership and provision of funding,
allowed historically engrained prejudice from local authorities to
prevent the provision of sufficient official and private sites with planning permission. In this context, the continuation of unauthorised
encampments, evictions and conflict with settled society was almost
inevitable.

Traveller responses

The limitations of the 1968 Act, and the subsequent decision of central government to leave site creation to private Traveller initiatives, resulted in at least one-third of caravan-dwelling Travellers having no authorised stopping place. These Travellers found themselves demonised, automatically tainted with associations of criminality, anti-social behaviour and fly-tipping:[75]

> We had a marvellous 999 call: 'The Travellers have gathered. Vehicles have pulled up on site ... There's lots of clothes on hangers being taken out'. It's an allegation of theft ... what they're actually doing is that they have a particular launderette that treats them decently, doesn't give them racial abuse, which they take all their washing to. And this is the washing coming home. Bringing your washing back from the launderette, if you're a Traveller gets you a 999 call.

Following allegations of fly-tipping in another case, an analysis of the waste demonstrated that it came from surrounding businesses.[76] In other instances, waste near Traveller sites has come from residents of local housing estates.[77] Despite such clear cases where the surrounding population have taken advantage of the presence of Travellers to engage in anti-social and criminal behaviour, travelling communities consistently have taken the blame.

Travellers who tried to take government advice to buy land frequently found themselves denied planning permission and evicted, while those on official sites often lived in what were little more than unpleasant ghettos, far removed from essential services and residential areas. The scarcity of stopping places and the climate of intolerance surrounding Travellers had a range of effects on them and their relationship with the settled community.

The worsening of Traveller–settled society relations, which have only ever been ambivalent at the best of times, has been both a cause and a result of the shortage of secure pitches. Changing socio-economic and physical environments also played their role in adversely affecting relations. Increasing home ownership and the importance of house price rises for individuals' investment strategies led to anxiety over any changes perceived to affect property values. Shifts in the structure of agricultural employment, the near-disappearance of hawking and other small day-to-day economic interactions and the increased focus by Travellers on fewer, but larger economic exchanges reduced everyday contact between Travellers and settled society. This was compounded by a belief that the work done by Travellers was shoddy and exploitative. Travellers themselves saw their 'profiteering' more in terms of a disjuncture of economic culture:

> we'll start at a ridiculously high price, knowing that the punter will knock us down, because he's been brought up to believe that we will try and rip him off … It's a game and normally both sides of the transaction know it, but it goes wrong now and then. You quote someone £500 for a £250 job and wait for the negotiation, but they say, 'Yes – go ahead.' What would you do?[78]

A mismatch in attitudes of some Travellers and settled society over what is 'reasonable' could be seen in other areas. By their own admission, Travellers on unauthorised sites tended to band together in larger groups for safety,[79] which left surrounding residents feeling intimidated. Constant harassment and discrimination on the part of the wider community led to the growth of anti-social behaviour from some Travellers, reinforcing what was already a vicious circle. This was a trend already identified in the early 1980s:

> … lack of access to any form of sites offering even temporary respite from continuous harassment and eviction must take its toll of the niceties of human behaviour. It is clearly unrealistic to expect conformist and cooperative behaviour from a group of people who are always about to be evicted. The insecurity engendered by not knowing how long a particular unauthorised site will be permitted to exist creates fundamental instability in the travellers' lifestyle which, if repeated too frequently, manifests itself in both their own and their children's behaviour.[80]

This dynamic was illustrated in phone calls made to the police relating to an unauthorised site: 'you have local residents standing at their windows observing the site *through their binoculars*, complaining about what they can see. Then they are surprised that some of the Traveller children make a "V" sign at them when they drive past … You treat any community that way, of course you get that response'.[81]

Hostility and discrimination experienced by Travellers also manifested itself in other ways. An unidentified number of Travellers simply gave up living on the road, and moved into houses, some cutting off ties with their Traveller community in order to reduce the chances of discrimination and rejection by neighbours.

Traveller agency was also expressed in more positive assertions of identity. Although detailed research remains to be done, the rise of the pan-European Gypsy evangelical movement can in part be understood in the context of the assertion of a distinctive culture and identity during a time of crisis.[82] Unlike earlier Traveller missionaries who tended to preach a 'Eurocentric discourse', the wave of evangelism which began in France in the late 1950s positively asserted Romany identities. The Bible was translated into various Romany languages, and evangelists presented 'the gospel in Romani colours and build up Romani congregations'.[83]

Other Travellers took a more secular route, and became engaged in political or social activism, aimed at fighting inequality within the system as a whole, or in particular areas, such as health or education. Although the Gypsy Council (renamed the Gypsy Council of Education, Culture, Welfare and Civil Rights in 1991) remained the largest organisation representing Travellers, a number of other organisations sprang up to respond to the continuing lack of representation of travelling communities. These tended to be aimed at particular sections of the travelling population, and while they were often successful in making links locally with statutory organisations working to a multicultural agenda, they were less successful in creating a national voice for all Travellers. In part this was due to a lack of unity both within and between different sections of the travelling community. For example, the Gypsy Council was seen as failing to represent the interests of all Travellers, resulting in the creation of a different Gypsy Council, as well as several organisations representing the different traditions within Britain's nomadic communities.[84]

This splintering took place in the context of the continued alienation of the majority of Travellers from formal political representation. Travellers continued to be under-represented on the electoral register and therefore seen as separate from, and often in opposition to, constituency politics. By the end of the twentieth century Traveller organisations and active individuals may have made major strides in getting their voice heard in particular sections of government, but were unable to move Traveller representation into the political mainstream.

The formation of the Gypsy and Traveller Law Reform Coalition in September 2002, by both Travellers and those from settled society, signalled a move towards a more inclusive approach to political representation within Travelling communities, and aimed at 'bringing together Travelling people from a range of ethnicities and backgrounds in recognition that the structural disadvantages experienced by the communities are identical'.[85] The Coalition campaigned for legal reform to tackle accommodation problems, working closely with the All Party Parliamentary Group for Traveller Law Reform. Its objectives included a return to the duty on local authorities to provide sites, and the Caravan Sites Security of Tenure Bill 2006. This aimed at providing equal security for Gypsies and Travellers living on local authority sites, compared to social housing tenants. In April 2006 the Coalition was reincarnated as the Traveller Law Reform Project, which continued its aim of legal change through parliamentary lobbying.[86]

Education and multiculturalism

The rise in Traveller politics and political intermediaries, while welcome, had limited impact on the majority of Travellers. Instead, most exhibited an 'ambivalence ... towards the various agents of the state' and the services they offered:

> Yes, they want their children to learn to read, but no, they do not necessarily want them registered, listed and irrevocably bound into the system of formal education. Yes, they want some kinds of preventive health care, but not others. Yes, they want to go to a regular doctor, but they are much happier turning up at Accident and Emergency departments when treatment is required.[87]

This ambivalence can be seen in Travellers' reactions to educational developments since the 1970s, when in line with more general multicultural and explicitly anti-racist policies, attempts were slowly made to create services that were not overtly assimilationist and proactively engaged with the needs of Travellers as a minority.[88] Even so, 'needs' were often still defined by professionals and LEAs rather than Travellers themselves, and the overarching context of a shortage of secure sites and discrimination often undermined the effectiveness of initiatives. Additionally, initiatives were commonly localised and patchy, and often reliant on specialised Traveller education staff for their success, rather than on radically challenging mainstream attitudes.

As recommended by the Swann Committee on the education of children from ethnic minority groups in 1985,[89] research was conducted on the educational experiences of children from numerically small minority communities who tended to be overlooked in debates that centred on South Asian and Afro-Caribbean pupils. This research considered Travellers alongside children of Cypriot, Vietnamese, Ukrainian and Italian heritage, as well as 'Liverpool blacks'. The findings demonstrated that although each group had unique issues, 'in respect of language and culture, racism and ethnic identity', and in their 'interrelation with academic performance, experience of schooling, and educational policies and practices', children from these communities had broadly similar experiences to those from larger minority groups. In some cases, and here Liverpool blacks and Travellers were both highlighted, experiences of discrimination were 'heightened to an extreme degree'.[90]

A review of available research suggested that only 40 per cent of Traveller children were in primary schooling and between 10 and 12 per cent in secondary education. These figures included attendances that varied from full-time to irregular: 'Unlike with other minority groups, the problem is not just one of the adequacy of education received but whether they received an education at all'.[91]

Part of the issue around attendance and access to schooling continued to be structural and was the result of frequent evictions from unauthorised sites, exacerbated in the 1990s by the introduction of the Criminal Justice Act. Research also showed that the historical reluctance of schools to admit Traveller children was reinforced by 'the perceived detrimental effect they may have on overall school performance and attendance results and consequently slippage in league tables'.[92]

Travellers' own opinions about the merits of formal education also continued to be a central factor in the reception of education: 'Their interest is essentially in the "three Rs" and the functional. Literacy is increasingly considered useful in helping them to cope with demands imposed by, and exploit opportunities offered by, the gorgio world'.[93] A view of Travellers' expectations of education being limited was challenged by Bhopal, whose work suggested that parents were keen to see their children finish secondary as well as primary school: 'Getting an education is important for everyone, but it's *more important* for us because we're different. We're Gypsies. If we get an education, then people will respect us and not call us … "dirty, stupid gypos."'[94]

The support of Traveller parents for extending the education of their children was both encouraged, and encouraged by, the development of specialist Traveller education units, which were part of LEA services and had emerged from the voluntary Traveller school programmes of the late 1960s and 1970s. By 1985, 65 out of 104 LEAs were making specialist provision of some type, either peripatetic teachers, through mobile units, or through dedicated teachers within mainstream education. By 1995 this had increased to 75 LEAs which between them employed 351 additional teachers, 170 classroom assistants and 54 educational welfare officers.[95] Traveller education services created distance learning resource packs and Traveller-focused educational material in addition to providing specialist support for children while mobile and in schools.[96] Despite these developments, which included many positive initiatives,[97] schooling for Travellers remained marginal, dependent on the attitude of the particular LEA and its approach not only to Travellers, but to anti-racist and multicultural education more generally.

In some areas a genuine commitment to anti-racism fed through into schools' work with Travellers, attempting to deliver support within a mainstream setting. One school in London appointed a coordinator who worked between primary and secondary schools, and actively aimed to help Traveller children overcome barriers upon entry:

> A few Travellers settle into the school and do well; others need remedial help with reading to facilitate the settling in process. Some Traveller children, however, feel that they suffer prejudice and victimisation from other children ... and they tend to react aggressively or to run out of school thoroughly upset. The school has a policy against racism and attempts to deal with pupils who perpetrate racist abuse. I have become something of a focal point for the Travellers in the school; hopefully they will come to me for help with problems rather than becoming aggressive or staying away from school.

This project coordinator further observed that Travellers were not the only children to have such difficulties within the system, which in itself created tensions: 'I have had to walk a diplomatic tightrope, as the school is anxious that Traveller pupils should not be treated substantially differently from other pupils. However, my very existence as the Traveller teacher indicates a measure of positive discrimination' as part of the school's commitment to a multicultural curriculum.[98]

Taylor's review of educational provision for Travellers in the late 1980s found that models of provision fell into three broad categories: placement in ordinary schools, separate school-based initiatives, and on-site schooling. For all these methods the same dilemma had to be addressed, one which applied to the education of all minority groups: on the one hand there was an expectation and a demand for minority children to be provided with an education that was of an equal standard to that given to the mainstream population. On the other, there were concerns that this could result in alienating children from their birth culture.

Liegeois, in his pan-European survey of educational provision for Gypsy and Traveller children, helpfully made the distinction between *education* and *school provision*. While Travellers, with a largely oral and dispersed culture, had little history of schooling, their social structure and culture always provided, and has continued to provide, for the education of their children: 'There are those – including the Gypsies – for whom *schooling is only a part* (and sometimes not even that) *of the education if their children*'. Since the 1970s in particular, more Traveller parents came to accept that literacy and numeracy were important skills in the modern world,[99] but saw these as a *supplement* to education received from within their own traditions, not as a replacement: 'Parents are perfectly conscious that it is they and not the school who will provide the child with the skills by which he will earn his living. There are many reasons behind this, including the poor quality of the schooling the Gypsy child receives ... prejudice ... [and] Gypsy preference for self-employment'.[100]

Therefore, neither increased settlement nor greater contact with the education system necessarily affected either attainment levels or children's experiences of schooling. A detailed study in the 1970s, of a secondary school in the south of England with 22 housed Traveller children on the roll, explored how the 'Gypsy problem' was perceived differently by the school and by the pupils and their parents. The children, although technically integrated, largely found themselves in the remedial classes, where they were seen as a 'troublesome group – regularly late or absent, frequently disruptive, generally uncooperative, quite lacking in motivation and grossly underachieving at all levels'. In addition to this, Traveller children were identified as exhibiting bullying and intimidatory behaviour. Ivatts explained their behaviour as the 'simple consequence of their intense dislike of secondary schooling, bolstered by a conviction that it had little relevance to them'. School interfered with family work patterns, deprived parents of the income and teenagers of the work experience they would normally receive as part of a more traditional Traveller life pattern. The Traveller children defended their 'bullying', stating that they only attacked other children after been taunted themselves: 'They calls us "dirty Gypsy"' – if they do, we 'it 'em, no messin', we bash 'em'.[101] An overwhelmingly negative experience of secondary education must not be seen as unique to Travellers: Paul Willis's classic, and roughly contemporaneous, study of the schooling of working-class boys in Sheffield found a strong counter-culture, which similarly saw schooling as profoundly alienating and irrelevant to their future world of work.[102]

Although there were debates and splits within Traveller education groups over the correct form of educational provision for Travellers,[103] two case studies indicate how similar structures could 'serve different, even opposite, policy goals'.[104]

The Central Region mobile resource unit in Scotland was established after research revealed the reason for most Traveller absenteeism was that they were 'afraid of the children being ostracised at school, or that they would be moved on from their unofficial roadside sites, while the children were at school'. The unit consisted of a number of vehicles and a mix of part-time and full-time teachers, who were divided between working in schools and in mobile classrooms, and three adult 'basic education' tutors. In a week they had contact with around fifty children, and actively aimed not only to promote Traveller culture but to foster a 'love of learning' beyond basic literacy and numeracy. In the long term the project aimed at 'integration, not segregation'. Between 1979 and 1983 the number of children enrolled in schools rose from 43 to 225, with families from other regions coming to access the service. The range of services, the sensitive nature of provision and active attempts to bridge the gap between Travellers and mainstream education all served to allow the scheme to become 'an instrument of acceptance, and of individual and collective progress'.[105]

The form of another scheme, based at an unnamed LEA in England, was similar in that it provided a mobile classroom. However, in this case the local authority had a tradition of rejecting Travellers: there were over one hundred Traveller children in the area but only one school admitted them, and specialist teachers were forbidden from visiting unauthorised sites. Two full-time teachers, who were appointed to staff the mobile classroom, 'felt sure that they were being used as an alternative to admission to school, or to provision of a multi-cultural policy in school'. Additionally, they believed injunctions placed on them not to engage in any politics, not to be funded to go on any courses or join any associations relating to

Travellers 'was indicative of the lack of support from the authority ... They felt unable to meet the clear demand from Travellers and felt isolated ... The purpose of this provision was segregation, not integration'. The scheme had some limited impact in that 5 per cent of Traveller children received 'ordinary' schooling, and a further 25 per cent had the chance of getting four to six hours a week instruction in the mobile unit.[106]

These cases demonstrate the continuity with earlier decades, with provision still being dependent on local initiatives and no consensus over the purpose of either schooling generally, or separate provision more specifically. They confirm that any one structure of education could either be inclusive or segregationist. As Liegeois cautioned, 'don't take things at face value. School in a caravan can either be a good or bad thing':

> the dichotomy need not be absolute: in either case the teachers involved may be doing their best to provide high-quality instruction; in either case they may draw largely on elements of the child's own culture both as a pedagogic device and as a means of recognising and validating that culture; in either case the teachers involved may approach their task with an attitude of respect; in either case they may take account of the wishes of the parents.[107]

The three decades following the introduction of the 1968 Act saw a number of developments, both positive and negative. Official sites with secure pitches were welcomed by many tired of constant eviction. They could create a space where Travellers were able to maintain their distinctive lifestyles, but were not without their problems. An absolute shortage of sites, poor location and design, and insecurity of tenure meant that residents were commonly physically isolated from the rest of the population, pitched with families they would normally choose to avoid, and unable to move on without risking losing their place. Additionally, designation was resented as being discriminatory towards Travellers as a group and for being awarded to local authorities who had made only scant provision. These shortcomings stemmed from policy being directed by local, rather than national, considerations, so that the creation of any site was dogged by popular prejudice, institutionalised racism and a supreme lack of political will.

Central government's decision in 1994 to remove any obligation on local authorities to provide sites and to place the responsibility for site creation on Travellers through the planning system further compounded the problem. Without proactively tackling the prejudice displayed towards Travellers, this policy culminated in evictions from private sites and continued heavy reliance by Travellers on unauthorised stopping places.

Travellers themselves were popularly blamed for continued shortcomings in site provision, which simultaneously caused and ensured their further marginalisation and vilification. For many, any advances in more appropriate and sensitive school provision were mediated through their continued marginal position, the experience of frequent eviction and a desire to maintain their own traditions. Additionally, attempts to target services at Travellers led in some cases to compartmentalised provision, with specialist officers or services developing a sound understanding of Traveller culture and needs, with mainstream provision remaining largely untouched.

Notes

1 National Gypsy Council, 'Annual Report of the National Gypsy Council', 1982, 14, ACPO archive.
2 Liegeois, *School provision*, 42.
3 For a more detailed exploration of the subject see D. Kenrick, 'What is a Gypsy?', in R. Morris and L. Clements (eds), *Gaining ground: Law reform for Gypsies and Travellers* (Hatfield, 1999).
4 D. Kenrick and C. Clark, *Moving on: The Gypsies and Travellers of Britain* (Hatfield, 1999), 149.
5 Kenrick, 'What is a Gypsy?', in Morris and Clements (eds), *Gaining ground*, 65–6.
6 Quoted in Taylor, *Worlds Apart?*, 355.
7 ACPO, letter from Kent to ACPO, 25 August 1978, and internal ACPO memo, 26 October 1978. The letter made it clear that the organisation did not accept it constituted racial discrimination, as the *Mills v. Cooper* (1967) judgment decided that Gypsy meant 'a person who leads a nomadic life without any fixed abode', rather than someone from the '*Romany race*' (original emphasis).
8 M. Lloyd and R. Morran, 'The case for change?', in R. Morris and L. Clements (eds), *Gaining ground: Law reform for Gypsies and Travellers* (Hatfield, 1999), 61 and 63.
9 Author's conversations with residents of Dale Farm and Gratton Puxon, August 2005.
10 Lloyd and Morran, 'The case for change?', 62.
11 Author interview with barrister, 8 April 2006.
12 ACPO, letter from Home Office to ACPO, 12 June 1968.
13 MHLG, *Gypsies and other Travellers*.
14 J. Cripps, *Accommodation for Gypsies: A report on the working of the Caravan*

Sites Act, 1968 (London, 1976), 7.

15 See Acton, *Gypsy politics*, 180–3, for discussion of this point.

16 ACPO, letter from Home Office to ACPO, 12 June 1968.

17 The whole issue of the caravan counts has always been controversial, with Traveller support groups in particular maintaining local authorities consistently under-counted in order to reduce their obligation to provide pitches. The problematic nature of the count was acknowledged in a report prepared for the Office of the Deputy Prime Minister, 'Counting Gypsies and Travellers: A review of the Gypsy caravan count system', Housing Research Summary 206, (London, 2003).

18 Kenrick and Clark, *Moving on*, 89–93.

19 *Ibid.*

20 TNA, HO45/10995/158231/9, evidence of Justice Bray to House of Lords Select Committee, 1910.

21 Sibley, *Outsiders*, 102.

22 Acton, *Gypsy politics*, 183.

23 National Gypsy Council, 'Annual report of the National Gypsy Council', 1982, 7.

24 DoE, circular 28/77, 25 March 1977, 'Caravan Sites Act, Part II, Gypsy caravan sites'.

25 Cripps, *Accommodation*, 11.

26 *Ibid.*

27 Okely, *Traveller-Gypsies*, 115–16.

28 Cripps, *Accommodation*, para. 3, 17.

29 Okely, *Traveller-Gypsies*, 117–18.

30 Sibley, *Outsiders*, 103.

31 Sibley, 'Persistence or change?', 66.

32 National Gypsy Council, 'Annual Report', 1982, 12.

33 Sibley, *Outsiders*, 115.

34 DoE, circular 28/77(April 1977).

35 *Ibid.*

36 ACPO, letter from HO to ACPO, 24 November 1978.

37 ACPO, G. Wibberley, 'A report on the analysis of responses to consultation on the operation of the Caravan Sites Act, 1968', 8.

38 ACPO, DoE memo, 'Gypsy sites policy in England', 1985.

39 Wibberley, 'Report', 11–12.

40 ACPO, DoE memo, 'Gypsy sites policy in England', 1985.

41 Quoted in Penal Affairs Consortium, 'Squatters, Travellers, ravers, protesters and the criminal law. An assessment of Part V of the Criminal Justice and Public Order Act 1994', (London, 1994), 4.

42 Okely, *Traveller-Gypsies*, 120–1.

43 Sibley, 'Persistence or change?', 67.

44 Okely, *Traveller-Gypsies*, 118–19.

45 See for example *Connors v. The United Kingdom*, 5.

46 Stockins, *On the cobbles*, 179.

47 The legal basis for this was set out in the House of Lords judgment,

Greenwich London Borough Council v. Powell (1989), 21 HLR 218.

48 The judgment was *Connors v. The United Kingdom*. Author interview with barrister specialising in Traveller cases, 8 April 2006.

49 Wibberley, 'Report', 14.

50 ACPO, DoE, 'The accommodation needs of long-distance and regional Travellers: a consultation paper', Feb. 1982, 3.

51 *Ibid.*, 4–5.

52 *Ibid.*, Appendix 1.

53 *Ibid.*, Appendix 3, précis of a conversation with a long-distance Traveller in January 1982.

54 *Ibid.*, 5–6.

55 ACPO, ACPO General Secretary to HO, 13 May 1982.

56 ACPO, letter from a Chief Constable to ACPO General Secretary, 14 April 1982.

57 Wibberley, 'Report', 21.

58 ACPO, ACPO General Purposes Committee to HO, 11 February 1986.

59 For a general introduction to this subject see F. Earle, A. Dearling, H. Whittling et al., *A time to travel? An introduction to Britain's newer Travellers* (Lyme Regis, 1994), and G. McKay, *Senseless acts of beauty: Cultures of resistance since the sixties* (London, 1996).

60 National Gypsy Council, 'Site provision in Britain: A short briefing paper', July 1992.

61 Section 39 gave powers to remove twelve or more vehicles that were illegally sited on land, or where the occupiers damaged property, used threats or violence.

62 Hawes and Perez, *The Gypsy and the state*, 117–18.

63 National Gypsy Council, 'Site provision'.

64 See P. Tain, *Criminal Justice and Public Order Act: A practical guide* (London, 1994) for a detailed discussion of the Act. Sections 61–2 dealt with removing trespassers from land, sections 63–7 with diverting people from proceeding to particular sites; sections 77–9 gave powers to local authorities to remove persons and vehicles unlawfully on land; and section 80 removed the obligation on local authorities to provide sites for Travellers.

65 Tain, *Criminal Justice*, 5.6.2.

66 Parliamentary Under-Secretary of State, quoted in *Connors v. the United Kingdom*, 9.

67 Quoted in Clark and Greenfield, *Here to Stay*, 80.

68 Lord Avebury, 'Preface', in Morris and Clements (eds), *Gaining ground*, xv–xvii.

69 Clark and Greenfield, *Here to Stay*, 97. For a list of evictions from privately owned sites since 2002 see www.travellersupport.org.uk/evictions.htm, accessed 21 August 2006.

70 www.gypsy-traveller.org/planning/index.htm, accessed 21 August 2006.

71 DoE 1/94, 'Gypsy sites and planning' and circular 18/94.

72 Clark and Greenfield, *Here to Stay*, 87.

73 Friends and Families of Travellers, 'Planning appeals and Gypsies and Travellers', 1998. See also www.gypsy-traveller.org/planning/index.htm, accessed 21 August 2006.

74 Office of the Deputy Prime Minister, 'Planning Policy Guidance, Note 1, General Policy and Principles', February 1997.

75 On the day that I write, the university sent round an email stating that Travellers illegally camped on campus were to be evicted, but in the meantime staff were advised to take extra security measures.

76 Author interview with barrister, 8 April 2006.

77 Clark and Greenfield, *Here to stay*, 168–9, also author conversation with Norfolk Traveller Education Service staff, autumn 2002.

78 Stockins, *On the cobbles*, 77.

79 *Ibid.*, 49–50 and ACPO, DoE, 'Accommodation needs', Appendix 3.

80 ACPO, DoE, 'Accommodation needs', 5.

81 Author interview with barrister, 8 April 2006.

82 This remains an area open for research. Primary sources on this subject include J. Ridholls, *Romany Revival* (London, 1980) and R. Dawson (ed.), *God's travelling children: Traditional Travellers coming to terms with their ethnicity* (Blackwell, Derbyshire, 2002).

83 D. Lazell, *Gypsy from the forest: A new biography of the international evangelist Gipsy Smith, 1860–1947* (Bridgend, 1997), 7.

84 For example, the Irish Travellers Movement in Britain, the Irish Traveller Movement, the National Romany Rights Association and the Scottish Gypsy/Traveller Association.

85 Clark and Greenfield, *Here to Stay*, 55–6.

86 M. Porter and B. Taylor, 'Gypsies and Travellers', in P. Thane (ed.), *A social history of equalities* (London, 2007), 25.

87 D. Hawes, *Gypsies, Travellers and the health service: A study in inequality* (Bristol, 1997), 6.

88 The same was true for other social issues. For the poor health of Travellers, their difficulties and agency in accessing services see R. Pahl and M. Vaille, *Health and health care among Travellers* (Canterbury, 1986); Hawes, *Gypsies, Travellers and the health service*; and G. Parry, P. van Cleemput and J. Peters *et al.*, 'The health status of Gypsies and Travellers in England: Summary of a report to the Department of Health' (Sheffield, 2004).

89 Lord Swann, *Education for all: The report on the education of children from ethnic minority groups* (London, 1985).

90 M. J. Taylor, *Worlds Apart? A review of research into the education of pupils of Cypriot, Italian, Ukrainian and Vietnamese origin, Liverpool blacks and Gypsies* (Windsor, 1988), xi.

91 *Ibid.*, 355–6.

92 K. Bhopal, 'Gypsy Travellers and education: Changing needs and changing perceptions', *British Journal of Education Studies* (2004), 50.

93 J. Butler, 'Gypsies and the personal social services', University of East Anglia Social Work Monograph, 17 (1983), 13.

94 Mrs Heart, quoted in Bhopal, 'Gypsy Travellers and education', 55. Original emphasis.
95 Office of Her Majesty's Chief Inspector of Schools, *The education of travelling children* (London, 1996).
96 For examples of cultural resource packs and publications for schools and Traveller children see S. Naylor and K. Wild-Smith, *Broadening horizons: Education and travelling children* (Essex, 1997), Wiltshire Traveller Education Service, *A horse for Joe* (Trowbridge, 1993); Norfolk Traveller Education Service, *1–10 Counting* (Norwich, 1993).
97 An analysis of good practice can be found in K. Bhopal *et al.*, 'Working towards inclusive education: Aspects of good practice for Gypsy Traveller pupils', DfEE Research Report RR238, and 'Gypsy Travellers and education: Changing needs and changing perceptions', *British Journal of Education Studies* (2004), 47–63.
98 T. Acton and D. Kenrick, 'The education of Gypsy/Traveller children in Great Britain and Northern Ireland', in Liegeois, *School provision*, 138.
99 ACERT, *'Education of Gypsy and Traveller children'*, 127. Original emphasis.
100 Liegeois, *School provision*, 65 and 137.
101 A. R. Ivatts, *Catch 22 Gypsies* (London, 1975), 6 and 18.
102 P. Willis, *Learning to labour: How working class kids get working class jobs* (Westmead, Farnborough, 1977).
103 For different accounts of the split of the National Gypsy Education Council and the formation of ACERT, see National Gypsy Council, 'Annual Report', 1982, 18–20, and Lady Plowden, *Looking back, moving forward* (London, 1982).
104 Liegeois, *School provision*, 117.
105 Acton and Kenrick, 'Education of Gypsy/Traveller children', in Liegeois, *School provision*, 115–17.
106 *Ibid.*, 116.
107 *Ibid.*, 117.

8

Conclusion

Contrary to popular depictions of 'Gypsies' in the twentieth century, Travellers' experiences – socio-economic, cultural and legislative – must be understood in the context of mainstream society, and not as a 'separate people'. As with the settled population they were affected by world wars, increased state intervention, regulation of the environment and lifestyles, the introduction of the welfare state, mechanisation, motorisation, multiculturalism and the rise in consumerism and standards of living. These profound shifts indicate just how closely Travellers' lives were bound up with the wider population.

At the same time the continuities in Travellers' experiences and relationship with the rest of Britain's population were of central importance. Up until 1968, Travellers never had a legally defined 'right to stop', ensuring they always existed on the margins of society, tolerated but rarely accepted. Continued nomadism was conditional on the attitudes of settled society, rather than on any understanding that as commercial nomads Travellers fulfilled certain functions within the economy.

Enduring in popular imagination was the image of the 'true Gypsy' as a eternal nomad, living in a horse-drawn, bow-topped caravan, in a rural area and engaged in traditional crafts. The precariousness of Travellers' position in society was illustrated in the fact that from this romanticised image stemmed a belief that any Traveller not conforming to this stereotype was not a Gypsy, and by extension had no right to a nomadic lifestyle. Since the nineteenth century, there was a gradual move away from romanticising Gypsies towards viewing them as social failures, preying on society and the benefits of the welfare state. While both images of Travellers were current throughout the twentieth century, there was a distinct falling away of the romantic view and a rise of the delinquency view. The decline of the visible markers of 'traditional' Gypsy lifestyle, which had become linked to notions of racial purity, led settled society to assume Travellers no longer had a separate 'racial' identity nor any distinctive cultural capital. Popular and state thinking alike failed to keep pace with Travellers, who adapted to motorisation, urbanisation and changing economic opportunities.

Consequences of this attitude were felt not only by individual Travellers, who received harassment and abuse for failing to live up to an unrealistic ideal, but also in the state's consistent belief that only perpetual nomads were genuine Gypsies. It was codified in law in the 1968 definition of Gypsies as people of a 'nomadic habit of life', and resulted in extreme cases in Travellers being denied their identity in the courts. Travellers not seen as 'true Gypsies' were depicted as social failures, needing intervention – educative, missionary, housing, or welfare – in order to allow them to take their proper place as functioning citizens. Developments in Britain were part of a pan-European trend of assimilation and containment, which saw a move away from racial definitions of hereditary nomads towards categorisations that defined Travellers as a social problem requiring reintegration into society.[1]

Entwined with settled society's inflexible image of Travellers were the structures through which the state interacted with Britain's travelling communities. Over the course of the twentieth century, government expanded its functions to exert influence over many aspects of its citizens' lives. The marginal position of Travellers, and the fact that many aspects of their traditional lifestyles conflicted with new state functions, meant they were more vulnerable to the negative aspects of these changes than most of settled society. Through control of physical space, behaviours and standards of living, government – backed by regulatory bodies and the police – regularised lifestyles and narrowed the definition of what was normal and acceptable. The expansion of the state into welfare provision, while providing material support for Travellers, was largely based on an understanding that they were less deserving of the benefits and more in need of the controlling aspects of welfare provision. Similarly, continued contestation of Travellers' ethnic status, based primarily on faulty understanding of what constituted a 'true Gypsy', succeeded in tempering the impact of the passing of race relations legislation on Travellers.

This is not to argue that the state adopted a concerted policy of repression towards Travellers. In fact central government, particularly in the first half of the century, prided itself on its impartiality and this led to it actively opposing legislation generated by local authorities, which it saw as unfairly targeting a particular minority group. Undermining this position were two trends: central government's almost complete lack of genuine understanding of, or indeed interest in, Traveller communities and their needs; and a structural reliance on local authorities for the implementation of regulations and the delivery of a majority of services.

The former meant that government felt able to argue with a clear conscience that legislative developments such as the 1936 Public Health Act and the Town and Country Planning Acts were not discriminatory and did not impinge on Travellers' lifestyles. The weakness of central government's position was increasingly revealed after 1945 when greater pressure on land, through house building and regulation, created a shortage of stopping places, which by the 1960s had escalated to crisis proportions in certain areas. Travellers were increasingly unable to buy their own land and legally live on it, or travel during the summer and find secure sites to over-winter.

Central government may have felt able to claim impartiality towards minorities, but it was local authorities who were delegated the responsibility of enacting legislation. Local harassment had always been much more of an issue for Travellers, although for much of the twentieth century this was localised, often inconsistent and frequently unsustained. It was through the creation of the planning system and official sites that local authority prejudice was given a virtual free hand. Central government repeatedly refused to take a lead in site provision, despite district councils and local residents consistently demonstrating virulent antipathy to the presence of Travellers in any form. By the end of the century this had caused an absolute shortage of legal caravan pitches that the 1968 Act had been designed to end. Additionally, Travellers were then blamed for unauthorised stopping places and for owning and living on land without planning permission.

It was also at the local level that most aspects of social and welfare provision were delivered. Through both education and housing policies local authorities demonstrated their reluctance to engage positively with Travellers' needs. While there were instances of schooling and welfare policies being used in a heavy-handed and assimilatory manner, their impact was often limited by deep contradictions. As with majority society's treatment of other minority groups, the desire to assimilate was counterbalanced by a reluctance to expend scarce resources and to allow the contact necessary to bring it about. Such attitudes could lead either to withholding services or imposing them on reluctant recipients, but at a lower standard than delivered to mainstream society. When Travellers did not respond in the appropriate manner, by becoming settled and educated citizens, for example, their behaviour was blamed for the 'failure' of policies. In this sense Travellers experienced the 'false promise of assimilation', whereby they were expected to become 'normal' yet largely denied the tools for doing so.

More common than direct attempts to integrate Travellers, was the practice of local authorities moving them out of their area rather than expending official time and money on long-term policies of settlement and 'rehabilitation'. In this sense the discrimination and prejudice exhibited in the localities by authorities and residents alike was largely self-defeating, in that it failed to meet their needs as much as it perpetuated the marginal position of Travellers. What ultimately dictated the relationship of Travellers to the state was the continuing lack of land for sites and lack of political will to provide them. Without these two factors, any attempts by the state to direct the lives and habits of Travellers were severely hampered by their continued, and increasingly enforced, nomadism.

Despite the pressures of the century, Travellers tenaciously maintained a distinct cultural voice and identity, reinforced through a continued commitment to self-employment and flexible economic practices and a guarded engagement with mainstream schooling and welfare services. From the late 1960s some of these trends were challenged by the twin developments of assertive Traveller activism, which started to demand rights and recognition, and the more general shift towards multicultural and anti-racist delivery of services. Travellers were hampered far more than other minority ethnic groups in reaping benefits of this new approach, due to their progressive de-racialisation over the course of the century in the eyes of settled society. Despite work by Traveller and race relations groups, government at all levels retained an ambiguous attitude towards recognising the separate and ethnic status of Travellers. Thus, while some specialist services emerged, in education for example, their impact was often limited and their understanding of Traveller culture was rarely integrated into mainstream service delivery.

Perhaps most significantly, acceptance of 'Traveller' as an ethnic identity separate from anachronistic lifestyle markers failed to permeate popular consciousness and the mainstream media.[2] Antipathy towards Travellers, always present to an extent in settled society, increased over the course of the century. A widening gap between the style of living of Travellers and the mainstream, a reduction in everyday, economic and unproblematic interactions and the growing physical isolation of Travellers on ghettoised official sites, all reinforced a sense of alienation. In popular imagination Travellers became delinquent predators on settled communities, bringing criminality, rubbish and anti-social behaviour, with their presence to be resisted at any price. Thus, at a time when other ethnic minority groups gained recognition and protection under race relation legislation, Travellers lost their separate identity status in popular imagination and only very slowly and partially gained it in law. In a very real sense, therefore, Travellers were, and continued to be, Britain's twilight citizens.

> ... 'real' Romanies are acceptable. But the problem is that unless you have two dangly earrings, a dancing bear tied up outside your barrel topped caravan and walk around bumping into things because you're busy staring into that crystal ball, then Jack and his gang don't accept you are a Romany. Of course I'm a real Romany. If I'm not that, what am I?[3]

Notes

1 Liegeois, *School provision*, 42.
2 For a discussion of the role of the media in perpetuating prejudice against Travellers see R. Morris, 'Nomads and newspapers', in Clark and Greenfield, *Here to stay*, 236–58.
3 Stockins, *On the cobbles*, 104. 'Jack' here referred to the then Labour Home Secretary, Jack Straw.

Select bibliography

Note on newspaper cuttings

Many of the newspaper cuttings referred to in the text come from two particular collections: the Dora Una Radcliffe collection at the Special Collections, Brotherton Library, Leeds University (http:leeds.ac.uk/library/spcoll/brocoll.htm) and the Gypsy Lore Society archive held at Sydney Jones Library, Liverpool University (http://sca.liv.ac.uk/collections/gypsy).

ACERT, *The education of Gypsy and Traveller children: Action-research and co-ordination* (Hatfield, 1993).

Acton, T., *Current changes amongst British Gypsies and their place in international patterns of development*, Proceedings of NGEC Conference, St Peter's College, Oxford, 26–28 March 1971.

——*Gypsy politics and social change: The development of ethnic ideology and pressure politics among British Gypsies from Victorian reformism to Romany nationalism* (London, 1974).

——'Academic success and political failure: A review of modern social science writing in English on Gypsies', Paper presented at Table Rondes des Etudes Tsiganes, Centre International d'Etudes Pedagogiques, Sevres, France (December 1977).

Acton, T. and G. Mundy, *Gypsy politics and Traveller identity* (Hatfield, 1996).

——*Romani culture and Gypsy identity* (Hatfield, 1997).

Adams, B., J. Okely, D. Morgan and D. Smith, *Gypsies and government policy in Britain: A study of the Travellers' way of life in relation to the policies and practices of central and local government* (London, 1975).

Adams, J. W. R., 'Gypsies and other Travellers in Kent: Report of the survey carried out 1951–2 by Kent County Council Planning Department', unpublished, Kent County Council, 1952.

Alder, S., *Work among the Gypsies: Being an account of twelve years mission work amongst the Gypsies* (Chobham, 1893).

Alexander, S., *St. Giles's Fair 1830–1914: Popular culture and the industrial revolution in nineteenth century Oxford* (Oxford, 1970).

Anderson, R., 'Education and society in modern Scotland, a comparative perspective', in R. Lowe (ed.), *History of education, major themes, vol. IV: Studies of education systems* (London and New York, 2000).

Angold, F. H., 'The Gypsy in the post-war world: An introduction to the question', *JGLS*, 23:3–4 (1945), 91–7.

Anon., 'The law as to the Gypsies', *Local Government Journal* (18 July 1896), 465.

Anon., 'Tent or workhouse?', *JGLS*, 3:3 (1909), 278–9.

Anon., 'Glad tidings from Gypsydom', *London City Mission Magazine*, 76 (1911), 173–82.

Anon., 'An Irish Tinker on the road: A glimpse into the life of Ireland's wanderers', *The Sphere* (15 December 1956), 462.

Association for Education in Citizenship, *Education for citizenship in secondary schools* (London, 1955).

Baldwin, S., 'England is the country and the country is England', in J. Giles and T. Middleton (eds), *Writing Englishness* (London and New York, 1995).

Barry, G., 'Schools for Gypsies', *Unesco Courier* (4 April 1958).

Bassett, P., 'A brief history of the Caravan Club of Great Britain and Northern Ireland', Centre for Urban and Regional Studies, University of Birmingham, and Institute of Agricultural History, University of Reading, 1980.

Baugh, G. C., 'Government grants in aid of the rates in England and Wales, 1889–1990', *Historical Research*, 65 (1992), 215–37.

Bauman, Z., *Modernity and the Holocaust* (Cambridge 1989).

——*Modernity and Ambivalence* (Cambridge, 1991).

——'Allosemitism: Premodern, modern, postmodern', in B. Cheyette and L. Marcus (eds), *Modernity, Culture and 'the Jew'* (Cambridge, 1998).

Beach, A. and N. Tiratsoo, 'The planners and the public', in M. Daunton (ed.), *The Cambridge Urban History of Britain, Vol. III, 1840–1950* (Cambridge, 2000).

Behlmer, G. K., 'The Gypsy problem in Victorian England', *Victorian Studies*, 28:2 (1985), 231–53.

Bellamy, C., *Administering central and local government relations, 1871–1919: The Local Government Board in its fiscal and cultural context* (Manchester, 1988).

Bercovici, K., *The Story of the Gypsies* (London, 1929).

Berlin, J., *The Gypsies of the New Forest* (London, 1960).

Berlin, S., *Dromengro: Man of the road* (London, 1971).

Bhopal, K., 'Gypsy Travellers and education: Changing needs and changing perceptions', *British Journal of Education Studies* (2004), 47–63.

Blunden, E., 'How much that we loved is going or gone', in J. Giles and T. Middleton (eds), *Writing Englishness* (London and New York, 1995).

Bognador, V., 'Power and participation', *Oxford Review of Education*, 5:2 (1979), 157–8.

Booth, C., *Life and labour of the people of London* (London, 1902).

Borrow, G., *Lavengro: The scholar, the Gypsy, the priest* (London, 1851).

——*The Romany rye: A sequel to Lavengro* (London, 1857).

Bourke, J., *Working class cultures in Britain* (London and New York, 1993).

Boyes, G., *The imagined village: Culture, ideology and the English folk revival* (Manchester, 1993).

Bradburn, E., *Dr Dora Esther Yates: An appreciation* (Liverpool, 1975).

Bradley, F. G., 'The control of moveable dwellings including the effects of the Town and Country Planning Act, 1947', *The Sanitarian*, 57:7 (1949), 202–4.

Brant, H., 'The Control of Holiday Camps', *Journal of the Royal Sanitary Institute*, 58:5 (1937), 113–14.

Branwell, G. B., *The tramp: A Romany in the fields* (London, 1929).

Brewer, E., 'Gypsy encampments in the heart of London', *Sunday at Home* (1896), 113–14.

Bridges, L., 'Tory education: Exclusion and the Black child', *Race and Class*, 36:1 (1994), 33–48.

Brown, I., 'Roms are Droms', *JGLS*, 7:3–4 (1928), 170–7.

Brown, J., 'Social control and the modernisation of social policy, 1890–1920', in P. Thane (ed.), *The origins of British social policy* (London, 1978).

Brubaker, R., *Citizenship and nationhood in France and Germany* (Harvard, 1992).

Burman, B. L., 'Gypsies: Free, romantic, mysterious', *Reader's Digest*, 70 (1957), 26–32.

Butler, J., 'Gypsies and the personal social services', University of East Anglia Social Work Monograph, 17 (1983).

Calder, A., *The people's war: Britain 1939–1945* (London, 1999 edn).

Camm, E., 'Hurtwood school', *JGLS*, 13:3 (1934), 221–2.

Carby, H., 'Schooling in Babylon', in Centre for Contemporary Cultural Studies, *The empire strikes back* (London, 1982).

Carew, F. W. (ed.), *Number 747: Being the autobiography of a Gypsy* (Bristol, 1891).

Casey, J. (ed.), *Gypsies of the New Forest* (London, 1960).

Church, R., 'The raggle-taggle Gypsies', in R. Church, *Green Life* (London, 1945).

Clark C., and M. Greenfields, *Here to stay: The Gypsies and Travellers of Britain* (Hatfield, 2006).

Clyde-Mackenzie, T., 'Some aspects of the slum problem', *Journal of the Royal Sanitary Institute*, 54:6 (1934), 323–30.

Collins, M., 'The sub-culture of poverty: A response to MacCarthy', in M. McCann, S. O' Siochain, and J. Ruane (eds), *Irish Travellers: Culture and ethnicity* (Belfast, 1994).

Connors, J. P., 'Seven weeks in childhood: An autobiography', in J. Sandford, *Gypsies* (London, 1973).

Cottaar, A., L. Lucassen and W. Willems, 'Justice or injustice? A survey of government policy towards Gypsies and caravan dwellers in western Europe in the nineteenth and twentieth Centuries', *Immigrants and Minorities*, 11:1 (1992), 42–66.

Cowles, F. I., *Gypsy caravan* (London, 1948).

——*Vagabond pilgrimage: Being the record of a journey from East Anglia to the West of England* (London, 1950).

Crabb, J., *The Gypsies' advocat:. Or observations on the origins, character, manner and habits, of the English Gypsies: to which are added many interesting ancedotes on the success that has attended the plans of several benevolent individuals who anxiously desire their conversion to God* (London, 1832).

Cripps, J., *Accommodation for Gypsies: A report on the working of the Caravan Sites Act, 1968* (London, 1976).

Croft-Cooke, R., *The moon in my pocket: Life with the Romanies* (London, 1948).

——*A few Gypsies* (London, 1955).

——*The happy highways* (London, 1967).

——'Affairs of Egypt, 1892–1906', *JGLS*, 2 (1908), 358–84.

——'Affairs of Egypt, 1907', *JGLS*, 2 (1908), 121–41.

——'Affairs of Egypt, 1908', *JGLS*, 3:4 (1909), 276–98.

——'Gypsies or potters of Natland, near Kendal', *JGLS*, 3:3 (1909), 283–4.

Crowther, M. A., 'The tramp', in R. Porter (ed.), *Myths of the English* (Cambridge, 1992), 91–113.

Cuttriss, F., *Romany life, experienced and observed during many years of friendly intercourse with the Gypsies* (London, 1915).

Dalton, H., *The fateful years* (London, 1957).

——*High tide and after: Memoirs, 1945–60* (London, 1962).

Davies, J., *Tales of the old Gypsies* (n.p., 1999).

Davin, A., *Growing up poor: Home, school and street in London, 1870–1914* (London, 1996).

Davis, J., 'Central government and the towns', in M. Daunton (ed.), *The Cambridge urban history of Britain, vol. III, 1840–1950* (Cambridge, 2000).

Dawson, R., *Crime and prejudice: Traditional Travellers* (Blackwell, 2000).

——*God's travelling children: Traditional Travellers coming to terms with their ethnicity* (Blackwell, Derbyshire, 2002).

De Baraclai Levy, J., *As Gypsies wander* (London, 1955).

——*Wanderers in the New Forest* (London, 1958).

Dodds, N., *Gypsies, didikois and other Travellers* (London, 1966).

Dunleary, P., *The politics of mass housing in Britain, 1945–75* (Oxford, 1981).

Eiber, L., 'The persecution of the Sinti and Roma in Munich 1933–1945', in S. Tebbutt (ed.), *Sinti and Roma: Gypsies in German-speaking society and literature* (New York and Oxford, 1998).

Ellis, H., *The criminal London* (London, 1895).

Evans, E., *Through the years with Romany* (London, 1946).

Evens, G. B., *A Romany on the trail* (Epworth, 1942).

——*A Romany in the country* (Epworth, 1944).

Fairfax, R., 'Stop hounding the Gypsies', *Yorkshire Life Illustrated*, 10:11 (1956), 30–1.

Farre, R. A., *Time from the world* (London, 1962).

Feldman, D., *Englishmen and Jews: Social relations and political culture, 1840–1914* (New Haven, CT, 1994).

——'Jews and the state in Britain', in M. Brenner (ed.), *Two nations: British and German Jews in comparative perspective* (Tubingen, *c.*1999).

——'Was modernity good for the Jews?', in B. Cheyette and L. Marcus (eds), *Modernity, culture and 'the Jew'* (Cambridge, 1998).

Field, F., *Inequality in Britain: Freedom, welfare and the state* (Glasgow, 1981).

Fings, K., H. Heuss, F. Sparing and H. Asseo, *From 'race science' to the camps: The Gypsies during the second world war* (Hatfield, 1997).

Fonseca, I., *Bury me standing: The Gypsies and their journey* (New York, 1995).

Foot, M., *Aneurin Bevan, vol. I* (London, 1962).

Fowler, S. (pseud.), 'My Gypsy patients', *The Countryman*, 41:1 (1950), 37–40.

Franklin-Gisborne, A. C., 'Caravan homes, 1959', *The Sanitarian*, 68:2 (1959), 94–116.

Fraser, A. M., 'The Gypsy problem: A survey of post-war developments', *JGLS*, 3:3–4 (1953), 82–100.

Freedan, M., 'The stranger at the feast: Ideology and public policy in twentieth century Britain', *Twentieth Century British History*, 1:1 (1990), 9–34.

Freeman, G. P., 'Migration and the political economy of the welfare state', *Annals of the American Academy of Political and Social Science*, 485 (1986).

Fryer, P., *Aspects of Black history* (London, 1993).

Gardner, P., '"Our schools, their schools": The case of Eliza Duckworth and John Stevenson', in R. Lowe (ed.), *History of education, major themes, vol. II: Education in its social context* (London and New York, 2000).

Garside, P., 'London and the Home Counties', in F. M. L. Thompson (ed.), *The Cambridge social history of Britain, 1750–1950, vol. 1: Regions and communities* (Cambridge, 1990).

Gentleman, H., 'The SDD and the travelling people of Scotland', in T. Acton (ed.), *Current changes amongst British Gypsies and their place in international development*, Proceedings of NGEC Conference, St Peter's College, Oxford, 26–28 March 1971.

Gentleman, H. and S. Swift (eds), *Scotland's travelling people* (Edinburgh, 1971).

Gibbins, H. E. J., *Gypsies of the New Forest and other tales* (Bournemouth, 1909).

Gmelch, S., *Nan: The life of an Irish Traveller woman* (London, 1986).

Godfrey, E., *The New Forest* (n.p., 1926).

Godfrey, F. L., 'The control of camping grounds in the interests of public health, with special reference to seaside camping grounds', *Journal of the Royal Sanitary Institute*, 54:7 (1935), 412–18.

Goodall, N., *A History of the London Missionary Society, 1985–1945* (London, 1954).

Grant, E. D., 'Some problems concerning hutted camps and temporary dwellings', *The Sanitarian*, 57:10 (1949), 339–40.

Groome, F. H., *In Gipsy tents* (East Ardsley, 1973).

Grosvenor, I., *Assimilating identities: Racism and educational policy in post-1945 Britain* (London, 1997).

——'A different reality: Education and the racialisation of the Black child', in R. Lowe (ed.), *History of education, major themes, vol. IV: Studies of education systems* (London and New York, 2000).

Hales, L. G., 'Control of moveable dwellings under planning schemes', *Journal of the Town Planning Institute*, Nov.–Dec. (1944).

Hall, C., *Civilising subjects: Metropole and colony in the English imagination, 1830–1867* (Cambridge, 1992).

Hall, G., *The Gypsy's parson: His experiences and adventures* (London, 1915).

Hancock, I. F., *The pariah syndrome* (Ann Arbor, MI, 1987).

Hansen, R., 'The politics of citizenship in 1940s Britain: The British Nationality Act', *Twentieth Century British History*, 10:1 (1999), 67–95.

Hanson, H., *The canal boatmen, 1760–1914* (Manchester, 1981).

Hardy, D. and C. Ward, *Arcadia for all: The legacy of a makeshift landscape* (London, 1984).

Harris, J., 'Political ideas and the debate on state welfare, 1940–1945', in H. Smith (ed.), *War and social change: British society in the second world war* (Manchester, 1986).

——'Society and the state in twentieth century Britain', in F. M. L. Thompson (ed.), *The Cambridge social history of Britain, 1750–1950, vol. III, Social agencies and institutions* (Cambridge, 1990).

Harvey, E., 'Wartime work of English Gypsies', *JGLS*, 21:3–4 (1942), 81–7.

Hasegawa, J., 'The rise and fall of radical reconstruction in 1940s Britain', *Twentieth Century British History*, 10:2 (1999), 137–61.

Hawes, D., *Gypsies, Travellers and the health service: A study in inequality* (Bristol, 1997).

Hawes, D. and B. Perez, *The Gypsy and the state: The ethnic cleansing of British society* (Oxford, 1995).

Hayes, N., 'Making homes by machines. Images, ideas and myths in the diffusion of non-traditional housing in Britain, 1942–54', *Twentieth Century British History*, 10:3 (1999), 282–309.

Healey, H. J., 'The need for and control of moveable dwellings', *Journal of the Royal Sanitary Institute*, 70:5 (1950), 560.

Heathorn, S., 'An English paradise to regain? Ebenezer Howard, the Town and Country Planning Association and English ruralism', *Rural History, Economy, Society, Culture*, 11:1 (2000), 113–28.

Himmelfarb, G., *The idea of poverty: England in the early industrial age* (New York, 1984).

Hodder, E., *George Smith (of Coalville): The story of an enthusiast* (London, 1896).

Holmes, C., 'The German-Gypsy question in Britain, 1904–6', in K. Lunn (ed.), *Hosts, immigrants and minorities: Historical responses to newcomers in British society, 1870–1914* (New York, 1980).

——*A tolerant country? Immigrants, refugees and minorities in Britain* (London, 1991).

Holroyd, M., *Augustus John* (London and Cape, 1975).

Howard, Dr, 'Report on the Gypsies and other Travellers in Hampshire' (unpublished, Hampshire Association of Parish Councils, 1960).

Hoyland, J., *A historical survey of the customs, habits and present state of the Gypsies; designed to develop the origin of this singular people and to promote the amelioration of their condition* (York, 1816).

Hughes, C., *West with the Tinkers: A journey through Wales with vagrants* (London, 1954).

Humphrey, W. O., 'The caravan problem: The effect of the new planning Act', *Town and Country Planning*, 16:64 (1948–49), 239–42.

Illich, I., *The right to useful employment* (London, 1978).

Ivatts, A. R., *Catch 22 Gypsies* (London, 1975).

Jefferies, R., *Field and hedgerow, being the last essays of R. J., collected by his widow* (London, 1904).

Jennings, R., *Men of the lanes: The autobiography of the tramps' parson* (London, 1958).

Joad, C. E. M., *A charter for ramblers* (London, 1934).

Johnson, R., 'Educational policy and social control in early Victorian England', in R. Lowe (ed.), *History of education, major themes, vol. II: Education in its social context* (London and New York, 2000).

Jones, D., *Crime, protest, community and policing in nineteenth century Britain* (London, 1982).

Jones, E. A., *Yorkshire Gypsy fairs, customs and caravans, 1885–1985* (Beverley, 1986).

Jones, G., *Social hygiene in twentieth century Britain* (Beckenham, 1986).

Joppke, C., *Immigration and the nation state: The United States, Germany and Great Britain* (Oxford, 1999).

Joshi, H. and B. Carter, 'The role of Labour in the creation of a racist Britain', *Race and Class*, 25:3 (1984), 53–70.

Joyce, N., *Traveller: An autobiography* (Dublin, 1985).

Keating, P. J. (ed.), *Into unknown England, 1866–1913* (Manchester, 1976).

Keenan, J. and D. Hines (eds), *In our own way: Tales from Belfast Travellers* (Belfast, 2000).

Keet-Black, J. (ed.), *The Sussex Gypsy diaries, 1898–1926* (Romany and Traveller Family History Society, n.p., 1999).

Kenrick, D. and S. Bakewell, *On the verge: The Gypsies of England* (London, 1990).

Kenrick, D. and C. Clark, *Moving on: The Gypsies and Travellers of Britain* (Hatfield, 1975).

Kenrick, D. S. and G. Puxon, *The destiny of Europe's Gypsies* (London, 1972).

Kornblum, W. and P. Lichter, 'Urban Gypsies and the culture of poverty', *Urban Life and Culture*, Spring (1972), 239–52.

Laing, E., *Moving stories: Traveller women write* (London, n.d.)

Law, B., *Times to remember: A further collection of the travelling people and their way of life* (Strensall, 1993).

Lazell, D., *From the forest I came: The story of Gypsy Rodney Smith* (n.p., 1970).

——*Gypsy from the forest: A new biography of the international evangelist Gypsy Smith, 1860–1947* (Bridgend, 1997).

Lee, S., *One in a million: A story of hardship, endurance and triumph in a Traveller family, 1938–* (Colchester, 1999).

Leitch, R. (ed.), *The Book of Sandy Stewart* (Edinburgh, 1988).

Leland, C., *The Gypsies* (Boston, 1924).

Lewy, G., *The Nazi persecution of the Gypsies* (Oxford, 2000).

Liegeios, J. P., *Gypsies and Travellers* (Strasbourg, 1987).

——*School provision for ethnic minorities: The Gypsy paradigm* (Hatfield, 1998).

Liegeois, J. P. and N. Gheorghe, *Roma/Gypsies: A European minority* (London, 1995).

Lombrosco, C., *Crime: Its causes and remedies* (London, 1910).

Loveridge, G., *Biography of Branwell 'Romany' Evans* (Huddersfield, 1995).

Lowe, R., 'The second world war, consensus and the foundation of the welfare state', *Twentieth Century British History*, 1:2 (1990), 152–82.

——*The welfare state in Britain since 1945* (London and New York, 1999).

Lowerson, J., 'Battles for the countryside', in F. Gloversmith (ed.), *Class, culture and social change* (Brighton, 1980).

Lucas, E. V. (ed.), *The open road: A little book for wayfarers* (London, 1905).

Lucassen, J. and L. (eds), *Migration etc.* (Frankfurt am Main, 1997).

Lucassen, L., 'A blind spot: Migratory and travelling groups in western European historiography', *International Review of Social History*, 38 (1993), 209–35.

Lucassen, L., W. Willems and A. Cottaar (eds), *Gypsies and other itinerant groups: A socio-historical approach* (Amsterdam, 1998).

Lunn, K. (ed.), *Hosts, immigrants and minorities: Historical responses to newcomers in British society 1870–1914* (New York, 1980).

McCann, M., S. O'Siochain, and J. Ruane (eds), *Irish Travellers: Culture and ethnicity* (Belfast, 1994).

McCormick, A., *The Tinkler-Gypsies* (London, 1907).

——'The Tinkler problem', *JGLS*, 12:3 (1933), 142.

McCulloch, G., *Failing the ordinary child? The theory and practice of working class secondary education* (Buckingham and Philadelphia, 1998).

McEvoy, P. A., *The gorse and the briar* (London, 1938).

McKay, G., *Senseless acts of beauty: Cultures of resistance since the sixties* (London, 1996).

McMillan, A., *Gipsy Hawkins: Shoeblack, cobbler, 'boy preacher', evangelist and soul winner* (n.p., 1939).

McNab, D. J. N., 'The shack dwellers of the New Forest: Their physical state and social characteristics', *Journal of the Royal Sanitary Institute*, 72:6 (1952), 720.

McVeigh, R., 'The specificity of Irish racism', *Race and Class*, 33:4 (1992), 31–47.

MacCarthy, P., 'The sub-culture of poverty reconsidered', in M. McCann, S. O'Siochain and J. Ruane (eds), *Irish Travellers: Culture and ethnicity* (Belfast, 1994).

MacColl, E. and P. Seeger, *I'm a freeborn man, and other original radio ballads and songs of British workingmen, Gypsies, prizefighters, teenagers – and contemporary songs of struggle and conscience* (New York, 1968).

——*Travellers' songs from England and Scotland* (London, 1977).

——*Till doomsday in the afternoon: The folklore of a family of Scots Travellers, the Stewarts of Blairgowrie* (Manchester, 1986).

MacDonagh, M., 'Nomadism in Irish traveller identity', in M. McCann, S. O'Siochain and J. Ruane (eds), *Irish Travellers: Culture and ethnicity* (Belfast, 1994).

Machin, G. I. T., 'British churches and social issues, 1945–60', *Twentieth Century British History*, 7:3 (1996), 345–70.

MacLaughlin, J., 'The evolution of anti-Traveller racism in Ireland', *Race and Class*, 37:3 (1996), 47–63.

MacRitchie, D., 'Irish tinkers and their language', *JGLS*, 1:6 (1908).

Mackintosh, J. M., *Trends of opinion about public health* (London, 1953).

Malleson, H., 'A sweet street sanctuary', *JGLS*, 4:1 (1911), 55–60.

——*Napoloen Boswell: Tales of the tents* (London, 1913).

Mandler, P., 'Against "Englishness": English culture and the limits to rural nostalgia, 1850–1940', *Royal Historical Society Transactions*, 7 (1997), 155–75.

Marsden, W. E., 'Rooting racism into the educational experience of childhood and youth in the nineteenth and twentieth centuries', in R. Lowe (ed.), *History of education, major themes, vol. III: Studies in learning and teaching* (London and New York, 2000).

Marsh, J., *Back to the land: The pastoral impulse in England, from 1880–1914* (n.p., 1982).

Marshall, T. H., *Citizenship and social class and other essays* (London, 1950).

Mayall, D., 'Itinerant minorities in England and Wales', Ph.D. dissertation, Sheffield University, 1981.

——*Gypsy Travellers in nineteenth century society* (Cambridge, 1988).

——'Defining the Gypsy: Ethnicity, "race" and representation', Paper to Leiden University Foundation Centennial Conference, September 1990.

——*English Gypsies and State Policies* (Hatfield, 1995).

—— 'Gypsy studies: A new era?', *Immigrants and Minorities*, 17:2 (1998), 57–67.

——*Gypsy Identities, 1500 to 2000: From Egipcyans and moon-men to the ethnic Romany* (London and New York, 2004).

Miller, P., 'Historiography of compulsory schooling: What's the problem?', in R. Lowe (ed.), *History of education, major themes, vol. II: Education in its social context* (London and New York, 2000).

——'Education and the state: The uses of Marxist and feminist approaches in the writings of histories of schooling', in R. Lowe (ed.), *History of education, major themes, vol. II: Education in its social context* (London and New York, 2000).

Mingay, G. E., *The Victorian countryside* (London, 1981).

Ministry of Housing and Local Government, *Gypsies and other Travellers* (London, 1967).

Mitchell, E. V., *The pleasures of walking* (Bourne End, Bucks, 1934).

Morris, R. and L. Clements (eds), *Gaining ground: Law reform for Gypsies and Travellers* (Hatfield, 1999).

Morwood, V. S., *Our Gypsies in city, tent and van* (London, 1885).

Murphy, T., *A history of the Showman's Guild, 1889–1949* (Oldham, 1949).

Murray, H., *Sixty years an evangelist: An intimate Study Of Gypsy Smith* (London, 1937).

Naylor, S. and K. Wild-Smith, *Broadening horizons: Education and travelling children* (Essex, 1997).

Neill, E., 'Conceptions of citizenship in twentieth century Britain', *Twentieth Century British History*, 17: 3 (2006), 424–38.

Newsam, Sir F., *The Home Office* (London, 1954).

Noonan, P., 'Policy making and Travellers in Northern Ireland', in M. McCann, S. O'Siochain and J. Ruane (eds), *Irish Travellers: Culture and ethnicity* (Belfast, 1994).

Office of Her Majesty's Chief Inspector of Schools, *The education of travelling children* (London, 1996).

Okely, J., 'Gypsy women: Models in conflict', in S. Ardener (ed.), *Perceiving women* (London, 1975).

——'Trading stereotypes: The case of England's Gypsies', in S. Wallman (ed.), *Ethnicity at work* (London, 1979).

——*The Traveller-Gypsies* (Cambridge, 1983).

——'An anthropological perspective on Irish Travellers', in M. McCann, S. O'Siochain and J. Ruane (eds), *Irish Travellers: Culture and ethnicity* (Belfast, 1994).

Orchard, D., *The life and story of May Orchard* (Exeter, 1995).

Pahl, R. and M. Vaille, *Health and health care among Travellers* (Canterbury, 1986).

Parry, G., P. van Cleemput and J. Peters *et al.*, 'The health status of Gypsies and Travellers in England: Summary of a report to the Department of Health' (Sheffield, 2004).

Pateman, C., 'The patriarchal welfare state', in A. Gutmann (ed.), *Democracy and the welfare state* (Princeton, 1988).

Patterson, S., *Dark strangers: A sociological study of the absorption of a recent West Indian migrant group in Brixton, South London* (London, 1963).

Pellew, J., *The Home Office, 1848–1914: From clerks to bureaucrats* (London, 1982).

Perkin, H., *The rise of professional society: England since 1880* (London and New York, 1990).

Petulengro, L., *Romany boy* (London, 1979).

Petulengro, X., *A Romany life* (London, 1935).

——*Romany hints for hikers; by Gipsy Petulengro* (London, 1936).

——*Britain through Gypsy's eyes* (London, 1937).

Phelan, J., *We follow the roads* (London, 1949).

——*Wagon wheels* (London, 1951).

Pierson, C., *Beyond the welfare state? The new political economy of welfare* (Pennsylvania, 1998).

Plowden, Lady, *Looking back, moving forward* (London, 1982).

Pollard, S. and C. Holmes (eds), *Essays in the economic and social history of South Yorkshire* (Barnsley, 1976).

Porter, M. and B. Taylor, 'Gypsies and Travellers', in P. Thane *et al.*, *Equalities in Britain, 1946–2006* (London, 2007).

Poulter, S., *Ethnicity, law and human rights: The English experience* (Oxford, 1998).

Puxon, G., *Roma: Europe's Gypsies* (London, 1987).

Rao, A. (ed.), *The other nomads: Peripatetic minorities in cross-cultural perspective* (Prospect Heights, 1986).

Reeve, D., *Smoke in the lanes* (London, 1958).

——*No place like home* (London, 1960).

——*Whichever way we turn* (1964).

——'The changing life of the Romany', *Country Life* (17 October 1963), 38–9.

Rehfisch, R. (ed.), *Gypsies, Tinkers and other Travellers* (London, 1975).

Reiss, C., *The education of travelling children* (London, 1975).

Ridholls, J., *Romany Revival* (London, 1980).

Robbins, D., 'Citizenship and nationhood in Britain', Working Paper, New Ethnicities Unit, University of East London, May 1995.

Roddis, R. J., *The law relating to caravans* (London, 1960).

Russell, M., *Five women and a caravan* (London, 1911).

Said, E., *Orientalism* (Harmondsworth, 1979).

Sampson, A., *The scholar Gypsy: The quest for a family secret* (London, 1997).

Sampson, J., 'The German Gypsies in Blackpool', *JGLS* (1907), 111–21.

——*The dialect of the Gypsies of Wales* (Oxford, 1926).

——(ed.), *The wind on the heath: A Gypsy anthology* (London, 1930).

Samuel, R., 'Comers and goers', in H. J. Dyos and M. Wolf (eds), *The Victorian city: Images and reality, vol. I* (1973).

——*East End underworld: Chapters in the life of Arthur Harding* (London, 1981).

——(ed.), *Village life and labour* (1975).

Sandford, J., *Gypsies* (London, 1973).

Saunders, P., J. Clarke and S. Kendall *et al.* (eds), *Gypsies and Travellers in their own words: Words and pictures of travelling life* (Leeds, 2000).

Scott, J. C., *Weapons of the weak: Everyday forms of peasant resistance* (New Haven, CT and London, 1985).

Semple, D., *Joy in living: An autobiography* (Glasgow, 1957).

Sexton, R. D., 'Travelling people in the United Kingdom in the first half of the twentieth century', Ph.D. dissertation, University of Southampton, 1989.

Seymour, J. (ed.), *The book of Boswell, autobiography of a Gypsy* (Harmondsworth, 1975).

Shaw, C. and M. Chaise (eds), *The imagined past: History and nostalgia* (Manchester, 1989).

Sibley, D., *Outsiders in urban society* (Oxford, 1981).

——'Persistence or change? Conflicting interpretations of peripheral minorities', *Environment and Planning D: Society and Space*, 4 (1986), 57–70.

Smith, B., *The whole art of caravanning* (London, 1907).

——*Caravan Days* (London, 1914).

Smith, G., *Gypsy life* (London, 1880).

——*I've been a' Gypsying, or rambles among Gypsies and their children in their tents and vans* (London, 1883).

Smith, R., *Gypsy Smith: His life and work* (New York, 1901).

——*From Gypsy van to evangelist* (n.p., 1909).

Smith, S. (ed.), *John Lings: Memories of a travelling life* (Newcastle-under-Lyme, 1992).

Southampton Committee, *For the amelioration of the state of the Gypsies; and for their religious instruction, and conversion: From August 1827 to May 1832* (Southampton, 1832).

Spence, L., 'The Scottish Tinkler-Gypsies', *Scotland's Magazine* (February 1956), 20–4.

Spring, J., 'Education as a form of social control', in R. Lowe (ed.), *History of education, major themes, vol. II: Education in its social context* (London and

New York, 2000).

Squires, P., *Anti-social policy: Welfare, ideology and the disciplinary state* (Hemel Hempstead, 1990).

Stables, G., *The gentleman Gypsy* (London, 1886).

Stanley, B., *Memories of the marsh: A Traveller life in Kent* (Romany and Traveller Family History Society, 1998).

Stapleton, J., 'Citizenship versus patriotism in twentieth century England', *The Historical Journal*, 48:1 (2005), 151–78.

Stedman Jones, G., *Outcast London: A study in the relationship between classes in Victorian society* (Oxford, 1971).

Stockins, J., *On the cobbles: The life of a bare-knuckle Gypsy warrior* (Edinburgh and London, 2000).

Stone, J. F. M. H., *Caravanning and camping: Experiences and adventures in a living-van and in the open air. With hints and facts for would-be caravanners* (London, 1912).

Strachey, J., 'The Gypsy scandal and the danger to the commons', *National Review*, 59 (1912), 459–72.

Strange, D., *Born on the straw: A Gypsy life* (London, 1968).

Strauss, D., 'Anti-Gypsyism in German society and literature', in S. Tebbutt (ed.), *Sinti and Roma: Gypsies in German-speaking society and literature* (New York and Oxford, 1998).

Street, B., *The savage in literature: Representations of primitive society in English fiction, 1858–1920* (London, 1975).

Swann, Lord, *Education for all: The report on the education of children from ethnic minority groups* (London, 1985).

Swinstead, J. H., *A parish on wheels* (London, 1897).

Symons, A., 'In praise of Gypsies', *JGLS*, 1:4 (1908), 295–9.

Szreter, S., 'A central role for local government? The example of late Victorian Britain', *History and Policy*, May (2002), www.historyandpolicy.org/archive/policy-paper-01.html.

Tabili, L., 'The construction of racial difference in twentieth century Britain: The Special Restriction (Coloured Alien Seamen) Order, 1925', *Journal of British Studies* 33 (1994), 54–98.

Tain, P., *Criminal Justice and Public Order Act: A practical guide* (London, 1994).

Taylor, B., 'Travellers in Britain: a minority and the state', *Historical Research*, 77:198 (2004), 575–96.

Taylor, B., J. Stewart and M. Powell, 'Central and Local Government and the Provision of Municipal Medicine, 1919–1939', *English Historical Review*, 122:496, 397–426.

Taylor, M. J., *Worlds Apart? A review of research into the education of pupils of Cypriot, Italian, Ukrainian and Vietnamese origin, Liverpool blacks and Gypsies* (Windsor, 1988).

Thane, P., 'Government and society in England and Wales', in F. M. L. Thompson (ed.), *The Cambridge social history of Britain, 1750–1950. Vol. 3, Social agencies and institutions* (Cambridge, 1990).

Thesleff, A., 'Report on the Gypsy problem', *JGLS*, 5:2 (1911), 81–107, and *JGLS*, 6:4 (1911), 266.

Thomas, D., *An underworld of war: Spivs, deserters, racketeers and civilians in the second world war* (London, 2003).

Thompson, E. P., *The making of the English working class* (London, 1963).

Thompson, F. M. L., 'Town and city', in F. M. L. Thompson (ed.), *The Cambridge social history of Britain, vol. 1: Regions and communities* (Cambridge, 1990).

Thompson, T. W., 'Affairs of Egypt, 1909', *JGLS*, 2 (1911), 113–34.

Thomson, M., *The problem of mental deficiency, eugenics, democracy and social policy, c.1870–1959* (Oxford, 1998).

Thurlow, R., 'The evolution of the mythical British fifth column, 1939–46' *Twentieth Century British History*, 10:4 (1999), 477–99.

Titmuss, R. M., *Problems of social policy* (London and Nendeln, 1952).

——'The limits of the welfare state', *New Left Review*, 27 (1964), 28–37.

Trentman, F., 'Civilisation and its discontents: English neo-romanticism and the transformation of anti-modernism in twentieth century culture', *Journal of Contemporary History*, 29 (1994), 583–625.

Tucker, D. E., 'Moveable dwellings', *The Sanitarian*, 54:11 (1946), 2831.

Vesey Fitzgerald, B., *Gypsies of Britain* (Newton Abbot, 1973).

Voet, R., *Feminism and citizenship* (London, 1998).

Vorspan, R., 'Vagrancy and the New Poor Law in late Victorian and Edwardian England', *English Historical Review*, 92 (1977), 59–81.

Wallace, D., *Walking, literature and English culture: The origins and use of the peripatetic in the nineteenth century* (Oxford, 1993).

Walton, J. K., 'Municipal government and the holiday industry in Blackpool', in J. Walton and J. Walvin (eds), *Leisure in Britain, 1780–1939* (Manchester, 1983).

Warren, J. L., *Gentlemen Gypsy* (London, 1899).

Watts-Dunton, T., 'The Tarno Rye', *The Athenaeum*, 3878 (1902), 243–6.

——'Gypsies and Gypsying', *Saturday Review*, 104 (1907), 695–6 and 724–6.

Webb, G. E. C., *Gypsies, the secret people* (London, 1960).

Weight, R. and A. Beach (eds), *The right to belong: Citizenship and national identity in Britain, 1940–60* (London, 1998).

Weylland, J. M., *Round the tower; or the story of the London City Mission* (London, 1875).

White, J., *The worst street in London: Campbell Bunk, Islington between the wars* (London and Boston, 1986).

Whyte, B., *The yellow in the broom* (Edinburgh, 1979).

——*Red rowans and wild honey* (Edinburgh, 1990).

Willems, W., 'The return of the Egyptian. The stigmatization of "Gypsies" in western Europe, 1783–1945', Working Paper for the New School of Social Research Centre for the Studies of Social Change, New York, 1993.

——*In search of the true Gypsy: From enlightenment to final solution* (London, 1997).

Williams, F., *Social policy: A critical introduction. Issues of race, gender and class* (Cambridge, 1989).

Willis, P., *Learning to labour: How working class kids get working class jobs* (Westmead, Farnborough, 1977).

Wilkinson, T. W., 'Van-dwelling London', in G. R. Sims (ed.), *Living London 3* (London, 1903).
Wilson, N., *Gypsies and gentlemen: The life and times of the leisure caravan* (London, 1986).
Winstedt, E. O., 'Gypsy civilisation',' *JGLS*, 1 (1908), 319–49.
Wood, M. F., *In the life of a Romany Gypsy* (London, 1973).
Woolmer, D. L., 'Gipsies in their Winter Quarters', *The Quiver* (1903), 530–5.
Wordie, R., 'A triumph of middle class idealism? Rural England and the folk movement, 1850–1979', *Twentieth Century British History*, 7:2 (1996), 262–70.
Yates, D., *My Gypsy days: Recollections of a Romani rawnie* (London, 1953).
Yegenoglu, M., *Colonial fantasies: Towards a feminist reading of Orientalism* (Cambridge, 1998).
Yeo, E. and S. (eds), *Popular culture and class conflict, 1590–1914: Explorations in the history of labour and leisure* (Brighton, 1981).

Parliamentary papers

Report of the Select Committee on the Temporary Dwellings Bill, 1887 (279).
Report from the Departmental Committee on Habitual Offenders, Vagrants, Beggars, Inebriates and Juvenile Delinquents (Scotland), 1895, C 7753.
Report of the Departmental Committee on Vagrancy, 1906, Cd 2852.
Report of the Inter-departmental Committee on Partial Exemption from School Attendance, 1909, Cd 4791.
Report of the Select Committee of the House of Lords on the Moveable Dwellings Bill, 1910 (H. of L. 146).
Report of the Departmental Committee on Tinkers in Scotland (Edinburgh, 1918).
Departmental Committee Report on Relief of the Casual Poor, 1930, Cmd. 3640.
Report of the Departmental Committee on Vagrancy in Scotland, 1936, Cmd 5194.
Report of the Select Committee on the New Forest, 1947, Cmd 7245.
Wilson, A., *Caravans as homes*, 1959, Cmnd. 872.
The Civil Service (England). Departments of State and Official Bodies Civil Service Commission, 1968, Cmnd 3638.

Internet sources

www.gypsy-traveller.org/planning/index.htm (accessed August 2006).
www.travellersupport.org.uk /evictions.htm (accessed August 2006).
Ward, C., 'The hidden history of housing', *History and Policy* papers, www.historyandpolicy.org/archive/policy-paper–25.html (accessed April 2006).

Index